The COLONIAL SUBJUGATION of INDIA

ALSO BY AMAR FAROOQUI

Early Social Formations (2001)

Smuggling as Subversion: Colonialism, Indian Merchants and the Politics of Opium: 1790–1843 (2005)

Opium City: The Making of Early Victorian Bombay (2006)

Sindias and the Raj: Princely Gwalior, c. 1800–1850 (2011)

Zafar and the Raj: Anglo-Mughal Delhi, c. 1800–1857 (2013)

The Establishment of British Rule: 1757–1813 (2014)

The COLONIAL SUBJUGATION of INDIA

AMAR FAROOQUI

ALEPH

ALEPH

ALEPH BOOK COMPANY
An independent publishing firm
promoted by *Rupa Publications India*

First published in India in 2022
by Aleph Book Company
7/16 Ansari Road, Daryaganj
New Delhi 110 002

ISBN: 978-93-91047-34-4

1 3 5 7 9 10 8 6 4 2

Printed in India.

For Amol,
without whose cooperation,
and the care he took of his parents during the pandemic,
this book would not have been possible

CONTENTS

CONTENTS

AUTHOR'S NOTE

The distinctive characteristic of the modern period of world history has been the advent of capitalism, and its ascendancy. This ascendancy coincided with the supremacy, till at least the early decades of the twentieth century, of a few colonial powers over the entire globe. The history of colonialism begins with the arrival of Christopher Columbus in the Caribbean Sea (1492) and the appearance of Vasco da Gama in the Indian Ocean (1498). The first event set in motion processes which led to the conquest of the American continent and the second resulted in the subjugation of various parts of Asia and Africa. For nearly three centuries, from circa 1500 onwards, Spain, Portugal, the Netherlands (Holland), England, and France were the main European nations engaged in colonizing non-European societies. Spain and Portugal were the dominant colonial powers in the sixteenth century. They divided the entire American continent, south of present-day United States of America, among themselves. Spanish control in America was more extensive than Portuguese. This part of the world, which came to be referred to as Latin America, remained under direct European rule till the early nineteenth century. In Asia, Portugal had several colonies, extending from coastal China to the Persian Gulf, while Spain ruled over the Philippines. The Portuguese virtually monopolized the trade between Asia and Europe along the all-sea route via the Cape of Good Hope throughout the sixteenth century.

The Dutch (i.e. the Netherlands) replaced the Portuguese as the dominant colonial power in the Indian Ocean in the seventeenth century. By the early decades of the seventeenth century the Dutch East India Company (formally named 'United East India Company', or Vereenigde Oostindische Compagnie in the Dutch language, abbreviated to VOC) had managed to gain control over the seaborne trade between Asia and Europe, using the Cape of Good Hope route. The most important commodity in the Asia–Europe trade at that time was Asian pepper (and some other spices such as cloves, nutmeg, and mace). The Dutch company was also important in the intra-Asian trade. The profits that the VOC earned from the intra-Asian trade enabled it to reduce its dependence on precious metal (bullion) for the purchase of Asian commodities for European markets. As there was hardly any demand for European commodities in Asian markets, the VOC had to pay for the goods it carried from Asia to Europe with bullion. This exchange was useful for Asian economies since Asia was deficient in the production of silver, which in this context should be regarded as a commodity.

Both the Portuguese and the Dutch resorted to violence on a large scale to establish their supremacy. Their ships sailed with large guns and other weapons capable of unleashing massive firepower. The Dutch used violence even more extensively than the Portuguese to establish control over trading networks in Asian waters. In the process they disrupted the traditional seaborne commercial networks of the Indian Ocean. As some of the Indonesian islands were major producers of spices, the Dutch colonized Indonesia, initially large parts of Java. From the 1650s onwards, the VOC, which had taken possession of the Cape of Good Hope (in present-day South Africa), encouraged European settlers to develop farming in the area around the Cape, thus beginning the process that eventually led to the white colonization of South Africa and the conquest of African people in the region.

At the beginning of the eighteenth century, England and France emerged as major colonial powers. The English East India Company (EIC) was incorporated in 1600, and the French company in 1664. However it was only by the end of the seventeenth century, following the decline of the VOC, that the English and French companies began to make their presence felt in the Indian Ocean. Southern India became a major arena of conflict between the two companies in the first half of the eighteenth century. This was part of a larger struggle between England and France for colonies. Throughout the century both were engaged in a global contest for supremacy, culminating in the Napoleonic Wars (c. 1800–15). With the defeat of Napoleon, the ascendancy of England (Britain) was assured for the next hundred years. From 1815, till the outbreak of World War I, Britain dominated the international capitalist economy. British naval dominance was unchallenged for most of this period, making it possible for Britain to acquire and control a vast empire. However, ultimately what made Britain the pre-eminent colonial power in the world was its economy. The industrialization of England from the mid-eighteenth century onwards had made its economy the most advanced in the world. It is not a coincidence that the first phase of the Industrial Revolution gathered momentum (1760–80) just around the time that the EIC conquered Bengal, along with Bihar (and parts of Orissa). The Battle of Plassey (1757), followed by the Battle of Baksar (1764), made the Company a major territorial power in India. Apart from the direct plunder of Bengal by the Company's servants, the EIC could now use the revenues of eastern India to purchase commodities such as cotton textiles for the home market without having to bring precious metals to India to pay for them. Thus began the regular flow of colonial tribute from India to Britain. British participation in the Atlantic slave trade (captives from Africa were transported across the Atlantic to the American continent as slaves to work on sugar, tobacco, and cotton plantations) too brought large earnings to its economy. By the nineteenth century Britain also had extensive territorial possessions in the African continent. Ultimately, however, the Indian empire was perhaps the most important component of its colonial domain. It needs to be underlined that British ascendancy was preceded by over two centuries of colonial intervention in Asia during the course of which the strength and independence of polities in the region were undermined—their economies subjugated, their military strength weakened, and their societies penetrated.

For over a century, from the middle of the eighteenth century down to the 1850s, the EIC was engaged in constant warfare to subjugate the Indian subcontinent. The entire subcontinent (excluding Nepal), along with Burma, constituted the British Indian empire. Whereas a substantial portion of the empire was administered directly, there were also the territories of 'native states', more than 500 in number, which were governed indirectly. These states too were integral components of the empire. What follows is a history of the formation of the Indian empire, the violence inflicted on the people of this part of the world to conquer it, and the instruments of coercion that were put in place to rule over it.

Resistance to colonial subjugation too has a long history. The revolt of 1857 was a significant moment in the continuous struggle against colonial rule. Following the brutal suppression of the revolt through a prolonged and widespread military offensive which amounted to the reconquest of a large part of the empire, the colonial state partially refashioned its instruments of coercion and practices of governance which enabled it to exercise control over the empire for another ninety years.

There was a qualitative change in the nature of the resistance during and after World War I. As the anti-colonial struggle acquired a mass character and ideological maturity grounded in a sophisticated understanding of colonialism as a system of exploitation, the colonial state responded by unleashing repression, while at the same time promoting divisive tendencies of which communalism was the most effective in damaging the radical potential of the national liberation struggle. These developments of the post-war period coincided with the decline and elimination of Britain's dominance in the international capitalist economy. Hence the desperation with which it sought out fresh allies in the Indian empire, bolstered princely rulers, and experimented with new strategies of imperial control such as offering concessions in the form of provincial autonomy and an infinitesimal share of power based on a severely restricted franchise. Democracy for Indians had little to do with citizenship; electoral politics helped to reinforce communal identities and promoted antagonisms. World War II and the mass upsurge which followed it brought about the collapse of colonial rule. Independence was accompanied by a horrific communal bloodbath which the colonial state, otherwise so effective in exercising control over a subject people for nearly two centuries, seemed helpless to prevent in its moment of flight. This book attempts to show that empire was anything but benign.

◆

A note on spellings: names of places in the Indian subcontinent are mostly those commonly used in the latter half of the twentieth century till the 1990s, when cities such as Cochin, Bombay, and Madras began to be renamed. Renaming is an ongoing process, at times contentious. The names and spellings used in the book are those with which people of my generation have been familiar. English language spellings of these places have been used. Many of these names and spellings were in use prior to 1947, though some spellings such as 'Cawnpore' (Kanpur), or 'Simla' (Shimla) and 'Poona' (Pune), were changed soon after Independence or a little later in the century. The current official name of the respective places has also been provided to make it easier for the reader to identify them, except places which have been renamed relatively recently. The erstwhile names and English spellings of the latter are often still in everyday use. Archaic spellings, such as 'Oudh/Oude' for Awadh (region/Mughal suba/kingdom/colonial administrative unit) have been avoided, unless required by the context. Moreover, Awadh corresponds to the pronunciation, and is used widely in scholarly writings. Subedar has been preferred to subadar or subedar, being closer to the everyday pronounciation. Punjab has been used instead of Panjab, as it continues to be used officially. Names of places outside the subcontinent, and their spellings, by and large follow the same principles. For names such as Sindia, the spelling which is closer to the pronunciation has been preferred.

I would like to express my gratitude to my colleagues in the Department of History, University of Delhi, discussions with whom over the years have helped shaped this work. Interactions with my students, whom I have had the opportunity to teach courses dealing with many of the themes discussed in the book, have been immensely useful for me. I am thankful to Prabhu Mohapatra, Partho Datta, and Anirudh Deshpande who spared time to go through portions of the manuscript and offered invaluable comments and suggestions. I am grateful to the editorial team of Aleph, especially Kanika Praharaj, who worked hard to improve upon the manuscript, saved me from many pitfalls, and have made it readable. Responsibility for errors remains mine alone.

ONE

ANTECEDENTS

The passage of a small fleet of Portuguese ships through the Arabian Sea at the end of the fifteenth century might not have appeared at that time as an event of much significance. Traffic along the route taken by the fleet was already quite heavy. A diverse trade in numerous commodities was carried out by seafaring vessels plying in Asian waters, along routes stretching from the South China Sea to the Red Sea and East Africa. However, the passage of the Portuguese fleet is central to the early history of colonial intrusion in the Indian Ocean. Portugal was to dominate the all-sea route between the Indian Ocean and Europe, via the Cape of Good Hope (at the southwestern tip of the African continent), for most of the sixteenth century. The viability of this route was established by the successful journey of Vasco da Gama (d. 1524) from Portugal to the west coast of India, and back, along this route. The passage of the fleet commanded by da Gama through the Arabian Sea marked the final lap of its outward journey.

Da Gama set out from Lisbon in 1497 leading a convoy of four ships on a journey along the Atlantic coast of Africa, then around the Cape of Good Hope—as this location came to be known—into the Indian Ocean, disembarking eventually at Calicut (Kozhikode) in Malabar shortly before the monsoon season of 1498. Calicut was a prominent centre of trade in spices, especially pepper. It was ruled at this time by a chieftain of the Nair Eradi clan who bore the title of Samudri (Samoothiri) Raja, generally rendered as 'Zamorin' in European accounts. The actual location where the Portuguese expedition landed

1

was the beach of Kappad, a short distance to the north of Calicut town. Surprisingly, the names of many of the Eradi rulers of Calicut are not easily forthcoming. They are usually referred to only by their title, i.e., Samudri or Samoothiri Raja, 'lord of the seas'.

Within a few years of the voyage of da Gama, the Portuguese were travelling regularly along this all-sea route between Lisbon and the Indian Ocean. The project for these voyages, including that of Vasco da Gama, had been initiated by the Portuguese state, and the route itself became a crown monopoly. The Portuguese commercial enterprise in Asia was conducted on behalf of the crown by the Casa da Índia, a state organization with headquarters in Lisbon. The Portuguese soon established 'factories' (feitorias) or trading posts, usually fortified, at strategic coastal locations in the Persian Gulf, the Arabian Sea, and the South China Sea for procuring commodities (mainly spices) for sale in European markets. The factories functioned as godowns where goods would be warehoused throughout the year awaiting shipment to Lisbon. Residential quarters of Portuguese officials, soldiers, and sailors too were located within these premises. More importantly, most of the factories served as naval bases. In this their coastal location was crucial. It was these bases that enabled the Portuguese to have a formidable military presence in Asia; this in turn allowed them to gradually subordinate Asian shipping to their interests. The factories also represented the initial permanent investment on the part of the Portuguese in Asia for facilitating their commerce.

Right from the beginning of the sixteenth century, the Portuguese had used their superior firepower to intimidate rulers and traders in Asia. Violence was the major new element they brought to the commercial world of the Indian Ocean. For instance, an armed conflict was triggered in 1500 during the second Portuguese expedition to Malabar due to their insistence that they be given priority in acquiring supplies for their cargo. When this demand was not conceded, fighting broke out, culminating in the bombardment of Calicut. Subsequently Vasco da Gama made another trip to Malabar in 1502, and finding that the Samudri Raja was unwilling to allow the Portuguese to trade on their terms, ordered a massive bombardment of the city. A large part of Calicut was destroyed in this action. The violence perpetrated on the Malabar Coast set the pattern for their dealings which were often indistinguishable from piracy. By the second decade of the century, the Portuguese had acquired several territorial possessions at strategic locations which enabled them to monitor and regulate shipping in Asian waters: Goa on the west coast of India in 1510; Malacca (close to Singapore) in the Malacca Straits, the main passage between the Indian Ocean and the South China Sea, in 1511; and Hormuz at the entrance to the Persian Gulf in 1515. Additionally, a fortified settlement came up in Colombo on the west coast of Sri Lanka in 1518. As the west coast of India increasingly became the main zone of Portuguese commercial activities in Asia, a series of factories-cum-naval bases were established all the way from the Gulf of Cambay (Khambat) in the north to Malabar in the south: Diu, Daman, Bassein, and Cochin (Kochi)—and, of course, Goa. The widely dispersed Portuguese colonial possessions in Asia, which included Macau in China (near Canton/Guangzhou) and Timor at the eastern extremity of the Indonesian islands, came to be collectively designated as the Estado da Índia (State of India) with Goa as its headquarters. The Estado da Índia functioned under the control of the Casa da Índia. The principal Portuguese colonial official in Asia, i.e. the viceroy, resided in Goa and had extensive administrative and military authority over the Estado da Índia.

In order to exercise effective control over Asian shipping, especially over sectors in which they were attempting to eliminate or minimize competition, the Portuguese evolved the notorious 'cartaz system' whereby Asian ships were forced to ply only along specified routes. Simultaneously, they were prohibited from carrying commodities such as spices which were sought by the Portuguese. Every ship had to carry a cartaz or passport issued by authorities of the Estado da Índia. The cartaz mentioned particulars of the ship, details of the voyage, and listed the cargo that was being transported. A fee was charged for issuing the cartaz; this became an additional source of income for the Portuguese. Moreover, ships were compelled to proceed via specified Portuguese settlements where they had to pay customs and other duties. These duties generated a large income which could then be used to purchase Asian goods. It needs to be underlined that ships plying without a cartaz or found to be contravening its terms (e.g., not operating along the route mentioned in the cartaz, carrying forbidden consignments, evading payment of duties) were captured and the crews killed or made captive. In other words, the Portuguese introduced, through the cartaz system, a sophisticated form of state-sponsored piracy in the Indian Ocean. They were able to enforce the system because of their naval military strength. It was this strength that also allowed them to control the all-sea commercial route between Europe and Asia throughout the sixteenth century.

Whereas the Cape of Good Hope route represented a significant shift in the Asia–Europe trade, the traditional sea-cum-land route through West Asia continued to operate despite colonial intervention. The Portuguese did try to close this route, but were not entirely successful. Their possession of Hormuz posed difficulties for the Persian Gulf route, but in the case of the Red Sea route their failure to occupy Aden or any other important strategic location at the entrance of the sea kept this artery open. One might mention in this context that Ottoman presence in West Asia made it difficult for the Portuguese to consolidate their hold in the region. In the second quarter of the sixteenth century there were a series of military engagements between the Portuguese and the Ottomans, both on land and sea, which created problems for Portuguese expansion in the Indian Ocean. Nevertheless, the activities of Arab and Gujarati traders, who had been prominent in the seaborne commerce of the Arabian Sea, received a setback due to the diversion of a part of the Asia–Europe trade to the Cape of Good Hope route. It has been estimated that by the latter half of the century nearly 75 per cent of the pepper available in European markets was being supplied by the Portuguese. Some of the pepper carried by Portuguese ships might have represented a net increase in supplies rather than a mere diversion.

For the Portuguese, India was the main source of pepper. Most of their supplies were procured from Malabar. In view of the hostilities they had generated during the course of their initial business transactions at Calicut and as a consequence of their ouster from it following the bombardment of the city, it became necessary for the Portuguese to search for some other location in the area from which they could obtain pepper. From 1503 onwards, Cochin, situated a short distance south of Calicut, became the principal centre of Portuguese commercial activities in Malabar. It was at Cochin that the Portuguese established their first fortified settlement in India.

The ruler of Cochin was nominally subservient to the Samudri Raja. At the time of the arrival of the Portuguese in Malabar he was attempting to assert his independence. The Portuguese played upon the tensions between the rulers of Calicut and Cochin, assisting the latter in throwing off allegiance to the Samudri Raja. By involving themselves in local political disputes the Portuguese managed to embed themselves in Indian society. Incidentally, Vasco da Gama passed away in Cochin in 1524 when he was in India for a third time. His body was initially interred in the historic church within the fort (St Francis Church); the remains were later taken to Portugal. Apart from Cochin, the Portuguese had establishments at Quilon (Kollam) and Cannanore (Kannur) in Kerala.

Towards the end of the sixteenth century the Portuguese monopoly on the Cape of Good Hope route began to be challenged by other European traders. Soon the Dutch replaced the Portuguese. The economy of the Netherlands was far more developed than that of Portugal and conditions were comparatively more favourable in the Dutch social formation for the growth of merchant capitalists. In fact, Portuguese commerce in Asia was partly sustained by the resources of its empire in America (Brazil). Trade in Brazilian commodities, such as sugar, provided some of the resources with which spices could be obtained in Asia. In the long run, however, modern commercial enterprise could only continue if it was linked to the growth of a strong class of merchant capitalists, something that did not happen in Portugal at this stage. A reflection of this weakness was that merchants from different parts of Europe bought up large quantities of spices from the Lisbon market and thus had the opportunity of pocketing a share of the profits from this lucrative trade. Moreover, Amsterdam in Netherlands became the pre-eminent centre of the international trade in precious metals.

The Portuguese just did not have the infrastructure for building a wide distribution network in Europe. In fact, the sale of Asian commodities carried in Portuguese ships to Europe was contracted to the leading sixteenth century merchant and banking concerns of the Fuggers and the Welsers based in the German city of Augsburg. As we have noted, the Asia–Europe trade via southern Africa operated as a crown monopoly. By the closing decades of the century the Portuguese state was finding it difficult to mobilize sufficient capital for investing in commercial voyages to Asia. It experimented with setting up a trading company but in the absence of a corresponding development of merchant capital these attempts remained unsuccessful.

The VOC was to dominate the Asia–Europe trade in the seventeenth century. This was a joint-stock company formed in 1602 in the Netherlands, and was given a monopoly over trade with the 'East Indies'. As a joint-stock company, the VOC was owned by several shareholders in accordance with their respective shares. This was a relatively new kind of business organization which was suited to ventures requiring a large outlay of capital and involving much risk. If there were losses, an individual shareholder's liability would be limited only to the extent of the share owned.

It may be mentioned that unlike Portugal, Netherlands was a republic: Republic of the United Netherlands. The republic included parts of present-day Belgium. As a political entity, the republic lasted for nearly two centuries (c. 1580s–1790s); today Netherlands is a constitutional monarchy. 'East Indies' broadly referred to all the geographical areas lying east of the Cape of Good Hope and, somewhat vaguely, west of the Pacific Ocean, though more specifically for the Dutch, East Indies referred to Asia.

In the opening decades of the seventeenth century the VOC was engaged in a tussle with the Portuguese, attempting to take over some of the strategic locations held by them in the Indian Ocean. On the other hand, the main focus of the VOC's attention for quite some time was Indonesia: many of the Indonesian islands, spread over a vast area between the Nicobar Islands in the west and the northern extremity of Australia in the east, were major producers of spices such as pepper, cloves, nutmeg, and mace. Much greater profits, up to several hundred times, could be made by obtaining nutmeg and cloves directly from their areas of production. In 1596, an exploratory Dutch expedition had arrived at Bantam (Banten, in western Java), an important market for spices. When prices of spices were found to be much higher than expected, the city was bombarded. Thus Dutch colonialism too commenced its career with the brutal killing of indigenous people in Asia. It is difficult to estimate the number of people who were slaughtered for the sake of a few sackfuls of pepper or nutmeg, but we do know that violence was resorted to regularly for procuring spices. This aspect of the history of Dutch enterprise is often overlooked by those who emphasize the VOC's managerial capabilities in explaining its success. An important reason for its success was its ability to send out numerically larger and better-equipped armed fleets as compared to the Portuguese. The Portuguese (and initially the English, who too were becoming active at this time) were unable to resist Dutch firepower.

There are two groups of islands in eastern Indonesia which produce three valuable spices, i.e., cloves, nutmeg, and mace (mace is the membrane that covers the nutmeg). Nutmeg—*Myristica fragrans*—(jaiphal in Hindi/Urdu, jaathikkaai in Tamil) has several culinary and medicinal uses. In the seventeenth century it was regarded as a miracle drug which could cure a wide range of diseases, including plague, and was much sought after. The two groups of islands which produced these rare spices are the Moluccas or Maluku (Amboyna/Ambon, Ternate, and Tidore are the major islands in this group) and the neighbouring Banda Islands. In the colonial era they were all collectively referred to as the Spice Islands. The Moluccas (not to be confused with the port of Malacca or Melaka) yield vast quantities of cloves, while nutmeg grows in abundance on the tiny Banda Islands. In the seventeenth century the Banda Islands were the only known source of nutmeg in the world. Along with pepper—which due to the much larger scale of the trade in it should be placed in a separate category—nutmeg, mace, and cloves (and Sri Lankan cinnamon) were the principal spices carried to European markets. Whereas pepper production was widely dispersed over a large area extending from southwestern India to Indonesia, cloves and nutmeg were obtained almost exclusively from the Spice Islands—hence the importance of these islands for the Dutch.

During the first two decades of the seventeenth century, the VOC gradually acquired control over the Moluccas, putting an end to the influence that the Portuguese had so far wielded in this remote corner of Indonesia. In 1621, the Banda Islands were conquered. The conquest of Banda was accompanied by massive violence in which virtually the entire local population was exterminated by the VOC. This genocide was not an impulsive act: the Company's directors (known as the 'Heeren XVII' or 'Gentlemen Seventeen', i.e. the council of seventeen, seventeen being the number of members of the board of directors) in Amsterdam had actually instructed its officials in Southeast Asia to 'repopulate' the islands. The prolonged resistance of the inhabitants of Banda to the reign of terror let loose by the VOC had prompted the directors to enunciate such a policy—the Dutch objective was to completely monopolize the entire yield of nutmeg so that it might have no competitor in European markets (a precondition for earning massive super-profits). Dutch settlers took over the production of nutmeg, using slave labour from neighbouring islands for the purpose.

Several of the petty chiefs of Banda had aligned themselves with the much weaker English in this struggle. Interestingly, the Dutch did not spare the English either. When servants of the fledgling EIC tried to gain a foothold on one of the smallest islands of the Banda group, Run (barely 3 kilometres wide), the VOC brutally wiped out most of them. An English captive who survived the ordeal recorded that while he and his companions were imprisoned in a dungeon built by the VOC on the island of Ai (one of the five islands of the Banda group) the Dutch guards 'pissed and **** upon our heads...and in this manner we lay, untill [sic.] such time as we were broken out from top to toe like lepers, having nothing to eat but durtie [dirty] rice, and stinking rainewater [sic.]'.[1] If such was the fate of white Europeans who challenged Dutch supremacy, one can easily imagine what would have befallen non-Europeans whenever they attempted to resist!

A more serious instance of violence against the English was the gruesome torture and killing in 1623 of the entire staff of the EIC, which included several Japanese guards, at Amboyna by the Dutch. This incident, known as the Amboyna Massacre

---

[1]Giles Milton, *Nathaniel's Nutmeg*, London: Hodder & Stoughton, 1999, p. 293.

(the details of which are much better known than those of the countless massacres of Asians and Africans by colonial powers), brought the two countries to the verge of war in Europe.

The VOC made Java the base of its operations in Southeast Asia. Here Jakarta in north Java became the seat of its Asian empire, and headquarters of its commercial enterprise in the region. The city was occupied in 1619. Jakarta was renamed Batavia by the Dutch; Batavia was named after the Batavi, an ancient Germanic tribe from which, according to prominent Dutch humanists of the early modern era such as Cornelius Aurelius and Erasmus, the inhabitants of the Netherlands were supposedly descended. This was the origin myth of the Dutch 'nation'. The name of the city, as was true of several other place names of the colonial period, had no relevance for the local populace. The existing town of Jakarta was completely destroyed on the orders of one of the most ruthless governors general of the VOC's territories in Asia, Jan Peiterszoon Coen (first tenure as governor general, 1618–23), and a new Dutch settlement then came up in its place. The Dutch consolidated their position in Southeast Asia by taking over Malacca from the Portuguese in 1641. For the next half-century, Southeast Asia was a preserve of the VOC. This ensured its *sole* access to supplies of spices, except, of course, pepper.

At a very early date, the VOC had resolved to aggressively engage in intra-Asian trade on a substantial scale. Earnings from this trade were to be channelized into the purchase of commodities for European markets, wherever the Company had to actually pay for these commodities or was unable to exercise coercion. Indian textiles were in great demand across Southeast Asia, especially the coarser cotton varieties for everyday use. These could be exchanged directly for spices, or indirectly through a complex series of exchanges involving several commodities. It was in this context that India became crucial for Dutch commerce. Gujarat and the Coromandel region were the two main producers of the varieties of cotton textiles that were in demand in Southeast Asian markets. In the first decade of the seventeenth century the VOC had already set up three factories on the Coromandel coast to obtain supplies of cloth. One of these was in Pulicat (1610), at the northern extremity of present-day Tamil Nadu, which became the administrative centre of their enclaves in the area till the end of the century. The Portuguese had maintained a presence in the Coromandel, but in their overall scheme of things commercial networks of the Bay of Bengal did not figure as prominently as those of the Arabian Sea. Pulicat itself had been wrested from the Portuguese by the VOC, and later, in 1658, the Dutch dislodged the Portuguese from another of their Coromandel outposts, Nagapattinam (located further south on the Tamil Nadu coast). In 1690, Nagapattinam became the headquarters of the VOC in Coromandel. Coromandel was the name by which the southeastern coastal area of the Indian subcontinent was known; the name has now fallen out of use.

Gujarat was the other major supplier of cotton textiles for Asian markets. Here the city of Surat was the principal centre of the extensive seaborne trade of the region. As the premier port of the Mughal empire, Surat was firmly under imperial control, rendering it difficult for European traders to insist on their own unreasonable methods in commercial dealings. European traders and sailors did occasionally resort to violence, but this was often the result of rivalries among themselves. It should be borne in mind that at the turn of the century there were fierce rivalries between the Portuguese, Dutch, and English. In 1618, the VOC received permission to set up a factory (obviously without fortifications or a military garrison) at Surat; within a few years there were several other Dutch outposts in Gujarat, all of which were subordinate to Surat. Unlike Malabar, where the Portuguese used their fortified position in Cochin to intimidate suppliers of spices and other commodities and obtain these at rates well below prevailing market prices, all European traders had to carry out their business in a competitive market at Surat. Mughal authorities kept a close watch on their activities and were in a position to enforce discipline. From the point of view of the Mughal state this trade was advantageous as, apart from the earnings that were accrued from various levied duties, it brought in large quantities of precious metal against which the textiles of Surat were purchased. This became a vital source of gold and silver for the empire, more so as the Indian subcontinent hardly had any source of these metals. As the century wore on, the trade became increasingly complex with the finer varieties of textiles being exported to Europe, and some of the spices from Southeast Asia being sold at Surat, partially replacing the inflow of bullion. Om Prakash has argued that from around the 1660s the 'bullion for goods' model gave way to a 'goods for goods and bullion situation'.[2] The implications of this situation, for our purposes, were that a market for Indian textiles was being developed in Europe, and that Surat was emerging as a leading destination for Southeast Asian spices which were then carried to other parts of the Mughal empire.

By the early 1630s, the VOC had brought Bengal and Orissa (Odisha) within the ambit of its activities. The Dutch discovered that raw silk produced in Bengal was in demand in Japanese markets where the VOC had acquired a toe-hold when it was allowed to set up a factory at Hirodo on the island of Kyushu (near Nagasaki) in 1609. The VOC's trade with Japan was briefly disrupted in the late 1620s, but resumed in 1633. The Portuguese, whose trade with Japan dated back to the mid-sixteenth century, were expelled in 1639. Subsequently, in 1641, the Dutch were ordered to shift their factory to Deshima, a small artificial islet connected to Nagasaki. Henceforth, the VOC was the only western trading concern allowed to carry

---

[2]Om Prakash, *The New Cambridge History of India: European Commercial Enterprise in Pre-Colonial India*, Cambridge: Cambridge University Press, 1998, p. 100.

on trade with Japan, and Deshima was the sole location to which it had access.

The importance of Japan lay in the fact that it was a leading international producer of silver, next only to South America in terms of its deposits at this time. By selling goods in Japan, the Dutch company could significantly augment its reserves of precious metal. Raw silk was one of the commodities that the VOC's ships carried to Japan. Later in the century, Bihar opium was added to its list of goods obtained from eastern India, for sale in Southeast Asia. Following the decline of the spice trade, fine cotton textiles from Bengal too began to be exported to Europe along with textiles from other parts of India. With its growing involvement in the commerce of Bengal, the VOC set up a factory at the port of Hugli (Hooghly), lying north of Calcutta (Kolkata). Earlier the Portuguese too had maintained a presence at Hugli but were expelled by the Mughals in 1632. The Dutch were allowed to establish a factory at the port in 1635. In 1656, the neighbouring settlement of Chinsura, then just a small village, became their headquarters in Bengal. The VOC also had factories at Agra, Patna, and Kasimbazar. The one area in which the Dutch were able to carry out considerable coercion was Malabar. Here they continued with the policies pursued by the Portuguese whom they finally supplanted in 1663 when they took over Cochin.

The seventeenth century witnessed changes in the Asia–Europe trade which eventually benefited, and were accelerated by, the EIC. In the latter half of the century there was a steady rise in the export of Indian textiles, and to some extent indigo. Spices, hitherto the mainstay of the trade, declined relatively and absolutely. Due to the Dutch stranglehold over Southeast Asian supplies of pepper, cloves, nutmeg, and mace, the EIC tried to make use of the possibilities provided by networks centred in India and subsequently China from where it sourced tea for England. Histories of the English and Dutch companies ran parallel to each other for some time, though the latter was by far the stronger of the two until the closing decades of the seventeenth century. The fact that the English company could carry out its activities with relative freedom in India, particularly in territories of the Mughal empire, and did not have to face the kind of obstacles that were placed in its way by the Dutch in Southeast Asia, presented it with a historical opportunity that it made good use of.

TWO

THE RISE OF THE EAST INDIA COMPANY

The weakening of Portuguese power in the Indian Ocean by the end of the sixteenth century had created a vacuum which the English and the Dutch tried to fill. Since the merchant capitalists of England were, as a class, much weaker at this stage than their Dutch counterparts, their progress was much slower in so far as their share of the Asia–Europe trade was concerned, at least till the 1680s. Towards the end of the 1590s, a group of English merchants based in London had succeeded in persuading the authorities to grant them special privileges, through a royal charter, for participating in the seaborne trade via the Cape of Good Hope. Not only were they seeking exclusive rights to trade in the 'East Indies', but also official sanction for taking out large quantities of precious metal from the country to finance their ventures.

The earliest scheme, proposed in 1527, for undertaking a transoceanic voyage from England to Asia was for a new route that would not involve going round the Cape of Good Hope. This was for a northwestern route through the Arctic Archipelago. Two preliminary English expeditions were launched in the Tudor era, during the reign of Henry VIII (r. 1491–1547), in search of a northwestern passage. These were unsuccessful, as would have been expected, given the enormous difficulties of the route. Nevertheless, the hope that such a route might be discovered by the English was not entirely abandoned. The scheme was seriously revived by the EIC at the beginning of the sixteenth century.

The formalities for the grant of a royal charter to what

came to be known as the (English) East India Company were completed towards the end of 1600. Despite the support of the English ruler, Queen Elizabeth I (r. 1558–1603) of the Tudor dynasty, it took the EIC some time to negotiate with various other statutory bodies such as the privy council (where they met with some opposition) before they could get the charter and send out a fleet of ships to Asia. The charter was initially valid for fifteen years; it was continuously renewed, with changes made to its terms from time to time, till 1853 when it received its final charter.

Even before the first charter had run its full course, a new charter was granted to the EIC by James I, who had succeeded Elizabeth as monarch of England in 1603. The charter was given in 1609, and unlike the first charter was 'perpetual' rather than for a fixed duration. Many of the subsequent charters were also perpetual. At the same time, for most of the seventeenth century, the Company had to face corporate challenges to its monopoly from rivals seeking to participate in the Asia–Europe trade. In 1637, a body known as the Courten Association managed to obtain a charter from Charles I (r. 1625–49) to trade in the East Indies. The Association was permitted to carry on its activities at those places where the EIC did not have a commercial presence, as for example in Goa and China. The competition that this led to caused serious problems for the EIC. In 1657, while England was briefly a republic (1649–60), a fresh charter was granted to the EIC by Oliver Cromwell, restoring its monopoly. Simultaneously, the stock of the Courten Association, as well as of several private ventures which had been instituted in the early 1650s, were united with the stock of the EIC. Charters of the latter half of the seventeenth century further strengthened the position of the Company. The crown was willing to grant more wide-ranging authority to the EIC for carrying out its operations in Asia mainly due to the willingness of the Company to extend generous loans to the respective monarchs.

However, it was not until the first decade of the eighteenth century that the EIC was able to fully secure its monopoly status. The last quarter of the seventeenth century was a difficult time for the Company, and it was almost in danger of losing the gains it had made since the 1650s. Several factors were responsible for the precarious situation with which it was faced in these decades. To begin with, there were renewed efforts to challenge the Company's monopoly. It was argued that the 1657 union had a fairly narrow basis which excluded a large number of possible investors. The fresh challenge to the EIC's privileges came during the despotic regime of its influential director, Josiah Child, who was governor of the Company for several terms during the 1680s, and continued to wield considerable power in the 1690s. Child's authoritarian attitude was resisted both within and outside the EIC, although this did not prevent the Company from obtaining a new charter in 1686 which further increased its powers in the context of its activities in India, as for instance minting coins in local currencies.

The major political changes in England that followed the Glorious Revolution of 1688, which established the supremacy of parliament over the crown, somewhat reduced the political influence of the EIC. Parliamentary intervention made it possible for a new company to be established despite stiff opposition from the 'old' company. The situation was further complicated by the formation of another company in Scotland. This company was authorized by the Scottish parliament to carry out trade with the East Indies. It should be borne in mind that whereas the crowns of England and Scotland had been united in 1603, i.e., the same monarchs ruled the two kingdoms, full-fledged union of the two only took place in 1707. Meanwhile, Scotland was governed as a separate country, and it was overshadowed by England. Eventually, the Scottish trading venture failed due to, among other factors, intense English hostility, leaving only the 'old' EIC, also known as the London EIC, and the 'new' EIC, or the English EIC, in the field. The London EIC was allowed to retain its former privileges till 1701; it also had investments in the English EIC. It was soon realized that competition between the two would be disastrous for English overseas commerce, particularly as the English EIC had to encounter opposition from the old company as it tried to gain a foothold in the East Indies. The latter already had a presence in the region as well as established trading networks which had evolved over a century. As for the new company, it was faced with serious financial problems as most of the capital it had raised when it was incorporated had been lent to the government. The loan had been the original condition for granting it a charter. Eventually a compromise was worked out. Steps were then initiated, under parliamentary and state supervision, to bring the two companies together. This was achieved in 1708–1709 with the formation of the United Company of Merchants Trading to the East Indies. The merger involved complex business arrangements for protecting the interests of shareholders of the London EIC and English EIC. These developments enabled more traders and financiers to participate in the increasingly lucrative trade in Asian merchandise. All subsequent charters were granted to the amalgamated company (united EIC), which continued to operate in India until 1858. From now on, all important changes relating to the privileges and structure of the EIC had to be authorized by acts of parliament.

◆

The voyage of the first fleet of the EIC comprising five ships, led by James Lancaster aboard the *Red Dragon*, commenced in April 1601. Lancaster was the admiral of the squadron while Henry Middleton, captain of the *Hector*, the second largest ship of the fleet, was second-in-command. Lancaster had considerable experience of long sea voyages; in the early 1590s he had undertaken a voyage to the Malay Archipelago as captain of a ship. Thus he was familiar with the route he was traversing. It was understood that the fleet would head straight to the Indonesian archipelago to procure spices, mainly pepper and cloves. Having sailed successfully via the Cape of Good Hope, it arrived at Sumatra, the large island in the western part of the archipelago. Here the English engaged in pepper transactions at numerous ports such as Acheh and Pariaman, and also obtained permission from some of the local rulers for conducting their trade on a recurring basis. A part of the fleet proceeded to Bantam, the leading pepper mart of Java; and to the Spice Islands to acquire a supply of cloves. One of the ships, the *Assention* (*Ascension*) was sent back to England ahead of the rest of the fleet with its cargo consisting of pepper, cloves, and cinnamon, and arrived safely in the middle of 1603. This marked the beginning of the EIC's regular voyages to Asian waters via the Cape of Good Hope route.

Interestingly, soon after the fleet under Lancaster sailed for the East Indies, the EIC was still willing to sponsor an expedition for discovering the hitherto elusive northwestern route to the East Indies. The northwest route, if discovered, was assumed to be easier to traverse. This in fact was not the case, as the latest expedition was to demonstrate. A navigator named George Waymouth had approached the EIC with a proposal to undertake the exploratory journey, a proposal that was accepted after some legal issues had been sorted out. These related to the prior claim of another English company, the Muskovy Company, which had obtained a charter from Elizabeth I in the 1550s. The continuing search for an alternative route was prompted by the length of the Cape route (it was assumed that the Arctic route would be shorter) and the obstacles created by the Portuguese who protected their monopoly through violent means. In May 1602, Waymouth set out with two small ships under his command. The expedition was unsuccessful, and Waymouth turned back due to the reluctance of his crew to continue with the voyage, arriving in England in September 1602. Henceforth, the East India Company would stick to the Cape route.

We have already seen how the Dutch through their

unrelenting hostility towards the English made it impossible for them to function in Southeast Asia. It was then that, by the mid-seventeenth century, the EIC began to vigorously explore other avenues. In the process it became critically dependent on its business links with India. By 1613, the EIC had a factory at Surat, preceding the VOC by five years. The Dutch were at this time concentrating on the Coromandel to get their supplies of cotton textiles for Southeast Asian markets. Yet India was initially incidental to the plans of the EIC. Its main objective was to procure spices from Southeast Asia for sale in Europe. Bantam in western Java, which was also the main base of the VOC's operations, was in the early decades of the century the headquarters of the EIC in Asia.

Even as Surat remained the chief establishment of the EIC in India, superseding Bantam in the 1630s as its Asian headquarters, the English company was expanding its activities in Coromandel during the 1630s and 1640s. The EIC had managed to acquire a small piece of territory on the coast in 1640 and soon fortified the site, naming it Fort St. George. The fort and the settlement that came up around it grew into the city of Madras (Chennai). In 1653, Madras was placed under a council chaired by a senior official who was designated president of the settlement: this made Madras a presidency. By the end of the 1650s, all the English settlements on the east coast, including Bengal, were placed administratively under the control of Madras. In the 1660s, on the west coast, the EIC got hold of a group of islands lying south of Surat. These islands were to develop into the principal urban centre of western India—Bombay (Mumbai). The Bombay group of islands was earlier under the Portuguese. Not very long after the Portuguese had occupied Goa they established themselves at Bassein, a short distance from the port of Surat, in the early 1530s. The seven islands that collectively came to be called Bombay (taking their name from the island of Bombay) are located in the Arabian Sea, south of Bassein. These islands remained territorial possessions of the Portuguese till the mid-seventeenth century when they were transferred to the English crown (in 1665). The EIC acquired the islands from the crown by extending a loan of £50,000 to the government, and against a token rent of £10 per annum. Thus, the Bombay group of islands came under the Company's control from 1668 onwards. In 1687, its headquarters in western India were shifted from Surat to Bombay. This was essentially an administrative arrangement since Surat continued to be the main centre of the seaborne trade on the northwestern coast till the first quarter of the eighteenth century when it began to decline as a result of problems resulting from the crisis in the Mughal empire around that time.

As yet, in the 1680s, the EIC's position was far from stable. Moreover, rather unwisely, it got involved in an armed conflict with the Mughals. As a result of the conflict, called the Anglo-Mughal War of 1686–90, the Company was temporarily dislodged from the west coast, and might have lost Bombay forever. The aggressive manner in which Josiah Child conducted the affairs of the Company at home had encouraged its officials in India to resort to violence and bullying more brazenly than usual in order to assert its presumed superiority, confident that their actions would be approved by their superiors in London.

There was a definite shift in the Company's business strategy under Child's command, with the directors opting for outright military confrontation in India. The key English functionary in the subcontinent at this time was a namesake of the EIC chief (though not related to him), John Child, who resided in Bombay as its governor, and additionally held charge of the Company's operations in southern and eastern India. In the late 1680s, the EIC management in London, with the sanction of King James II (deposed in 1688), formally launched an offensive on two fronts. The objective of the offensive was to simultaneously extend the Company's influence in Bengal and on the west coast. It sought to achieve this aim by exhibiting its naval prowess, commencing in 1686 with an attack on the important port of Hugli, where the EIC had maintained a regular presence since 1651 (see chapter III).

The Company was certainly in no position to take on the Mughal war machine at this stage. Mughal officials reacted by ousting the EIC from eastern India and the Coromandel and closing down all its factories in the regions. The Hugli factory had already been abandoned. With the arrival of armed ships in the Bay of Bengal, to reinforce the fleet sent out earlier, the English attempted in 1688 to capture the port of Chittagong at the eastern extremity of the Bengal coast. According to the scheme devised in London, a fortified settlement in Chittagong would be the main location in the region for the EIC's trade. Dacca (Dhaka) in eastern Bengal was the capital of Mughal Bengal for most of the seventeenth century, and a major centre of trade and textile production. The famed muslin of Dacca was manufactured in the surrounding areas and soon became a much sought-after article for export to Europe.

The plan for the invasion of Chittagong was a complete failure. In the west, intensified attacks by English vessels targeting Mughal shipping in the Arabian Sea called forth harsh measures to curb the Company's piratical raids. The imperial authorities ordered a siege of Bombay, resulting in the destruction and depopulation of the settlement. Lasting for fifteen months, from early 1689 to the middle of 1690, the siege and its consequences came to be blamed on the incompetence of John Child. The blockade and occupation of Bombay was carried out by a strong force led by Sidi Yaqut Khan (his full name rarely appears in most accounts of the siege), who owed allegiance to the Mughals. Yaqut Khan was based in the impregnable fortress of Janjira located off the Konkan coast, south of Bombay. The Europeans and their Indian and creole Indo-Portuguese dependents were confined to the Fort at the southern tip of Bombay island. A large proportion of those who took refuge in the Fort were civilians. Many of the soldiers deserted the EIC, going over to Yaqut Khan, further weakening the English. Ultimately, the Company had to surrender unconditionally to the Mughals. Aurangzeb (r. 1658–1707) issued orders imposing a huge indemnity as the price for allowing the Company to engage in trade, and admonishing them for their defiance of Mughal authority.

Reports of the debacle in Bombay were immediately suppressed. The systematic cover-up by senior functionaries of the EIC has meant that the events of the Anglo-Mughal War have been referred to in the vaguest terms in narratives of the early history of the Company's activities in India. A typical example is the mention it receives in a much-cited work, *The Cambridge History of India*.

> Into the war with the Moghuls, which resulted from the troubles in Bengal, the English on the western coast entered only after a long hesitancy and in a feeble manner. The seizure of some Moghul vessels brought about a rupture towards the end of 1688, with the consequence that the factors at Surat were imprisoned. Child in retaliation captured a number of richly freighted ships. Thereupon ensued a siege of Bombay by the Moghul forces, until in 1690 the English put an end to the war by a humiliating submission involving the payment of a considerable sum. Child, whose dismissal was one of the conditions of peace, died just as the negotiations were reaching a conclusion.[1]

More recent research has shed light on the catastrophic outcome of the EIC's misadventure, and process of erasure from the historical record of the siege which 'has figured little in histories of the early East India Company, even though it

---

[1]*The Cambridge History of India, Vol. IV: The Mughul Period*, Cambridge: Cambridge University Press, 1929, p. 103.

helped precipitate one of the worst crises in the entire history of the Company'.[2]

It took quite some time for the Company to recover from the setback of the war.

◆

Meanwhile, another European competitor had appeared on the scene. In France, the Compagnie des Indes Orientales (East India Company) was founded under royal patronage in 1664. Though the Compagnie underwent some changes in its nomenclature and organization, the overall pattern of control, wherein the state had a decisive say in its affairs, remained constant throughout. Given the weakness of merchant capital in France, the new company was not in a position to engage in trade between Europe and Asia very actively during the first few decades of its existence. It was only at the beginning of the eighteenth century that the French East India Company emerged as a major rival to the EIC in India. The Dutch Company had ceased to be a significant player by the turn of the century. Between the 1720s and 1750s the French and the English were locked in a fierce battle to dominate the colonial enterprise of the Indian subcontinent.

The Compagnie made sluggish and unsteady progress till the end of the 1710s. In 1674, a trading post had been set up at Pondicherry (Puducherry) on the Coromandel coast, near Madras. This eventually became the headquarters of its possessions in India. In Bengal, the French had a settlement at Chandernagore (Chandannagar) from 1690 onwards. Chandernagore is located a short distance north of Calcutta. Besides, the French company purchased textiles from Surat for sale in Europe. The Compagnie's commercial activities began

---

[2]Margaret R. Hunt, 'The 1689 Mughal Siege of East India Company Bombay: Crisis and Historical Erasure', *History Workshop Journal*, Vol. 84, Autumn 2017, p. 150.

gathering momentum in the 1720s and by the following decade both the Dutch and the English were becoming worried about French competition. The French company was now a profitable business concern. In the latter half of the 1730s, the quantity of bullion which the French company was carrying to Asia exceeded that of the EIC. The quality of textiles exported from Pondicherry was often better than the fabrics sold by the EIC in European markets.

An ongoing international conflict between Britain and France intensified the struggle between the English and French companies in India in the 1740s and 1750s. Both sought to enhance their influence in southern India by fostering factional quarrels among regional and local elites, and offering support to rival candidates in succession disputes in the Deccan, and in the principality of Arcot, comprising parts of north and central Tamil Nadu. Arcot town is located in northern Tamil Nadu (district Vellore). The political situation in Tamil Nadu was quite fluid in this period. Mughal possessions in the region had been administered from Arcot since the closing years of Aurangzeb's reign. Karnatak (or, more precisely, Karnatak Payanghat), which was the official nomenclature for these possessions, encompassed portions of present-day Tamil Nadu and Andhra Pradesh–Telangana. Karnatak was anglicized to 'Carnatic'. Carnatic (which is the term we shall use in the following discussion), *did not*, it should be noted, refer to what is now the state of Karnataka but indicated in eighteenth century colonial usage a loosely defined geographical area broadly corresponding to present-day Tamil Nadu. Arcot had actual control over small patches of this large territory, though Arcot was sometimes used interchangeably for the entire Carnatic.

Tanjore (Thanjavur) in central Tamil Nadu was under a Maratha dynasty of the Bhonsle clan. The founder of the dynasty, Venkoji (also known as Ekoji; c. 1675–84), was closely related to Shivaji. Large portions of Tamil Nadu were under the rule of poligars (palaiyakkarars) who were warrior chieftains who had acquired control over their respective localities in the centuries following the decline of the Vijayanagara empire. In the eighteenth century they were an important feature of the political landscape of Tamil Nadu.

Under Pierre-Benoît Dumas, governor of the Indian territories of the Compagnie from 1735 to 1741, the French company started intervening in local political conflicts so as to extend the scope of its influence. In return for some help given to the ruler of Tanjore in 1738, Dumas requested that Karaikal, located south of Pondicherry, be ceded to the French. Some differences over monetary compensation for the cession were quickly sorted out when the de facto chief of Trichinopoly or Trichy (Thiruchirapalli) Husain Dost Khan, better known as Chanda Sahib, intervened to ensure the transfer, paving the way for cooperation between Chanda Sahib and the French. Both were soon using each other to further their territorial ambitions. Chanda Sahib was nominally subject to the authority of Arcot. He was instrumental in the southward expansion of Arcot, in central Tamil Nadu, and further south in the Tinneveli (Tirunelveli) region.

In 1742, Joseph François Dupleix was appointed to succeed Dumas, and remained governor till 1754. He is the most prominent figure in the history of French colonial expansion in India. He was stationed in Chandernagore as superintendent from 1731 to 1741 before his promotion to the post of governor of all the territories of the French company in India. Dupleix's appointment coincided with the outbreak of a series of military conflicts in Europe which are together referred to as the War of Austrian Succession (1740–48). France and England were supporting different candidates as heirs to the Habsburg throne in this war. In 1744, France went to war with England. Several other European powers were drawn into the fight. Obviously, in India, the French company and the EIC were arrayed against each other, leading eventually to a full-blown war, the First Carnatic War (1746–48). During the course of this war the

French were able to capture Madras in 1746. This placed the EIC in a precarious position in the Coromandel. Major differences between Dupleix and another important colonial official, Mahé de La Bourdonnais, prevented the French from consolidating their position. Pondicherry itself was besieged by a British naval force in 1748. The siege lasted for forty days, but ended in disaster for the British force which eventually retreated. The successful resistance of Pondicherry reinforced the reputation of Dupleix as an able military leader. Meanwhile, the war had ended in Europe in 1748 and with this there was a brief interval in the Anglo-French conflict in India. Following protracted negotiations between the two sides, Madras was handed back to the EIC in 1749.

The next phase of the struggle between the two rivals, the Second Carnatic War (1749–54), coincided with fierce disputes over succession in the Mughal Deccan, and simultaneously in Arcot. These were the main political entities in those areas of south India in which the French and the English operated; both were nominally part of the Mughal empire. The Mughal subas of the Deccan collectively constituted a fully autonomous political entity. In the early 1720s, Nizam-ul-Mulk Chin Qilich Khan (Asaf Jah I), the then pre-eminent noble at the Mughal court, had relocated permanently from Delhi to the Deccan to consolidate his position as independent ruler of Mughal territories in the region. He may be regarded as the founder of the state of Hyderabad, whose rulers bore the hereditary title of 'nizam'. In the discussion which follows, we shall refer to the rulers of Hyderabad, belonging to the dynasty of Asaf Jah, by their title of nizam. This is the title by which they came to be known generally in the colonial period.

The Nizam-ul-Mulk governed the Deccan from Aurangabad. The capital of this nascent state was shifted to Hyderabad under Asaf Jah II (r. 1762–1803), around 1763. Significantly, the Nizam-ul-Mulk did not repudiate his allegiance to the Mughal emperor, Muhammad Shah (r. 1719–48); Muhammad

Shah passed away a few weeks before the Nizam-ul-Mulk's demise in June 1748. The latter had maintained that the Deccan subas were still very much part of the Mughal empire, and acknowledged the sovereignty of the emperor. On the one hand there was little possibility of the Mughal court actually intervening in the affairs of the south, and on the other Asaf Jah was keen to retain links with the north so that Hyderabad could 'draw upon the remaining administrative, military and cultural resources of the now increasingly defunct Mughal Empire in order to build itself up'.[3]

The death of Asaf Jah created a political vacuum which the French and the English rushed to fill by exploiting a dispute over succession. There were two contenders for the position of nizam: Nasir Jang (second son of Asaf Jah) and Muzaffar Jang (a grandson of Asaf Jah, i.e. the son of one of his daughters). Nasir Jang became the nizam following the death of Asaf Jah. He was immediately challenged by Muzaffar Jang who had the support of the French company. As might have been expected, the English were in the opposite camp, lending strength to Nasir Jang. The new nizam was assassinated in 1750.

The conflict at Hyderabad overlapped with a tussle at Arcot where Chanda Sahib aspired to supplant the incumbent ruler Anwaruddin Khan (1744–49). Anwaruddin governed Arcot as its subedar on behalf of the Nizam-ul-Mulk, although the principality owed its origins in the 1720s as a virtually independent state to Saadatullah Khan (d. 1732). Saadatullah Khan had been the Mughal diwan of Karnatak Payanghat. In the 1720s–30s, he established himself as the ruler of northern Tamil Nadu, with his seat at Arcot. Most of the European companies (English, French, Dutch, etc.) had their fortified settlements on the Coromandel coast in the Arcot territories. Hence the historical significance of the principality. In 1744,

[3]Munis D. Faruqui, 'At Empire's End: The Nizam, Hyderabad and Eighteenth-Century India', *Modern Asian Studies*, Vol. 43, No. 1, 2009, p. 35.

Anwaruddin succeeded in replacing the Navaiyat dynasty of Saadatullah Khan. Anwaruddin was an appointee of the Nizam-ul-Mulk while Chanda Sahib was related to the Navaiyats. The latter had been captured by the Maratha chief Raghoji Bhonsle in 1741 during a military campaign, and was released from captivity in 1748. Upon his return he asserted his claim to the subedari of Arcot, seeking to oust Anwaruddin in alliance with the French. Chanda Sahib and the French company had been allies since the 1730s. Chanda Sahib's claim had some basis, given the role he had played in the late 1730s in extending the influence of Arcot in the Carnatic. His long absence had reduced his political importance which he was now attempting to regain.

In 1749, Anwaruddin was killed at the battle of Ambur. This was an encounter in which the ruler of Arcot was fighting against the combined forces of Muzaffar Jang, Chanda Sahib, and the French. Chanda Sahib now declared himself the ruler or subedar of Arcot. On the other hand, the English championed the cause of Muhammad Ali, one of the sons of Anwaruddin. In a sense the French and the English were fighting a series of interrelated proxy wars which are collectively referred to as the Second Carnatic War. Their manoeuvres heightened tensions as they tried to push the respective candidates whom they were backing to be increasingly aggressive, assuring them of military assistance. The war engulfed large parts of southern India.

The slaying of Nasir Jang in December 1750 led Dupleix to move swiftly to ensure the succession of Muzaffar Jang as the nizam. Accompanied by a large contingent of French troops under the command of Charles de Bussy, Muzaffar Jang proceeded from Pondicherry towards Hyderabad. De Bussy was the key military officer of Dupleix's team and played a significant role in the French expansionist drive down to 1758. It was the English conquest of Bengal in 1757 that eventually destroyed the prospects of a French empire in India.

When Muzaffar Jang was in turn assassinated in February

1751, de Bussy backed Salabat Jang, the younger brother of Nasir Jang, as the successor. Obviously by now the French had established complete control over Hyderabad, control that they exercised through de Bussy. Salabat Jang's succession (unlike that of Nasir Jang or of Muzaffar Jang) was confirmed by the Mughal emperor, which gave to it more legitimacy. The French company received extensive grants in Tamil Nadu and the authority to govern a vast, somewhat undefined, area extending up to Madurai. More importantly, the new nizam ceded a few districts to the French company, prominent among which were Guntur, Rajahmundry, and Ellore (1753). These districts, located along the Seemandhra/Andhra coast would later be transferred to the EIC and were administratively designated as the Northern Circars (sarkars).

The Arcot issue was however not yet resolved. While the French were busy in Hyderabad, English forces had launched a massive offensive against Chanda Sahib, hoping thereby to check growing French influence in the region. Arcot and Trichinopoly were besieged, and successfully occupied. Then, in 1752, Chanda Sahib perished during the course of the conflict. This helped the EIC to establish its supremacy over the Carnatic. Their ally, Muhammad Ali, was acknowledged as the nawab (governor). The Wallajah family, to which he belonged, retained the title of nawab of Arcot (but not the territories) throughout the period of British rule.

Under the circumstances it would have appeared to contemporary observers that there was a stalemate in India. The two companies were therefore encouraged by well-wishers in Europe to arrive at a negotiated settlement. Representatives of the French and English companies commenced their dialogue in 1753. One outcome of these talks was the recall of Dupleix. The process leading to the recall had of course begun earlier when his policies came in for criticism by shareholders of the French company. It was felt that he had been instrumental in the escalation of hostilities between the English and the French.

His removal was thus considered essential. Charles Godeheu, a director of the French company, was sent out to India with wide-ranging powers to sort out the problems created by the Anglo-French struggle in Carnatic. He was given extensive authority, including that of imprisoning Dupleix if such a measure became necessary! Further, he was to report on the Indian affairs of the Compagnie. Dupleix's tenure ended in 1754. He returned to France having spent nearly thirty-four years in India. The English and the French agreed to a ceasefire in south India in the same year, terminating the Second Carnatic War (though not Anglo-French rivalry).

The story of French colonial intervention in India does not end here. The endgame of the Anglo-French contest was played out during the Third Carnatic War. De Bussy, we should remember, was still a force to be reckoned with in Hyderabad, and the Third Carnatic War was really a touch-and-go affair, which either side might have won. The result finally went in favour of the EIC because of its conquest of Bengal. It has been suggested that the removal of Dupleix, who remained very bitter about the matter till his death (1764), robbed the French of an outstanding chance to build an empire in India. This amounts to overestimating the role of the individual in shaping history. We ought to keep in mind that England was on the verge of an industrial take-off in the 1750s. The loot and plunder of Bengal contributed in no small measure to sustaining the first phase of the Industrial Revolution (c. 1760–80). One is not entirely certain that the French economy would have had such an opportunity.

The Third Carnatic War (1756–63) was an offshoot of the Seven Years' War in Europe (1757–63), which in turn was part of an international conflict among western powers for colonies, although it involved issues related specifically to European politics. The war in Europe was a continuation of the War of Austrian Succession. Some of the unresolved issues of the earlier war provided a reason for Prussia to launch a military offensive in which Austria was its main target. England, which was diplomatically allied with Prussia, too got involved in the conflict. Since France was an ally of Austria, the former also jumped into the fray. The English and the French were now at war wherever the two had been seeking to wrest colonial possessions from each other, especially in North America and India. In India there were two theatres of war: Bengal and Carnatic. We shall take up the story of Bengal in the following chapter. Suffice it to say here that with the outbreak of hostilities between England and France, the EIC's forces in Bengal occupied Chandernagore, thereby crippling the commercial operations of the French company. It was against this backdrop that the French government sent a senior military officer Thomas Arthur de Lally-Tollendal as commander general of colonies in the East Indies with instructions to inflict maximum damage on the English. De Lally-Tollendal was given sweeping powers and had under him a large military force. Nevertheless, his command did not extend to the sea; the French naval forces were under Admiral d'Aché.

De Lally-Tollendal reached India in April 1758. De Bussy had already taken over English factories on the Orissa coast and annexed a large stretch of territory in the area, between Ganjam and Masulipatnam; de Lally-Tollendal's campaigns did not meet with much success. Madras was besieged by the French towards the end of 1758. The attempt to capture it was given up within a few weeks. De Lally-Tollendal continued to conduct campaigns sporadically till the beginning of 1760 when he was finally defeated at Wandiwash (Vandavasi, in Tiruvannamalai district of present-day Tamil Nadu). With the rout of the French in the battle of Wandiwash, the English company was able to establish its ascendancy over large parts of peninsular India.

In June 1758, shortly after de Lally-Tollendal assumed command, de Bussy was ordered by him to move out of Hyderabad to render assistance with military operations in Carnatic. He participated in the fighting at Wandiwash, where he was captured by the English and subsequently released. Much later, in 1783, de Bussy was appointed governor general of French colonial possessions in India. He passed away in Pondicherry in 1785.

Scholars generally agree that recalling de Bussy was an unwise step because the French lost the strategic advantage they had gained through their hold over Hyderabad. They were never to regain their position in the state after de Bussy's departure. De Bussy's influence in the Hyderabad state, lasting for nearly eight years, had made it possible for the French company to penetrate and undermine the independence of the state. This was done by using the resources of Hyderabad itself, thus minimizing the cost of colonial expansion. De Bussy's Hyderabad model was to provide the inspiration for the English company's 'subsidiary alliance' scheme for colonial subjugation, which will be discussed in a later chapter.

The English followed up their success at Wandiwash by occupying Pondicherry in 1761. In a final act of humiliation, de Lally-Tollendal was made captive and transported to England as a prisoner of war. Upon his return to France a terrible fate awaited him. Already the Compagnie, and the government, had placed the entire blame for the comprehensive defeat of the French squarely on de Lally-Tollendal to deflect criticism of their own failings. Upon his arrival in Paris, de Lally-Tollendal was immediately thrown into prison. In 1766, he was tried for treason, found guilty, and sentenced to execution. He was hauled through the streets in a most humiliating manner while being taken to his place of execution, and beheaded.

When peace was restored in Europe in 1763, Pondicherry and other settlements were restored to France under the provisions of the Treaty of Paris (1763). However, the possibility of a French empire in India was over. In Hyderabad, Salabat Jang was deposed by his younger brother, Asaf Jah II (also known as Nizam Ali), in 1762. Asaf Jah II emerged as the staunchest ally of the EIC in southern India. During a military campaign prior to the engagement at Wandiwash, English forces had occupied the Northern Circars. These districts constituted the first extensive stretch of territory acquired by the EIC in the region and were incorporated into the Madras Presidency. By the end of the Third and final Carnatic War the English company had become a territorial power in south India, and had established pre-eminence at Hyderabad. The most substantial gains, of course, were made in eastern India. The success of the EIC in the Battle of Plassey (Palashi) in 1757 brought Bengal and Bihar (and some areas of northern Orissa) under its control.

THREE

BEGINNINGS OF EMPIRE

The search for supplies of raw silk for its Japan trade took the Dutch company to Orissa, and thence to Bengal. This was the era of Shah Jahan (r. 1628–58). Immediately after the expulsion of the Portuguese from Hugli in 1632, the VOC began exploring possibilities of setting up a base in Orissa, mainly to procure raw silk. Simultaneously, the EIC too made an appearance in the province. We can see that rival European companies kept a close watch both on local and regional politics, as well as on each other. In 1633, the VOC established its first factory in Orissa at Hariharpur (Jagatsinghpur), a port on a tributary of the Mahanadi River, giving access to the Bay of Bengal. The same year an EIC delegation led by one of its employees named Ralph Cartwright travelled to Cuttack to petition the provincial governor for permission to engage in trade in Mughal Orissa. Cartwright managed to obtain the requisite authorization, along with exemption from custom duties. The Company promptly proceeded to set up a factory at Hariharpur, and shortly afterwards another at Balasore. It soon extended its business to Bengal, where a factory was set up in the 1650s at the port of Hugli. Although trade in Bengal goods gradually increased, for the time being it lagged far behind the EIC's commercial dealings in Gujarat and the Coromandel. Cotton textiles and raw silk were the main commodities purchased from Bengal for the European market during the latter half of the seventeenth century.

Towards the end of the seventeenth century the EIC established another trading outpost on the banks of the Hugli river, which later became its headquarters in eastern India—Fort William. This outpost was the nucleus of the settlement that grew into the city of Calcutta, the beginnings of which may be traced back to the Company's possession of the villages of Sutanuti, Govindapur, and Kalikata. The three villages, over which the Company had acquired talluqdari rights by the 1690s, together constituted the site at which the fort and the surrounding settlement developed.[1]

The EIC gained a lead over their European rivals in the region because it was able to claim, since as early as the 1650s, duty exemptions. How it had managed this is not entirely clear, but initially some deception was involved. By the end of the century the English had obtained proper sanction from the relevant Mughal official for 'duty-exempt status' in eastern India against the payment of 'an annual tribute of Rs 3,000'.[2] It has been estimated by Om Prakash that in the decade 1711–20, the VOC would have paid a sum of about Rs 1.2 lakhs (by contemporary standards) as customs duties in Bengal. If we assume that the EIC would have had to pay an equivalent sum in the absence of the concession, this figure should give us a rough idea of the 'differential advantage' that it enjoyed. The concession was further confirmed through a farman, or royal decree, issued to the EIC by Emperor Farrukhsiyar (r. 1713–19) in 1717.

The EIC's charter had made it the sole entity authorized to engage in trade between the East Indies and England. This implied that no individual, including employees of the Company

[1]Talluqdars were landed magnates who derived their authority from the state (and their own ability to mobilize armed force locally), with the responsibility to ensure the collection of land revenue payable by villages of their respective estates. They wielded almost unlimited power over the inhabitants of their estates. Strictly speaking, they were not the owners of all the land which was part of the estate and did not possess 'ancient' rights, though they took away a fairly large share of agrarian produce for themselves.
[2]Prakash, *European Commercial Enterprise in Pre-Colonial India*, p. 134.

stationed in Asia, could undertake any commercial activity privately. Company servants could not buy or sell goods on their own account. However, limited private trade was permitted, mainly within Asia. The EIC's involvement in the intra-Asian sector was not as extensive as that of the VOC. Company employees accumulated private profits by shipping commodities such as textiles and sugar from Bengal to Surat and the Persian Gulf. Private trade by servants of the Company contributed to the growing presence of the English in the commerce of eastern India. Curiously, Calcutta-based English traders were able to successfully operate in the western Indian Ocean (Persian Gulf and Red Sea) well into the middle of the eighteenth century while their geographically better located counterparts based in Surat or Bombay failed to do so. Gradually, by the third quarter of the century the Bengal trade shifted its orientation towards the eastern Indian Ocean. In other words, English enterprise in eastern India was continuously vibrant for an entire century before the Battle of Plassey.

The EIC's trade, combined with the private trade of its servants, cumulatively reduced the revenues of Bengal due to the systematic misuse of exemptions allowed by the Mughal state. As the English penetrated the economy of the suba, they claimed privileges that had not been officially granted to them, thereby undermining the finances of the province to a considerable extent. Much has been made of a supposed distinction between the export trade of the EIC on the one hand, and the export-cum-inland trade of its servants, in narratives of the genesis of the conflict between the English and the provincial government of Bengal. It is not as though the Bengal administration was trying to differentiate legally between the Company's official trade and the personal earnings of its servants—a matter that would have concerned the EIC alone. What was a matter of worry was the unscrupulous manner in which both were together swindling Bengal by withholding the payment of duties.

The Mughal suba of Bengal had become more or less autonomous by the 1720s. It was ruled by the family of a prominent official of the Aurangzeb era, Murshid Quli Khan (d. 1727). Murshid Quli Khan and his immediate successors acknowledged the formal suzerainty of the Mughal emperor. They regularly sent a share of the revenues of the province as tribute or peshkash to the emperor, though the quantum of the tribute dwindled over a period of time. The family of Murshid Quli Khan was replaced by that of Alivardi Khan in 1740. Alivardi Khan was a key figure in the chief establishment of Bengal. The domain of the governor or nâzim of Bengal, whose seat of authority was by this time at Murshidabad, included Bihar and (nominally at least) Orissa. Alivardi Khan had held several leading positions at the provincial level, including charge of Bihar, before he unseated the incumbent nâzim or nawab and took over.

Alivardi Khan's rule ushered in an era of political stability which has been misread in some writings on the eighteenth century in terms of regional economic prosperity. The decline of the Mughal empire is supposed to have benefited provincial elites such as those of Bengal. This is an oversimplification for two reasons. First, Alivardi Khan had come to rely heavily on bankers for revenue collection which enabled a few financial concerns to make huge profits through what actually amounted to usury. The most important of these banking firms was that of the famous Jagat Seths which rose to prominence under Murshid Quli Khan. The business was established by Manikchand (Oswal) and his father, who had migrated from Rajasthan to Patna where Manikchand initially set up his banking concern. The firm had branches at several places, including Delhi and Dacca. Manikchand was soon involved in high finance, providing credit to Mughal provincial functionaries and arranging for the transfer of imperial revenues from Bengal to Delhi. In recognition of his services, he received the title of 'Seth' from emperor Farrukhsiyar (titles by the emperor were still much sought after). Following the death of Manikchand in 1714, his nephew, and adopted son, Fatehchand became the head of the Murshidabad branch of the firm. Fatehchand had been groomed by Manikchand for carrying on the business at what was by now the most important location of the banking house. Fatehchand enlarged his financial empire by acquiring a grip over the revenues of Bengal through his proximity to Alivardi Khan. In the early 1720s, Emperor Muhammad Shah bestowed on Fatehchand the more distinguished title of 'Jagat Seth' as a mark of royal favour. The title was a recognition of his pre-eminent status as a banker. Fatehchand and his successors are better known by the ceremonial title of Jagat Seth, as is their business concern. During the first half of the eighteenth century the interests of a powerful section of provincial elites in Bengal were intertwined with those of the Jagat Seths.

Besides, colonial trade had made deep inroads into the economy so that large earnings actually accrued to European traders and private companies. The resulting vulnerability of the state made it easier for European traders to defy its authority. Thus, whenever steps were taken to prevent the EIC and its servants from misusing their concessions they tried to use a combination of intimidation and bribes to evade the payment of duties. The high stakes that private English traders had in the export trade of Bengal made them more and more aggressive. In order to procure cloth at cheap rates they forced suppliers and producers (through their agents or gumasthas) to sell at unremunerative prices. Not only were they undercutting Indian traders but each other and their employer, the EIC, as well.

The growing contradictions between the European traders and sections of the ruling class in Bengal, of which the bankers had become a vital component, escalated into a major conflict soon after the death of Alivardi Khan in 1756. In a bid to enhance their influence at the Murshidabad court the English fomented intrigues that would place their allies in positions of power. Among their allies they could count the banking house of Jagat Seth, which due to its hold over the finances of the state already had considerable clout at the court. As for the leading officials at the court, the EIC had cultivated ties with Mir Jafar and Rai Durlabhram Som. Mir Jafar was a brother-in-law of Alivardi Khan and commanded some of the contingents of the army; Rai Durlabh held charge of the diwani or revenue department. Commercial and military rivalry with the French made it all the more necessary for the English to engage in schemes for grabbing a share of political power. The steady growth of French commerce at Chandernagore (and the continuing presence of the VOC) lent urgency to such an agenda.

The conquest of Bengal is often erroneously referred to as a 'revolution' in colonial writings. What 'revolution' implies in this context is succinctly stated by P. E. Roberts (author of perhaps the most outstanding university-level textbook on the political history of the Company period, though written entirely from a colonial perspective): 'The revolution of 1756–7 was not primarily or solely the conquest of an Indian province by a European trading settlement. It was rather the overthrow of a foreign (Muhammadan) government by the trading and financial classes, native (Hindu) and British; both the latter gained commercially, though the British took the predominant part in the actual events and alone succeeded to the political sovereignty. The fall of the Muhammadan power was precipitated by its internal dissensions.'[3] In this formulation, Roberts gives a religious colour to the events in Bengal. What Roberts was articulating represented the consensus among colonial historians on the issue by the early twentieth century, and became useful for contemporary communal mobilization.

◆

[3] P. E. Roberts, *History of British India Under the Company and the Crown*, Oxford: Oxford University Press, 1921, third edition, 1952, p. 130.

Alivardi Khan was succeeded by his grandson Siraj-ud-daula. Mounting tensions between the EIC and Nawab Siraj-ud-daula set in motion events that culminated in the Battle of Plassey. Seeking to discipline the Company and its servants, Siraj-ud-daula drove the English out of Calcutta in June 1756 when they refused to comply with instructions not to strengthen the defences of Fort William. While most of the Company's servants had evacuated the fort before it was occupied by the nawab's forces on 20 June, there were some who had stayed behind. They were captured and imprisoned in a small room (the so-called 'black hole' of colonial accounts) where they spent the entire night. Many of the captives are supposed to have died of suffocation. The exact number of prisoners, or of casualties, is not known. Neither do we have much information about the actual dimensions of the 'black hole'. The 'authorized' colonial version of the incident, as it appeared in later textbooks, was that 'a hundred and forty-six English prisoners, one of them a woman, were forced to spend the night of an Indian summer in the military punishment cell of the fortress, a room of about eighteen feet square. One hundred and twenty-three perished in the inferno...'.[4] Among the survivors of the tragedy was John Holwell, commandant of the fort at the time of its surrender. He is the author of the only detailed account of the incident that has come down to us. Holwell's impact was more far-reaching. Versions contained in all contemporary sources can be traced back to him. In the words of Partha Chatterjee, who has recently undertaken an exhaustive reappraisal of the incident, these 'are not independent pieces of evidence but rather the result of consultations with Holwell or a reading of his various descriptions of the event'.[5] The grossly exaggerated colonial narrative of the incident became the justification for the

[4]Ibid., p. 133.
[5]Partha Chatterjee, *The Black Hole of Empire: History of a Global Practice of Power*, Ranikhet: Permanent Black, South Asia edition, 2012, p. 19.

conquest of Bengal. Plassey became necessary, it was repeatedly asserted, because of the terrible suffering endured by those incarcerated in the 'black hole'.

Indeed Calcutta was far too valuable to be given up without a fight. Troops were sent out from Madras led by an officer named Robert Clive, backed by a royal naval force commanded by Charles Watson, to recapture Fort William. The subsequent infamy of Clive has allowed Watson to slide into obscurity (he died in Calcutta in August 1757). Clive and Watson successfully occupied Calcutta in January 1757. A sham peace was then concluded with the nawab by which the privileges of the EIC were restored. Meanwhile, Clive was involved in secret negotiations for removing Siraj-ud-daula. Mir Jafar and Rai Durlabh agreed to be part of this conspiracy. They were to be given military assistance in return for large payments to the Company and personally to its servants. The dealings were so murky that Clive double-crossed the chief go-between, a prosperous merchant by the name of Amirchand (Amichand/Omichund). He even forged the signature of Watson on a document when he found the naval officer to be a reluctant accomplice in one of his schemes. The overall plan seems to have been coordinated by the Jagat Seth firm which actually possessed the resources for making immediate payments to the Company.

Once the plot was in place, the Company's troops marched, in the third week of June 1757, northwards from Calcutta in the direction of Murshidabad. Siraj-ud-daula's army confronted them at Plassey, located about 50 kilometres south of his capital. A military engagement took place on 23 June in which the Company's forces were able to easily overwhelm their opponent. The greater part of the nawab's army did not participate in the fighting on the instructions of Mir Jafar and Rai Durlabh. Siraj-ud-daula was put to death after the battle. Mir Jafar became the new nawab. This marked the beginning of British rule over Bengal and some parts of Bihar, though it took some time for the EIC to consolidate its position as the de facto ruler of eastern India.[6]

The EIC's incessant demands for money and territory, and constant interference, made it impossible for Mir Jafar to run the government. Further, he does not seem to have been a particularly competent person. In another factional manoeuvre, Mir Jafar's son-in-law, Mir Qasim, was acknowledged as the nawab in October 1760 (Clive had returned to England, temporarily, in February). Mir Qasim too faced similar problems, but unlike Mir Jafar he decided to resist the Company's unreasonable demands. He began by enforcing rules pertaining to the payment of customs and transit duties, checking the blatant evasions and malpractices of the English company and its servants. This was necessary not just for restoring the authority of the state, but more importantly for realizing adequate revenues to strengthen the army. Mir Qasim was determined to challenge the EIC militarily if it continued to defy the nawab's government. This was the last serious attempt to salvage Bengal from colonial depredation and led to the showdown at Baksar (Buxar). In the words of P. J. Marshall, Mir Qasim's 'three years as Nawab [1760–63] were...to prove to be the most determined effort ever made to establish an independent state in eastern India'.[7]

Mir Qasim strengthened his hold over the finances, undertook reorganization of the army, and carried out a purge of pro-EIC elements. He moved his court from Murshidabad to Munger in Bihar (east of Patna). This reduced the EIC's meddling in day-to-day administrative matters. The Company's officials had, for

[6]Whereas substantial portions of territory situated in present-day West Bengal and Bihar, and Bangladesh, were subordinated by the EIC following the Battle of Plassey, it was over a period of several years that the entire region was incorporated into its Indian empire. Besides, the Company's control extended to some tracts of Orissa lying north of the river Subarnarekha. Most of Orissa, south of the river, was under the Bhonsle rulers of Nagpur.
[7]P. J. Marshall, *East Indian Fortunes: The British in Bengal in the Eighteenth Century*, Oxford: Oxford University Press, 1976, p. 85.

instance, constantly interfered with bureaucratic appointments which had been strongly resented by the nawab. One should bear in mind that the machinery of the state was not entirely under the control of the English after 1757, as is often assumed. It took them several years to dismantle the pre-colonial edifice. Even then they had to retain certain features of the nawabi regime: the position of the nawab itself was not dispensed with till the nineteenth century.

With Mir Qasim's capital located at Munger, Bihar became the main zone of conflict. By the middle of 1763, the EIC had managed to bring about another realignment whereby Mir Jafar was once again recognized as nawab by the pro-English faction. The EIC formally declared war against Mir Qasim in July 1763. A wider conflict developed as Mir Qasim forged an alliance with the recently installed Mughal emperor Shah Alam (r. 1759–1806) and Shuja-ud-daula, Mughal subedar or provincial governor of Awadh (1754–75). For reasons that we need not go into here, Shah Alam (Ali Gauhar) had been in exile in eastern India since 1758. Upon receiving information of the assassination of his father, Emperor Alamgir II, in 1759, he had declared himself emperor. The succession was recognized by most of those who mattered in the politics of those regions of the subcontinent that had been encompassed by the Mughal empire in the early eighteenth century.

In view of his shaky position in northern India, Shah Alam was keen to acquire a base for himself in the eastern provinces of the empire. For nearly two years after his accession the wandering emperor was occupied with military operations for this purpose, mainly in Bihar but in Bengal as well. The situation in Bihar was rather fluid at this time; the EIC's hold over it was tenuous, as was that of Mir Qasim and other Mughal potentates. Shuja-ud-daula was among the Mughal potentates with an interest in the area, the more so as the eastern boundaries of his domain, Awadh, lay close to Bihar. Consequently, he aligned himself with Shah Alam for extending the boundaries of Awadh eastwards. Shah Alam formally appointed Shuja-ud-daula as the imperial vazir and together the two devoted their energies to acquiring control over Bihar which inevitably led to a conflict with the Company. They were soon joined by Mir Qasim.

The tussle between the two sides culminated in the Battle of Baksar (October 1764). Baksar, contrary to textbook descriptions of the episode, was certainly not a major military confrontation. During the monsoon season of 1764, Shuja-ud-daula, accompanied by Shah Alam, had set up his camp at Baksar where he had withdrawn after an unsuccessful assault on Patna (Patna was under the Company's control). On 23 October, fighting at Baksar commenced with heavy artillery fire from both sides. While the cannonade progressed, Shuja led a fierce cavalry charge against English troops, forcing them to flee. A large number of the Company's men perished in this onslaught. At this point the English noticed that a detachment of their troops was out of the opponent's reach. Taking these men with him, the EIC commanding officer (Hector Munro) stealthily approached the deserted houses located on the outskirts of the township of Baksar. Moving along the main street, the English soldiers took by surprise the contingent which Shuja had stationed behind these residential structures. For some time utter chaos prevailed and eventually a section of troops loyal to Shuja fell back. Other contingents however went on fighting. Many of Shuja's fighting units were trapped elsewhere in a position from which it was difficult to attack the enemy, and a disorderly retreat ensued leading to heavy losses among the Awadh combatants. Yet Shuja, not entirely convinced that the Company had won a decisive victory, stayed on in his camp for a while. The emperor on the other hand behaved as though he were indifferent to the outcome of the battle, which in any case he did not consider to be of critical importance. Mir Qasim's political career, however, ended with Baksar.

The EIC was not entirely confident that it could defeat Shuja in an extensive war. Thus, shortly after the battle, officials of the Company made overtures of friendship to the emperor. From Baksar, Shah Alam had proceeded to Banaras and thence to Allahabad. Meanwhile, the Company indicated that it was willing to come to an understanding with the vazir. Negotiations began in right earnest when Clive returned to India in May 1765 for his second term as governor of Bengal. In August that year he travelled to Allahabad to pay his respects to the emperor. Then, shuttling between Allahabad and Banaras (where Shuja had set up his headquarters), he persuaded the emperor and his vazir to grant the diwani of Bengal, Bihar, and Orissa to the Company. This implied that the EIC would have the right to manage the revenues of these three Mughal administrative units. The principal argument in favour of the Company was that revenues could not be collected properly without its assistance since the administration had collapsed. And if the provincial government did not have a sufficiently large income, the emperor could not receive his share of the revenues of these subas. Significantly, during the consultations with Clive, Shah Alam refused to concede that he had been defeated at Baksar.

The farman granting the diwani of Bengal, Bihar, and Orissa to the EIC was received by Clive at a formal durbar held by the emperor at Allahabad on 12 August 1765. Established protocol was scrupulously followed on the occasion, to which Clive willingly submitted. An important condition laid down in the decree was that the Company would ensure the payment of 'twenty-six lacs of rupees a year, for our royal revenue which sum has been appointed from the Nawab Najm-ud-daulah Bahadur and remit the same to the royal sarkar'.[8] Najm-ud-daula, nawab of Bengal (1765–66), had succeeded his father Mir Jafar (who passed away in early 1765) to the subedari of the eastern provinces of the empire and had already been officially

[8]K. K. Datta, *Shah Alam II and the East India Company*, Calcutta: The World Press, 1965, p. 39.

recognized by the emperor through a royal communication issued under his private seal a few months before the diwani decree was finalized.

◆

With the conquest of Bengal began the process of the subjugation of the entire Indian subcontinent, a process that continued for the next hundred years and even beyond (the conquest of Burma was not completed till the mid-1880s). As we have seen in the previous chapter, the EIC had used its coastal settlements as bases for expansion into the interior. The Company continued to systematically weaken local/regional polities elsewhere by intervening in their disputes, as they had done in Bengal. Apart from being engaged in devising means for the appropriation of the resources of Bengal, for much of the latter half of the eighteenth century the British concentrated their energies on establishing effective control over south India through either direct annexation or indirect subordination of political entities in the region.

From the late 1760s down to 1799, the Company's expansionist drive in south India was fiercely resisted by the state of Mysore under Haidar Ali and his son Tipu. This was one of the reasons why the British were eager to strengthen their alliance with Hyderabad which, as we have noted, had already been reduced to a junior partner of the Company after the Third Carnatic War. Haidar Ali began his career as a military officer in the Mysore army. He rose to prominence during the struggles of the 1740s in southern India. Having successfully intervened at several critical moments to defend Mysore during various regional conflicts, he emerged as the principal commander of the state's army by the end of the 1750s, and de facto ruler of the state in 1761. Within the next two decades, Mysore became the leading state of the region with an army that could effectively challenge the EIC. The state's borders extended to the river Krishna in the north; its territories encompassed much of present-day Karnataka, large portions of Andhra, most of western Tamil Nadu barring the extreme south, and northern Kerala.

Mysore and the surrounding countryside were part of the Vijayanagara empire in the late medieval period. By the end of the sixteenth century the area became autonomous with the decline of Vijayanagara rule. The petty chiefs of Mysore, belonging to the Wodeyar family, originally owed their allegiance to Vijayanagara. Throughout the seventeenth century the Wodeyars expanded their domain, till by the time of Chikka Deva Raja (r. 1673–1704) it extended to most of the central portion of inner south India, roughly corresponding to present-day Karnataka excluding the sea coast. This expansion was carried out on the basis of a series of local alliances, all of which could not be sustained in the face of the southward thrust of the Mughal empire. The state survived by acknowledging the overlordship of the Mughal emperor.

With the collapse of Mughal authority in the early decades of the eighteenth century, Mysore too began facing problems. Its territories intersected with those of Hyderabad, Arcot, and the Marathas. Therefore, it was invariably drawn into disputes among these powers, and those of the European companies as well. The Second Carnatic War, which engulfed large parts of south India, witnessed rival armies crisscrossing Mysorean territories. Haidar Ali appears in history against the backdrop of this conflict. He got involved in campaigns linked to the Hyderabad succession tussle and more earnestly in those for the control of Arcot. It was during these campaigns that he seems to have come in contact with the French through de Bussy's subordinates. The tilt towards France had become more pronounced by the early 1750s; ties between Mysore and France acquired greater depth in the latter half of the century, particularly after the French Revolution.

Once the French had been confined to Pondicherry and a few tiny enclaves on the east coast at the end of the Third

Carnatic War, Haidar Ali concentrated his energy on driving the British out of southern India. For the rest of his life, he was primarily engaged in fighting the EIC and simultaneously building a powerful and territorially extensive kingdom of Mysore. From claiming some of the areas that were part of the Arcot ruler's realm, Haidar Ali moved towards claiming nawabship of the entire Carnatic region, something that was incompatible with the political ambitions of the incumbent nawab, Muhammad Ali. It may be recalled that the EIC had lent its support to Muhammad Ali in his conflict with Chanda Sahib. Haidar Ali was aligned with Chanda Sahib.

The EIC was, of course, the main target of Haidar Ali's military offensive. He inflicted defeat on the British in two successive wars, the First and Second Anglo-Mysore Wars. The first war began in 1767 and ended in 1769 when Haidar Ali's forces reached the outskirts of Madras, compelling the Company to sue for peace on his terms. This was a severe blow to the Company's prestige. The second war (1780–84) was a fiercely fought military contest ranging over a vast area stretching from Mangalore on the west coast to Arcot in the east. In one of these engagements, the battle of Pollilur (Pullalur, near Kanchipuram) in September 1780, in which the Mysore army was led by Tipu, the EIC suffered massive losses—'the severest blow', it was noted at that time, 'that the English ever sustained in India'.[9]

Haidar Ali passed away in December 1782 while the war was in full swing. He was succeeded by Tipu Sahib (later, Tipu Sultan) who continued the fight against the Company with extraordinary vigour and succeeded in checking British expansionist designs in south India for the time being. Incidentally, it has been pointed out that 'sultan' was not a title used by Tipu, but was part of his name and that 'Tipu',

[9]Thomas Munro, cited in Mohibbul Hasan, *History of Tipu Sultan*, Delhi: Aakar Books, 2005 (reprint of second edition, 1971), p. 15.

contrary to popular belief, does not mean tiger.[10] The 'tiger motif' which came to symbolize Tipu, specifically his challenge to the British, seems to have evolved after he became the ruler of Mysore: 'The tiger motif was ubiquitous on the uniforms and weapons used by his soldiers, and on Tipu's coins, flags, and throne. An enduring curiosity for more than two hundred years has been a mechanical tiger—now displayed in the Victoria and Albert Museum in London—which can be seen devouring a British soldier while emitting snarls, to the accompaniment of the victim's wails.'[11] The 'mechanical tiger' toy was carried to London after the final Anglo-Mysore war (1799) for display at the EIC's museum located at its headquarters in Leadenhall Street in London where it instantly became the most prominent attraction. The solidity of its manufacture is attested to by the fact that it endured countless demonstrations of its functioning for the pleasure of visitors for over a century before it was accidentally, and irretrievably, damaged in the 1940s. The mechanical tiger was but one small item constituting the Company's collection of objects plundered from Mysore, which included the priceless jewelled homa bird which had adorned the canopy of Tipu's masnad, his throne. A large part of the immense booty was also disbursed among various private collections. A substantial portion of the Company's official collection is today housed in the Victoria and Albert Museum (London), a major repository of colonial artefacts in England.

In 1787, Tipu was to declare himself badshah after repudiating the overlordship of the Mughal emperor Shah Alam. Kate Brittlebank has argued that already by the mid-1780s Tipu was asserting his authority without reference to the emperor.[12] This was to be seen in the omission of Shah Alam's name from coins struck by Tipu, and the insertion of

[10]Hasan, *History of Tipu Sultan*, pp. 6–7.
[11]Chatterjee, *Black Hole of Empire*, p. 93.
[12]Kate Brittlebank, *Tipu Sultan's Search for Legitimacy: Islam and Kingship in a Hindu Domain*, Delhi: Oxford University Press, 1997, p. 65.

Tipu's name in the khutba (Friday sermon) instead of that of the emperor as was customary. In other words, Tipu projected himself as the legitimate ruler of an independent kingdom. An impressive victory at Mangalore, which brought the war to an end in 1784, gave him a stature that lent credibility to his claim to being an absolute monarch.

There has been considerable discussion in the past few decades about the extent to which Mysore under Haidar Ali and Tipu can be regarded as having become 'modern'. We know that Haidar Ali had begun reorganizing the army, especially the cavalry and artillery. He introduced new technology of which the deadly Mysore rockets are a prominent example. These were missiles comprising an iron tube fastened to a bamboo rod. The propellant (gunpowder) was packed into the iron tube. When fired, these rockets could attain a range of nearly 2 kilometres. Taken aback by the effectiveness of these rockets the British were motivated to innovate in this field leading to the development of improved versions by the first decade of the nineteenth century.

Military reorganization went hand in hand with streamlining of the revenue collection apparatus. The role of intermediaries was substantially reduced so that the burden on the peasants was somewhat diminished and the state was able to appropriate a larger share of the produce. This made possible the drive towards centralization which was the principal objective of measures initiated under Haidar Ali and continued by Tipu. An important purpose of acquiring greater centralized control over the state's share of the produce was to have access to enlarged resources for maintaining a well-equipped standing army, trained in accordance with modern principles of drill and deployment. These modernizing tendencies intensified in Tipu's reign with the ruler himself contributing to them through a series of state-sponsored schemes. An impetus was given to trade in a wide range of commodities with the state directly participating in commercial activities. Manufacture was encouraged as a matter of conscious policy. Further, Tipu seems to have been much more aware than many of his contemporaries in Asia of trends in global politics. For this reason he attempted to forge international alliances by sending embassies to Turkey and France. His relationship with France became more cordial after the revolution in which his sympathies lay with the Jacobins. This does not necessarily mean that Tipu endorsed Jacobin radical ideals (though he did become a member of the 'Jacobin Club' that was established in Mysore); his declarations in favour of the Jacobins should be read as a political move to enlist the support of France in his struggle against the British.

Partha Chatterjee has characterized Tipu as an 'early modern absolute monarch'.[13] He argues that instead of downplaying the worth of Tipu's interventionist strategy, we need to appreciate the possibilities that were created by his decisive personal involvement in almost all aspects of administration: '...the absolutist early modern tendency responded to the new historical conditions of uncertainty and instability not by reasserting a conservative dogma of dynastic legitimacy but rather by stressing the personal qualities of effective and decisive leadership displayed by the prince. The absolutist element in this early modern tendency was, in this sense not an element of conservative restoration; it was potentially revolutionary.'[14] In the end, of course, unrelenting colonial aggression stifled the possibilities for modernization that were inherent in this progressive development.

Given that Mysore was the main obstacle to British expansion in south India, the destruction of the state became a matter of great urgency for them. This objective was accomplished between 1789 and 1799 through the Third and Fourth Anglo-Mysore Wars. The third war (1789–92) began when Governor General Charles Cornwallis launched an offensive against

[13]Chatterjee, *Black Hole of Empire*, pp. 85–93.
[14]Ibid., p. 93.

Mysore to prevent it from extending its territory in Kerala. The Company managed to enlist the support of Hyderabad and the Marathas against Tipu in the effort. The rulers of the states of Travancore and Cochin in south Kerala were already hostile to Mysore. Tipu was compelled to fight simultaneously on several fronts which overstretched his military resources. The war resulted in his losing nearly half of his kingdom, besides having to pay a heavy indemnity. The territories ceded by Tipu were shared between the British, the Marathas, and Hyderabad. The Company thus acquired control over north Kerala (Malabar) while Mysore lost its access to the sea. The EIC also got some districts in Tamil Nadu, which were added to the Madras Presidency. The task of subjugating Mysore was completed by Richard Wellesley who became governor general in 1798. Wellesley was sent out with a mandate to ensure British ascendancy over the Indian subcontinent. Napoleon Bonaparte, who was now in power in France, had just begun preparing for an invasion of Egypt, announcing his intention to significantly expand the French colonial empire in Africa and Asia. There were reports in circulation to the effect that Tipu had asked the French for military assistance to expel the British from India. The possibility of an alliance between Tipu and Napoleon was sought to be pre-empted by sending troops to invade Mysore in 1798. This marked the beginning of the final Anglo-Mysore war. The invasion was preceded by Wellesley's insistence that Tipu agree to a humiliating treaty that would have made him a subservient ally of the British, something that was unacceptable to the ruler of Mysore. A massive offensive was then launched by Wellesley. Mysore was attacked from both the east and west simultaneously.

In the fierce fighting that ensued, Tipu died valiantly defending his capital Seringapatam (Srirangapatna) during the culminating battle of the war (4 May 1799). It might be asked whether, notwithstanding his personal courage and his numerous successes on the battlefield, Tipu had a thorough understanding of advances in modern warfare. A British officer who took part in the battle, later commented that Tipu 'fell in the defence of his capital; but he fell, performing the duties of a common soldier, not of a general'.[15]

His corpse, bearing several marks of injury, was discovered under a heap of bodies of soldiers who had perished in the intense fighting, and immediately subjected to abuse. Once the town had been captured there was a mad scramble for the riches of the conquered kingdom. The pillage, on a scale that was virtually unprecedented, continued for several hours after Seringapatam was occupied, giving an opportunity to each European soldier to amass a mini-fortune. Every house was plundered. Tales of the fabulous wealth that some of these soldiers are supposed to have carried back with them to England, in the form of rare jewels or other valuable objects, later found their way into literary productions such as Wilkie Collins's bestseller *The Moonstone* (1868) and became an integral part of British imperial imagination. *The Moonstone* is a famous detective novel, one of the first of this genre in the English language, which has as its central theme the theft of a valuable diamond (the 'moonstone' of the title), belonging to a young woman in mid-nineteenth century Victorian England. The diamond, of Indian provenance, is supposed to be sacred, and for generations has been guarded by three (Indian) priests. It had been carried to England following the battle of Seringapatam by an officer who had taken it as his share of the booty from Tipu's palace. In the story, successors of the three priests who had been killed at Seringapatam while trying to protect the diamond, travel to England to retrieve it and play an important role in the plot. The novel opens with a chapter entitled 'The Storming of Seringapatam', and describes the manner in which the imaginary gem came into the possession of its fictional

---

[15]Mark Wilks, quoted in Rajmohan Gandhi, *Modern South India: A History from the 17th Century to Our Times,* Delhi: Aleph Book Company, 2018, p. 110.

owner John Herncastle. Collins used well-known paintings and published material for the description, which may perhaps even be read as a critique of the violence and plunder that had ensued after the fall of the capital of the Mysore kingdom.

> I got to an open door, and saw bodies of two Indians (by their dress, as I guessed, officers of the palace) lying across the entrance, dead. A cry inside hurried me into a room, which appeared to serve as an armoury. A third Indian, mortally wounded, was sinking at the feet of a man whose back was towards me. The man turned at the instant when I came in, and I saw John Herncastle, with a torch in one hand, and a dagger dripping with blood in the other. A stone, set like a pommel, in the end of the dagger's handle, flashed in the torchlight, as he turned on me, like a gleam of fire. The dying Indian sank to his knees, pointed to the dagger in Herncastle's hand, and said in his native language—'The Moonstone will have its vengeance yet on you and yours!' He spoke those words and fell dead on the floor.[16]

At the end of the war a large portion of the state's territory was annexed by the Company, with some areas being handed over to Hyderabad as a reward for its assistance in the war. A weak and much diminished Mysore was allowed to survive with a descendent of the Wodeyar dynasty, which Haidar Ali and Tipu Sultan had supplanted, as its ruler. Henceforth, the ruler of the 'native' state of Mysore was projected as the premier 'Hindu' princely ruler of the British Indian empire. For most of the nineteenth century, the truncated territories of Tipu's erstwhile kingdom were actually administered by colonial officials.

Within a few years of the subjugation of Mysore, the territories of Arcot and several other petty-states in the Tamil Nadu region (including the Maratha-ruled state of Tanjore

---

[16]Wilkie Collins, *The Moonstone: A Romance*, London: Penguin Classics, 1998, p. 14.

which had long supported the British) were taken over and attached to the Madras Presidency. The British had to carry out a series of military campaigns in central and southern Tamil Nadu between 1799 and 1805 to crush the resistance of powerful local chiefs, the poligars. The poligars have been referred to as 'little kings' (petty rulers who needed the formal sanction of an overlord to legitimize their authority) by Nicholas Dirks in his classic study of the only indigenously-ruled state that survived in Tamil Nadu, the state of Pudukottai, which rendered vital help to the Company in these campaigns.[17] The poligars refused to submit to colonial rule, which necessitated an all-out war against them after Tipu had been dealt with. The two wars against the poligars have been called India's 'first war of independence' by K. Rajayyan, the major historian of these conflicts.[18] The most outstanding of the poligar anti-colonial leaders was the legendary Kattabomman who proved to be the staunchest of the Company's adversaries. The First Poligar War (1799) was fought mainly against Kattabomman, in and around Tinneveli. The Second Poligar War which raged till circa 1805 resulted in the final suppression of other anti-British poligars. British rule was fully established in southern India by the early years of the nineteenth century. However, resistance in various forms continued. In 1806, a mutiny broke out among infantry units of the Company's army stationed in the fort of Vellore in north Tamil Nadu (near Chennai). It may be mentioned that surviving members of the royal family of Mysore had been imprisoned in the fort after Tipu Sultan was killed.

The uprising was linked to widespread discontent against the EIC in south India, although a recent study maintains that it was definitely not related 'to other local insurgencies in south

[17]Nicholas B. Dirks, *The Hollow Crown: Ethnohistory of an Indian Kingdom*, Indian edition, Hyderabad: Orient Longman, 1989 (first published, Cambridge, 1987), pp. 193–97.
[18]K. Rajayyan, *South Indian Rebellion: The First War of Independence (1800–1801)*, Mysore: Rao and Raghavan, 1971.

India at that time'. According to James Frey, 'there is no direct evidence suggesting that the Vellore Mutiny and the other Madras Army disturbances of 1806–1807 were anything other than sepoy protests, fairly limited in scope, and also confined to particular battalions, disturbances, whose primary cause is to be found in the problems of the early colonial military system.'[19] Nevertheless, Frey's own discussion brings out the connections between the events at Vellore and the dislocation caused by imperialist wars in south India. To begin with, the Company's Indian troops or sipahis had been engaged in uninterrupted fighting for over sixty years, from the 1740s to 1805. They were constantly marching from one battlefield to another, making do with improvised accommodation—living in 'increasingly shabby tents for years at a time' rather than in regular cantonments.[20] There had been no time even to standardize the uniforms of sipahis. After 1799, stricter discipline was enforced, modifications were made in the uniforms with a view to eliminating variations, while at the same time service conditions deteriorated. Growing dissatisfaction among the soldiers was articulated in terms of opposition to the introduction of headgear which supposedly resembled a kind of hat worn by Indo-Portuguese drummers and was for this reason seen as indicating lowly status. The factors underlying the Vellore mutiny were, however, complex, as Frey himself notes. Textbook accounts of the uprising have focused exclusively on the question of the new headgear, with the additional suggestion that its design was somehow intended to make the sipahis look like Christians! Such a narrative trivializes the grievances of the sipahis.

Several sections of society in south India had not reconciled themselves to the conquest of Mysore and Tanjore, or the

[19]James W. Frey, 'The Sepoy Speaks: Discerning the Significance of the Vellore Mutiny', Gavin Rand and Crispin Bates, eds., *Mutiny at the Margins: New Perspectives on the Indian Uprising of 1857* (Volume 4: *Military Aspects of the Indian Uprising*), New Delhi: Sage, 2013, p. 4.
[20]Ibid., p. 5.

subjugation of Hyderabad, Travancore, and Arcot. The mutiny at Vellore was not an isolated incident; discontent spread to all these areas in its wake. We should bear in mind that the upheavals of 1806–1807 coincided with the final stage of the suppression of recalcitrant poligars. The Vellore uprising was, more specifically, the outcome of a possible attempt to reinstate Tipu's descendants as the rulers of Mysore. Considering that the EIC had struggled with the problem of recruiting adequate numbers of soldiers in south India throughout the latter half of the eighteenth century, it is not surprising that it should have eagerly admitted into its army sipahis from disbanded contingents of Indian polities in the region, including Mysore. Frey notes that there existed a 'Mysorean cell' in one of the Company's 'native infantry' units which was in regular touch with members of the exiled royal family, or at least their personal servants. Significantly, the unit in question, 'the 1/1st Native Infantry' could have been infiltrated by sympathizers of the Tipu regime as it 'had been one of the units that took part in the storming of Seringapatam in 1799, and it remained in Mysore for years, afterward, finding most of its new recruits locally'.[21]

It was these soldiers who took the lead in the mutiny which began on the night of 9/10 July 1806. British officers in the fort were attacked and in the fierce fighting that went on for several hours there were heavy casualties on both sides. Tipu's family barred the entry into the palace where its members were lodged (situated within the premises of the fort), and it would appear that they did not have anything to do with the assault directly. Reinforcements were quickly rushed to Vellore which joined the contingents in the town to put down the uprising ruthlessly. Rebels, or those suspected of having assisted them, were killed indiscriminately. Many of them were pursued into the countryside, captured, and summarily executed. The situation remained fairly grave till the end of

[21]Ibid., pp. 10–11.

the year necessitating extensive enquiries in places as far away as Quilon on the Kerala coast. In the surcharged atmosphere several units were disbanded. Eventually, the male members of the immediate family of Tipu Sultan were transported to Calcutta as their presence in the south was considered risky. It was feared that they might become the rallying point for mobilization against the Company's rule. The governor of Madras Presidency, William Bentinck, was censured by being recalled from his posting. For several years afterwards he was engaged in publishing lengthy tracts seeking to justify his handling of the crisis in south India. This points to the seriousness with which the 1806 mutiny was taken in Britain.

FOUR

TERRITORIAL EXPANSION

Among the expansionist strategies evolved by the EIC after the subjugation of Bengal, one of the most widely used was that of the 'subsidiary alliance'. This was first perfected in the context of Hyderabad (the main elements of the model having been assembled by the French in the 1740s). The state had already been subordinated to British colonial interests in the 1760s when Asaf Jah II became the ruler with the Company's support. The EIC's resident at Hyderabad emerged as a powerful figure in the political structure of the state in the following decades.

Before commencing final military operations against Mysore, Richard Wellesley had concluded a treaty with Hyderabad that firmly tied its ruler to the Company's cause. This treaty inaugurated what has been called the 'subsidiary alliance system', but was a culmination of a longer process whereby the independence of the state had been gradually curtailed over nearly half a century. Subsidiary alliance implied the acknowledgement of the supremacy of the British and the surrender of control over foreign relations and the army to the colonial power. A key component of the 1798 treaty with Hyderabad, which was to be a feature of similar treaties with other states too, was that the Company had to be paid regularly for maintaining armed contingents in the state over which the state exercised no control. This was ostensibly for the 'protection' of the state, though actually such an arrangement meant that the Company could augment its military strength by using the resources of Hyderabad. The state was thus divested of its army, at the same time having to bear the expenses of its own occupation. After the Fourth Anglo-Mysore War an even more debilitating treaty was imposed on Hyderabad in 1800. The state had to hand over some of its territory for the maintenance of its British-controlled military force, the strength of which was increased at this stage. Henceforth, political entities of the Indian subcontinent were to be offered the option of submitting peacefully by becoming part of the subsidiary alliance system, or of a military contest if they resisted colonial domination. In the case of a major state like Awadh, as we shall see, collaboration with the British and acceptance of subsidiary treaties did not prevent eventual outright annexation.

The story of the absorption of the kingdom of Awadh, which gave to the Company control over the fertile plains of northern India, is a story of conquest by trickery and intimidation. The territories of the kingdom were acquired by the British in several stages spread over a period of nearly ninety years. The process commenced with the defeat of Shuja-ud-daula at Baksar in 1764 and culminated with the annexation of the remnants of the state in 1856. In 1773, Shuja-ud-daula agreed to station British troops in his state against the payment of a subsidy (Treaty of Banaras). This arrangement became the means by which the Company steadily drained Awadh of its resources, leaving it utterly ruined. Shuja-ud-daula's son and successor, Asaf-ud-daula (r. 1775–97), had to constantly strive to find the means to pay for the maintenance of the British force stationed in Awadh while coping with threats of annexation. By the end of the eighteenth century, the Company had made deep inroads into the polity of the state. The real turning point came in 1797 when, after Asaf-ud-daula's death, the Company successfully asserted its right to determine his successor by withholding recognition to his son and heir Wazir Ali who was not inclined to accept British domination. Wazir Ali had to abdicate at the beginning of 1798 and was exiled to Banaras where he continued defying the Company, even mobilizing resistance against it. An armed insurrection launched by him in January 1799 led to the killing of the governor general's agent stationed in Banaras. Wazir Ali was subsequently captured and placed in rigorous confinement in Fort William (Calcutta), in a cage-like structure that was 'bomb-proof'.[1] The brutal imprisonment of the deposed ruler of Awadh was an indication of the severity with which the British tried to suppress any resistance to its sway over the state.

Wazir Ali had meanwhile been replaced by Sadat Ali (r. 1798–1814), the eldest surviving son of Shuja-ud-daula, as the ruler of Awadh. The new ruler was more pliant in his attitude towards the British. In 1801, he was coerced to hand over to the Company more than half the territories of the state. These included the low-lying region of present-day Uttarakhand; Bareilly and tracts around it; and large portions of western, central, and eastern Uttar Pradesh (present boundaries). This marked the beginning of the formation of the United Provinces, named Uttar Pradesh after Independence (from which Uttarakhand has recently been separated). Awadh was reduced after 1801 to what later became the Lucknow and Faizabad divisions (which included the districts of Sitapur, Unnao, Bahraich, Raebareli, Sultanpur, and Gonda—apart from Lucknow and Faizabad) of the United Provinces. The state was now surrounded by British-ruled territory on three sides. To the areas detached from Awadh were added the north Indian possessions of Daulat Rao Sindia (ruler of the Gwalior state) occupied in 1803, to constitute the colonial administrative unit awkwardly named 'Ceded and Conquered Provinces' formed in 1805. To this administrative unit were added the hills and high mountains of Uttarakhand conquered by the British during the Anglo–Nepalese War of 1814–16. The Ceded and Conquered

[1]John Davis, *Vizier Ali Khan, or the Massacre of Benaras: A Chapter in British Indian History*, London: Spottiswoode & Co., 1871 edition (first published, 1844), p. 73.

Provinces were reorganized as the North-Western Provinces during the 1830s. The story of the final annexation of a drastically truncated kingdom of Awadh will be taken up later.

◆

With southern India and Bengal firmly under its control, the Company turned its attention to the Marathas who had not entirely recovered from the major setback they suffered in the Third Battle of Panipat (1761) when their forces were decisively defeated by Ahmad Shah Durrani, ruler of Afghanistan. The debacle at Panipat had shattered the prestige of Peshwa Balaji Baji Rao and physically removed from the scene his eldest son Vishwas Rao, who perished on the battlefield. After the death, in 1772, of Madhav Rao, who had succeeded Balaji Baji Rao after the latter passed away in 1761, a prolonged war of succession for the peshwaship ensued. Raghunath Rao, Balaji Baji Rao's brother, as one of the contenders dragged a willing East India Company into this conflict giving the British a handle to interfere in Maratha politics. Apart from the implications that this had for the Maratha position vis-à-vis the British, this struggle further eroded the peshwa's authority. The story of the Company's involvement in Maratha affairs at this juncture is a complicated one, particularly as it overlapped with an intense factional quarrel within the Company's establishment in India. There were serious disagreements among policymakers about the tactics to be adopted for reducing the Marathas. In the course of several military contests, between 1775 and 1782, usually referred to as the First Anglo-Maratha War, the Company was able to partially undermine Maratha polity. It required another sixty years for the military strength of the Marathas to be completely destroyed. The initial phase of the Anglo-Maratha struggle ended with the Treaty of Salbai (1782) with no spectacular gains for the British, something that is greatly lamented in colonial historiography. Nevertheless, they obtained a toehold in Maratha polity. This allowed them to intervene in a conflict between Peshwa Baji Rao II (r. 1796–1818) and the Holkar chief Yashwant Rao (r. 1799–1811), leading to the Second Anglo-Maratha War of 1803–1805. The conflict was an offshoot of the struggle between Yashwant Rao and Daulat Rao Sindia (r. 1794–1827) for control over Pune. In mid-1801, the Holkar army had occupied Ujjain, the seat of the Sindias; a few months later, in October, Sindia forces sacked neighbouring Indore, which was the capital of the Holkars. Then in 1802 Yashwant Rao defeated the combined forces of Baji Rao and Daulat Rao at Pune which resulted in the Company's intervention in the dispute on an appeal from the peshwa. The price extracted by the British for extending their support to Baji Rao was that he had to accept a subsidiary alliance which deprived him of control over military and foreign affairs (Treaty of Bassein or Vasai, December 1802). The next year, he was restored to peshwaship under British auspices.

The Second Anglo-Maratha War was a major military confrontation, encompassing large parts of the subcontinent. This was a war, as Randolf Cooper has argued, that the Company found hard to win. Contrary to the portrayal of it in colonial historiography as an entirely one-sided contest in which the British were bound to be victorious due to their military superiority, Cooper's detailed study of the war reveals that Yashwant Rao and Daulat Rao—the two main opponents of the Company—were defeated not because they were militarily inferior but because of a combination of various factors that included the wholesale desertion of European officers of Maratha (especially Sindia) contingents during the course of the war. In fact, Maratha artillery was quite superior to British artillery.[2] Senior military officials of the Company underestimated the strength of their opponents and were taken

[2]Randolf G. S. Cooper, *The Anglo-Maratha Campaigns and the Contest for India: The Struggle for Control of the South Asian Military Economy*, South Asian edition, New Delhi: Cambridge University Press, 2005, pp. 291–99.

aback at the firepower unleashed against its army in the two key battles of the war, Delhi and Assaye, which took place, respectively, on 11 and 23 September 1803. Both these battles could have gone either way. Ultimately the British succeeded due to a combination of war, espionage, and diplomacy—not because they had a clear military advantage. The Sindia army along with the forces of the ruler of Nagpur came close to defeating the British in the Battle of Assaye (September 1803), one of the two decisive battles of the Maratha war. The British were led by Arthur Wellesley, the future Duke of Wellington: 'Arthur Wellesley would later remember [the battle] as one of the hardest he had ever fought, and altogether tougher than his later confrontation with Napoleon at Waterloo.'[3]

The first phase of the war ended in December 1803 with the signing of the Treaty of Sarje-Anjangaon between Daulat Rao Sindia and the East India Company. Under the provisions of the treaty, Daulat Rao lost most of his possessions in northern India, including Delhi, besides some isolated outposts in western India. A treaty was also concluded with Raghoji Bhonsle, the Maratha chief of Nagpur, who had participated in the war as an ally of Daulat Rao. This treaty brought to the British some additional territory in Orissa and Bengal. The war with Yashwant Rao Holkar continued till 1805. This, the second phase of the war, ended on a disastrous note for the Company. The most outstanding event of this phase was the crushing defeat inflicted by Yashwant Rao on a British force under Colonel William Monson at Mukandwara Pass near Kota in July 1804. The British lost five infantry battalions and six companies of artillery in the battle. The Second Anglo-Maratha War actually ended in a stalemate, the tangible gains for the British being their ascendancy at Pune and the acquisition of some territory mainly in northern India. There was one noteworthy prize that

[3]William Dalrymple, *The Anarchy: The East India Company, Corporate Violence, and the Pillage of an Empire*, London: Bloomsbury, 2019, p. 370.

came their way, though its significance was largely symbolic. Following the defeat of Sindia's contingents at the Battle of Delhi (Battle of Patparganj), the city was occupied by the Company's army led by Gerard Lake. The administration of Delhi and its adjoining areas was taken over by the British, and Emperor Shah Alam was placed under their 'protection'. The emperor's authority was confined mainly to the Red Fort. Actual administrative control over Delhi and the surrounding areas was in the hands of the British resident at the imperial court. Earlier, Shah Alam had appointed Mahadji Sindia as de facto imperial regent (vakil-e-mutlaq) in 1784 and the administration of the Delhi region had been entrusted to him at that time. The Company's officials now replaced Sindia officials. In recognition of the Mughal emperor's status as the sovereign, the British upheld his de jure authority. Right up to 1857, proper respect was accorded to the emperor in keeping with this status. This was reflected in adherence to established court etiquette. For instance, token tribute or nazr was presented to the emperor on important occasions. The presentation of nazr was a public acknowledgement by the Company of the sovereign status of the Mughal emperor.[4] Control over the emperor facilitated the legitimization of the Company's authority.

[4]See Amar Farooqui, *Zafar and the Raj: Anglo-Mughal Delhi, c. 1800-1850*, New Delhi: Primus, pp. 4–7.

FIVE

EVOLUTION OF THE COLONIAL STATE

The East India Company's all-powerful court of directors, with its headquarters at Leadenhall Street in London, controlled and supervised the entire range of the Company's operations in Asia, down to the minutest detail. The court of directors comprised twenty-four members who were elected by the court of proprietors. In the eighteenth century (till the early 1770s) shareholders with minimum £500 stock were entitled to vote in the court of proprietors. The court of directors was ultimately answerable to the court of proprietors (or, general court) whose main concern was that the Company should remain a profitable venture so that shareholders could earn large dividends. Day-to-day functioning of the Company was conducted through various committees of the court of directors. In India, the possessions of the EIC were grouped into three administrative units: Madras Presidency (territories located in southern India); Bengal Presidency (territories located in eastern India); and Bombay Presidency (territories located in western India). Each presidency was under a president/governor. British victory in the Battle of Plassey had made the Bengal Presidency, from its vast territorial extent, the pre-eminent administrative unit of the Company. Simultaneously, there was a manifold increase in the political, military, and administrative functions of the Company.

By the beginning of the 1770s a consensus had emerged in British politics that parliament ought to exercise some measure of control over the EIC's Indian possessions. It may be mentioned here that this was a time when imperial policies began to be seriously questioned against the backdrop of problems that Britain was facing in keeping its American colonies under control. It is no coincidence that the incident referred to as the Boston Tea Party, which was the prelude to the American Revolution, occurred in the same year as the enactment of the first major piece of legislation for the 'better Management of the Affairs of the East India Company'—the Regulating Act of 1773. The 1773 Act provided the basic framework for colonial governance in India, and at the same time modified some features of the Company's organizational structure. It recognized the precedence of the Bengal Presidency ('Presidency of Fort William in Bengal') over the two other presidencies. A governor general (earlier designated governor) was appointed for administering the territories of Bengal, Bihar, and Orissa. He was to be assisted by a council comprising four members. All civil and military authority was vested in the governor general and his council. The Act specifically named the first governor general (Warren Hastings) as well as the four initial members of the council (John Clavering, George Monson, Richard Barwell, and Philip Francis). Each had a five-year term. The presidencies of Madras and Bombay were placed under the overall supervision of Fort William. Copies of the Company's correspondence relating to India were to be submitted regularly to the British government in order to enable it to monitor the management of the empire.

The numerical composition of the council (four members in addition to the governor general) constituted under the 1773 Act rendered the governor general vulnerable in case three of the members combined to oppose him. This is precisely what happened. Of the four newly appointed members, three—Francis, Monson, and Clavering—regularly voted against Hastings on virtually every major issue. This was a reflection of the council's serious differences over policies to be pursued by the Company for preserving and extending its authority. Francis was the leader of the anti-Hastings faction in the council. Opposition by the Francis group made it difficult for the governor general to function, at least till 1776 when Monson died. Luckily for Hastings, Clavering died the following year, and Francis departed for England in 1780 after being wounded in a duel with Hastings. In England, Francis joined the campaign against Hastings, publishing several pamphlets (anonymously) to expose him. He became a member of parliament in 1784 and actively assisted with the trial in impeachment proceedings against Hastings. Among the issues on which Francis had a sharp difference of opinion with Hastings in the Fort William council was that of land revenue policy. He had proposed a scheme for a permanent settlement, which was to provide the inspiration for the land revenue settlement introduced under Cornwallis in the Bengal Presidency in 1793 (see Appendix, p. 285).

The Company's organizational structure was streamlined under this Act by restricting the voting rights of shareholders. This was done firstly by limiting the vote to those who held minimum £1,000 worth of stock. Besides, the shareholder had to be in possession of the stock for at least one year in order to qualify for voting. Members of the court of directors were to be elected for a period of four years. One fourth of the members were to retire every year, and stay out of office for a minimum duration of one year before they could seek re-election. It needs to be emphasized that the Company owed its existence to a royal charter granted to it by the English monarch in 1600 and renewed from time to time. It was therefore ultimately subject to the authority of the monarch/government. Moreover, the Company was in dire need of credit just when its activities began to be scrutinized in the late eighteenth and early nineteenth centuries and had applied to the government for a large loan. This made it difficult for it to resist demands for some kind of parliamentary control over its functioning. In other words, the Regulating Act was linked to the British Parliament's sanction for the loan.

The 1773 Act had several anomalies which were sought to be rectified through a subsequent legislative measure, enacted in 1784 (Pitt's India Act). The most important feature of the 1784 Act was the introduction of a permanent mechanism for monitoring, on behalf of parliament, the administration of the Indian empire. A body consisting of six members, who were designated as 'commissioners for the affairs of India', was constituted for the purpose. This body, generally known as the 'board of control', became the main instrument till 1858 for parliamentary supervision over the Indian empire. The board of control included two high-ranking cabinet ministers. The senior commissioner (president of the board of control) presided over the functioning of the board. The president of the board of control was often referred to as the Indian minister. However, it should be noted that it was the court of directors that actually governed the Indian empire, even as the board of control had the power to override its decisions. Normally, instructions would be sent out to India by or via the court of directors, but the 1784 Act contained provisions for conveying orders of the board, whenever necessary, directly to Fort William through a 'secret committee' bypassing the court of directors. The secret committee was a separate and privileged channel of communication between the board and senior company functionaries in India, consisting of a small number of directors. Within India itself, the governor general's council was reconstituted by reducing its strength from four to three. More powers were concentrated in the hands of the governor general so that his authority might not be constrained by the council. The Madras and Bombay presidencies were subordinated to Bengal in unambiguous terms. Thus, Pitt's India Act made the governor general a very powerful colonial official and centralized the Company's colonial government, though centralization was not always possible in practice.

Towards the end of the eighteenth century there was growing opposition to the EIC's monopoly over the commerce with India and China. Private traders were keen to share in the profits of this commerce and resented their exclusion. With the expansion of the cotton textile industry, Lancashire manufacturers wanted to develop overseas markets for their products. The EIC's interests were at variance with those of the Lancashire manufacturers since the Company was mainly engaged in importing Asian commodities into Britain rather than selling British manufactured products in Asia. Towards the end of the eighteenth century it was focusing mainly on the import of Chinese tea and silk. The Indian empire was vital for procuring these commodities. The 'trade triangle' devised by the Company involved the supply of opium and raw cotton from India to China (opium was a banned substance in China, but was smuggled under the protection of the Company); the purchase of tea and silk from China with profits earned from the sale of opium and raw cotton; and the import of this tea and silk into Britain. Lancashire cotton textiles had no place in this scheme of things. Of course by now the Company's earnings were no longer confined to its commercial profits. It had access to the resources of its territories in India. Additionally, the greatly enlarged scope of the Company's activities—political, administrative, military, commercial, technical—necessitated the cooperation of several sections of British society. By the beginning of the nineteenth century, the Indian empire was no longer the concern of just a handful of merchant capitalists. With 'free trade' becoming the dominant economic doctrine in Britain, it was even more difficult for the government to resist demands for the termination of the Company's monopoly.

The Company fiercely contested the proposal to abolish its Indian monopoly when its charter came up for renewal in 1813. It mobilized many of its senior functionaries living in retirement in England, the aged Warren Hastings for example, to oppose the proposal. It also tried to enlist public support for its cause by deviously arguing that unrestricted access to India would lead to large scale emigration eventually resulting in European settlers demanding independence from the mother country as had happened in the case of the American colonies. The Indian empire would thus be lost to Britain. In the early decades of the nineteenth century there was a debate over the desirability of encouraging European settlement in India. Though the Company was strongly against this idea, there were some, including a few of its own leading officials, who thought it would help in the dissemination of the achievements of Western civilization. We should bear in mind that British subjects required the Company's permission to reside in India. This permission was not easily granted. And even when it was, they could not own land in the Company's Indian territories. Parliament was, on the other hand, unconvinced of the Company's arguments and the Charter Act of 1813 put an end to its monopoly over India.

The Company still retained its monopoly on trade with China, with the tea trade as the key component, for another twenty years, before the Charter Act of 1833 abolished the Company's monopoly over the China trade. The 1833 Act however had a larger significance. Most of the provisions of this elaborate legislative measure pertained to arrangements for governing the Indian empire. The framework evolved in 1833 was to continue almost unchanged down to 1858, and some elements were retained in the latter half of the nineteenth century.

The charter gave to the Company the authority to govern the Indian empire for another twenty years, till 1854, when the charter was to come up for renewal (the 1833 Act came in force in 1834). With the abolition of the monopoly of trade with China, the Company ceased to be a commercial concern. All its business activities were wound up. Henceforth, it was to be only a political–administrative body. This did not amount to a loss for its shareholders who were guaranteed an annual dividend of 10.5 per cent by the British government. The dividend was paid out of the revenues of the Indian empire, and amounted to £6.3 lakh per annum. Ultimately, it was the people of India who had to shoulder the burden of paying dividends to the shareholders of the EIC. For the time being it would suffice to note that the Act contained a provision by which at the end of forty years the Company's shares could be bought by the British government at double the nominal price of each share (£200 for each share of £100) and the Company could then be dissolved. This provision ensured that the EIC would survive at least down to 1874.

The Charter Act of 1833 also introduced some administrative changes, for instance the formation of a fourth presidency (Agra Presidency) by splitting the Bengal Presidency into two. This experiment was a short-lived one and in 1836 the presidency was reconstituted as the North-Western Provinces, under a lieutenant governor. Later in the century the territories of the truncated kingdom of Awadh would be attached to the North-Western Provinces, to form the United Provinces of Agra and Oudh, usually referred to as the United Provinces. The Act also removed restrictions on British settlement in India. The 1813 Act, while abolishing the Company's monopoly of trade, had imposed restrictions on long-term residence by private British individuals in India. A licence had to be obtained from the Company for residing in India. The Company had the authority to deport anyone back to Britain. It used this power to get rid of some of its critics, particularly British journalists. The most well-known case is the deportation in 1823 of the editor of the *Calcutta Journal*, James Buckingham. Under the provisions of the Charter Act of 1833 British settlers could henceforth acquire land in India.

More importantly, some crucial changes were made in the composition and functioning of the governor general's council. The council was given wide legislative powers. So far the three presidency councils had made 'regulations' within the framework of laws laid down by the British Parliament. There were separate regulations for each of the three presidencies. These had to be registered with the respective Supreme Courts of each presidency before they could be enforced. This at times led to disagreements between the executive and the higher judiciary. At the same time, a great deal of confusion was caused due to the multiplicity of laws applied in courts— Muslim, Hindu, customary, English. One of the objectives of the changes introduced by the Charter Act, pertaining to law-making, was to do away with the overlapping jurisdiction of the Company's judicial machinery and the Supreme Courts (which administered English law and had jurisdiction over Europeans; they were constituted by the crown). Besides, the Act centralized the process of framing laws, giving to the laws and regulations framed by the governor general's council the force of statutes. The council became the main legislative body in India. Presidency governments could submit drafts of legislation to the council for consideration. Of course, the British Parliament continued to be supreme in this matter and laws made by the council could not override laws made by parliament.

Since the making of laws required legal expertise, a provision was made for adding a 'law member' to the council. The council, which originally (1773) consisted of four members, was at this time (since 1784) a body of three members other than the governor general. The law member became the fourth member and his presence was supposed to be essential when the council was deliberating upon any legislation. The law member was not supposed to attend meetings of the council when it deliberated upon other matters. The law member could not be appointed from among servants of the EIC. This two-fold function of the council, executive and legislative, had significant implications for subsequent constitutional developments. Thomas Macaulay was the first law member to be appointed to the governor general's council. Macaulay had played an important role in drafting the 1833 charter. In order to do away with the multiplicity of laws, the process of codification and systemization of law was initiated by the Act. A law commission was set up for the purpose; the four-member commission was headed by Macaulay.

Due to the several problems it faced, progress on codification was slow. Almost single-handedly Macaulay compiled a penal code, and the first draft was finalized in 1837. English law was the basis of the code. It took more than twenty years before it could be enacted (Indian Penal Code, 1860).

The Charter Act of 1833 further strengthened the authority of the board of control, and gave more powers to the president of the board of control. Moreover, the governor general was henceforth to be known as the 'governor general of India'.

◆

In the latter half of the eighteenth century, the East India Company's non-military personnel (writers, factors, junior merchants, senior merchants), and occasionally its military officials, were increasingly saddled with administrative and judicial responsibilities to govern the Company's expanding empire. The non-military personnel mentioned above were covenanted servants of the Company, those who had been recruited in Britain on the recommendation of some member of the court of directors and had signed a covenant or bond at the time of their formal appointment. The covenanted servants, as distinct from the less privileged uncovenanted servants, filled the highest civilian positions in the directly administered territories of the British Indian empire. Simultaneously, some features of the Mughal bureaucracy were incorporated into the Company's governing apparatus. In the words of Marshall, 'In the years after 1765, the functions of a late Mughal provincial state, as the British understood them, were engrafted onto the organisation of a trading company.'[1] The Company's military service was a distinct and separate branch of employment.

As we have seen, the EIC's servants posted in Asia had, from a very early date, combined their commercial role with

[1]P. J. Marshall, *Bengal: The British Bridgehead: Eastern India 1740–1828*, Cambridge: Cambridge University Press, 1988, p. 100.

political and military functions—as the servants of the VOC too had done before them. Following the conquest of Bengal, and more so with the grant of diwani, extensive administrative, particularly revenue, functions were added to the political and military responsibilities of the Company's personnel. By the end of the eighteenth century, steps were being taken to streamline the appointment of administrative, judicial, and diplomatic personnel of the Company. Service conditions were improved, rules for promotion (henceforth strictly on the basis of seniority) were formalized and salaries were enhanced.

The Charter Act of 1793 created the basic framework of a 'civil service' for governing the Indian empire, although the transformation of the Company's commercial establishment into a modern bureaucracy was a long drawn out process. Some of the most important changes took place during the mid-1850s. Till almost the end of the nineteenth century, the uppermost level of the bureaucratic apparatus of the colonial state was staffed almost entirely by Europeans. The 1793 Act formally reserved higher positions of the civil service for covenanted servants of the Company (hence the nomenclature covenanted civil service). All employees sent out from Britain were required to sign a covenant or bond at the time of their appointment. This covenant made it binding upon the employee to submit himself absolutely to the discipline of the Company. By signing it he agreed to various conditions such as not accepting any private gifts or presents. Covenanted servants started their career as 'writers' (essentially copying clerks to begin with), rose to be 'factors' and could then be promoted to the position of 'junior merchant' or even 'senior merchant'. Senior merchant was the highest rank in the Company's managerial hierarchy. The civil service was blended with this structure as appointments for administrative purposes were made from among the covenanted servants. From 1793 onwards those appointed to posts with a salary of £500 and above per annum were required to have been in the Company's service in India, as covenanted servants, for a minimum of three years; six years in the case of those drawing £1,500 and above; nine years in the case of those with a salary of £3,000 and above; and twelve years in the case of those with a salary of £4,000 and above. Prior to 1793, district collectors were entitled to a commission of 1 per cent on the revenue collected in their respective areas of jurisdiction subject to a maximum of Rs 27,500 per annum. The collector was the principal colonial official at the level of the district. A minimum of twelve years of service had to be put in for promotion to the post.

Since there was no way in which an Indian could fulfil these requirements, Indians were automatically excluded from the covenanted civil service. The Charter Act of 1793 formalized this exclusion, already decreed through an order issued by Cornwallis who was governor general at this time. In fact, since the directors of the Company had the sole privilege of nominating appointees and were unlikely to extend their patronage to Indians, the covenanted civil service remained closed to the subject population throughout the period of the Company's rule. It may be mentioned here that the Company's service had three branches at this time: civil, military, and marine.

Towards the end of the eighteenth century it had become obvious that civil servants needed some professional training in order to perform their administrative functions efficiently. The first move in this direction was the founding, in 1800, of Fort William College (College of Fort William) in Calcutta at the initiative of governor general Wellesley. This institution was to have a chequered future. Since Wellesley had not obtained the proper authorization of the court of directors for setting up the institution, it was not accorded official recognition as a centre for training probationers. The governor general's scheme entailed a three-year course of study for fresh recruits (junior servants who had already been stationed in India for a few years prior to the setting up of the college too were eligible for enrolment). These recruits would have been between the ages of sixteen and eighteen upon arrival in India. A major objective of the institution was to teach 'Oriental' classical and regional languages, primarily Persian, Arabic, Sanskrit, Hindustani, Bengali, and Marathi. Islamic and Hindu law were also important components of the curriculum. Among the leading scholars associated with Fort William College one might mention John Gilchrist, William Carey, Henry Colebrooke, and John Baillie. Many of them were pioneers of 'orientalist' studies in India (and Britain) and were also associated with the Asiatic Society founded in 1784. Colebrooke, for instance, had introduced English speakers to Vedic texts. Along with William Jones and Charles Wilkins, he was part of the first group of British scholars who in late-eighteenth-century Calcutta emerged as the intellectual leaders of orientalism.

The college employed a large number of Indians (munshis, pandits, maulvis) who were experts in their respective languages and had mastery over legal and/or sacred texts. Wellesley had spelt out the details of the project in a comprehensive note written in 1800. By 1805 he had successfully implemented most of the key proposals contained in his note. In an equally lengthy note addressed to the court of directors (1802) Wellesley had forcefully argued against closing down the college. He was able to salvage the project in a modified form. It was henceforth to serve as an institution of advanced Oriental learning (languages and law) for junior servants, mainly those posted in the Bengal Presidency. Instead of the fixed three-year duration of the course of study, a more flexible programme was introduced whereby students could leave as and when they successfully cleared examinations in the languages they had opted for and passed in the compulsory subjects. The European and Asian scholars who had been brought together at the college constituted, during the first quarter of the nineteenth century, an intellectually vibrant body for the creation of colonial knowledge. 'By 1805 the college had become a veritable laboratory where Europeans and Asians worked out new transliteration schemes, regularized spoken languages into precise grammatical forms, and compiled dictionaries in languages relatively unknown in Europe.'[2] The college was instrumental in publishing dictionaries, grammar textbooks, and translations. It possessed a rich collection of Oriental texts, the nucleus of which was a portion of the fabulous library of Tipu Sultan that had been taken as booty after the Fourth Anglo-Mysore War. The library of Tipu Sultan contained

> many curious and interesting manuscripts, of which the following is a summary: Korán, 44 vols; commentaries on Korán, 41; Prayers, 35; Traditions, 46; Theology, 46; Súfyism (mystic writings), 115; Ethics, 24; Jurisprudence, 95; Arts and Sciences, 19; Philosophy, 54; Astronomy, 20; Mathematics, 7; Physic [sic.], 62; Philology, 45; Lexicography, 29; History, 118; Letters, 53; Poetry, 190; Hindí and Deccani Poetry, 23; Hindí and Deccani Prose, 4; Turkish Prose, 2; Fables, 18. ...With the exception of one precious Korán, which was forwarded to Windsor Castle [England], the greater part of this library was transferred to the newly-founded College at Fort William, Calcutta.[3]

Tipu's rich collection included a codex of the *Padshahnama* personally signed by Shah Jahan. It should be borne in mind that the texts were classified by colonial officials, whose perceptions are reflected in the way they understood the subject matter of the texts.

Fort William College lasted in its altered form till the 1830s when it was almost entirely abandoned with the decision to withdraw support to Oriental learning during the tenure

[2]David Kopf, *British Orientalism and the Bengal Renaissance: The Dynamics of Indian Modernization, 1773-1835*, Berkeley: University of California Press, 1969, p. 67.
[3]Lewis B. Bowring, *Rulers of India: Haidar Alí and Tipú Sultán and the Struggle with the Musalmán Powers of the South*, Oxford: Clarendon Press, 1893, p. 202.

of William Bentinck. Nevertheless, remnants of the college lingered on for another twenty-five years. The expertise that was available at the residual institution due to its association with Indian scribes and scholars was too valuable to be entirely discarded. It continued to be of use to British officials for improving their language skills, for translation of texts, and for compilation of dictionaries. The college was finally closed down in 1854.

The court of directors had, while rejecting Wellesley's original scheme under which Fort William College was to be the primary institution for training of probationers, simultaneously announced its resolve to establish such an institution in England. Towards this end the East India College was founded in 1806 at Hertford Castle located near London, shifting in 1809 to a grand new building at Haileybury, also close to London. The East India College was commonly referred to as Haileybury College. Candidates nominated by the Company's directors had to undergo their training as probationers at the East India College for two years (four terms of six months each) before proceeding to India. They then had to spend some time at Fort William College in the manner outlined above.

An entrance exam had to be cleared by nominated candidates before they were admitted to Haileybury. Throughout the period in question this was a mere formality, although by the 1830s examinees were being tested more rigorously leading to quite a few failures. Initially, however, almost all the candidates managed to get through. They were expected to have attended school and were required to produce a certificate to that effect. Essential qualifications were a rudimentary knowledge of accounting and neat handwriting. Bernard Cohn has pointed out in his essay on the recruitment of civil servants during the Company era that contrary to what is generally assumed, a relatively small percentage of the candidates were at this stage products of elite public schools. Of the 155 new recruits between 1809 and 1820, only twenty-three had certificates from such schools in England. A couple of candidates had attended preparatory courses such as those offered by the East India Company College School, which were designed to coach civil service aspirants.[4] The East India Company College School was one among several private initiatives for imparting basic instruction that would facilitate admission to Haileybury. At the beginning of the nineteenth century, applicants had to be between sixteen and twenty-one years of age (before this the minimum age for recruitment was sixteen and twenty was the maximum).

It seems that Haileybury was academically a fairly mediocre institution. The quality of teaching was just about average; trainees did not have to study too hard. Moreover, students did not gain much specialized knowledge about India. This was partly because there was lack of clarity among decision-makers about the kind of training that would be suitable for the trainees. Undue importance was given to the learning of classical languages (Sanskrit, Persian, and/or Arabic). By themselves they were unlikely to be of much practical use to newly appointed civil servants. Even Fort William College had begun placing greater emphasis on regional languages (vernaculars), but the Hailebury curriculum privileged classical languages, particularly Sanskrit. Passing the Sanskrit examination was an essential requirement for graduation. This was largely due to the influence of Sanskrit scholars such as H. H. Wilson who were instrumental in shaping the syllabus. The faculty of the college included Thomas Malthus who taught history and political economy here for nearly three decades, and was actively involved in the day-to-day functioning of the institution. Malthus was appointed in 1805 and continued in his post till his death in 1834. He had already established his reputation as a scholar

[4]Bernard Cohn, 'The Recruitment and Training of British Civil Servants in India, 1600-1860', *An Anthropologist Among Historians and Other Essays*, New Delhi: Oxford University Press, 2001 (first published, 1987; second edition, 1988), pp. 534–37.

with *An Essay on the Principle of Population* (1798) before he joined the college. There was a supporting staff of three Indian instructors who assisted with the teaching of languages. Indians were gradually dispensed with in later years. It may be mentioned that some of the vital teaching material was sourced from Fort William College. At the end of two years, and after clearing the compulsory Sanskrit examination, trainees were formally appointed as covenanted servants and then set out for India.

Positions at the middle level of the civil service, referred to as the uncovenanted service, were filled, as the nomenclature indicates, by employees of the Company who had not signed any covenant or bond. These were usually drawn from the European expatriate community in India (traders, planters, etc.), sons or other male relatives of covenanted servants, or those of mixed European–Indian descent known at this time as Eurasians. The uncovenanted service was an inferior service, recruitment to which was made entirely in India. Uncovenanted officials occupied positions such as those of deputy collectors, sub-deputy collectors (this position was specific to Bengal), and deputy magistrates, at the subdistrict level. Although the salaries were fairly adequate, at least from the second quarter of the nineteenth century, there were few opportunities for promotion, and unlike the covenanted servants these employees were not entitled to a pension. An important perquisite that covenanted servants enjoyed was that of long leave (furlough) to allow them to go home for up to three years after they had put in a certain number of years of service (about ten years in the second quarter of the nineteenth century). Covenanted servants were entitled to a special allowance during their stay in Europe. Uncovenanted servants did not enjoy this privilege. As the functions of the government expanded in the nineteenth century, it became necessary to employ an increasing number of uncovenanted servants, and during the course of the century a large number of these positions were opened up to Indians as well. Moreover, key administrative officials at levels below the district but above the village, as for instance tahsildars, all of whom were Indian, came to be categorized as uncovenanted servants.[5] This is an indication of the fluidity which marked the categorization of civil servants at lower and middling levels of the bureaucracy in the early nineteenth century.

◆

The district was the basic administrative unit through which the colonial state exercised control over the Indian empire. The key official in the district, from the 1770s onwards, was the collector who presided over the revenue collection machinery. This was his primary job. Initially, the collector also had judicial responsibilities, and functioned as the district magistrate as well. In his capacity as magistrate he looked after law and order. Subsequently, these offices were separated when it was found that collectors were unable to pay due attention to the combined tasks of collector, judge, and magistrate. As a matter of fact, collectors had a huge workload relating to their revenue functions alone, for which reason at a later stage (in the 1830s) deputy collectors began to be appointed to assist them. Further, the judicial functions of civil servants were gradually separated from executive functions, supposedly on the basis of western principles, though in the colonial context this was a deception in the absence of the development of democratic institutions. Nevertheless, most of the judicial work at the district level was handled by civil servants. Covenanted servants spent a lot of their time attending to cases brought before judicial courts.

Indians played a vital role in the routine administrative functioning of the colonial state at lower levels. In the districts this implied that revenue, law, and order, together with sundry administrative responsibilities in tahsils (subdivisions of districts; subdistricts) and villages, devolved upon 'natives'. The tahsildar

[5]The tahsildar was the principal executive official of the tahsil (subdistrict).

was the main Indian revenue and executive official at the tahsil level, and wielded considerable power. He had some police functions as well till the first decade of the nineteenth century. Tahsildars were given a commission on the revenue collected by them. Whereas tahsildars and other tahsil and village functionaries such as patwaris, qanungos, and chaukidars were Indians, district collectors and magistrates were exclusively British during this period. Needless to say, under Company rule it was impossible for non-Europeans to hold positions at the upper or middle levels in the provincial or presidency governments.

◆

While the civil service was crucial for running the Indian empire, the army was essential for enlarging and securing it. The Company's charter gave to it the authority to raise its own army, something that it started doing in right earnest during the first half of the eighteenth century when it was engaged in conflicts with the French in southern India. Apart from recruiting Europeans as soldiers, usually from among marginalized sections of society, the Company began recruiting a large number of Indian troops from various parts of the peninsula. The subjugation of several Indian states in the latter half of the century, beginning with the conquest of Bengal, placed at the disposal of the Company both soldiers as well as financial resources of the erstwhile states. We have seen that some of the disbanded troops from Tipu's army were inducted into the EIC's army in south India.

It was now possible to form a large army and to use it to conquer more territory which in turn would make possible the further expansion of the military strength of the EIC. The model of military organization that evolved in the eighteenth century was to remain unaltered in its essentials till the end of colonial rule. This was a model in which ordinary soldiers (sipahis or 'sepoys') were Indian while officers were European. From the point of view of the British, the Company's army was a private army. Enlisting in it was one of the options available to those in Britain who aspired to a military career as officers. Young men from England were usually not interested in being ordinary soldiers or 'privates'. Privates invariably came from very poor families, and were recruited in the royal (king's) army.

The royal army and the Company's army were separate formations; they were merged after the revolt of 1857. Two additional points need to be made here. First, that in the initial phase of its existence, the Company had to rely almost completely on the military support of the royal army (and even more so the royal navy) to safeguard its interests, and subsequently used the British Army whenever its own military resources were insufficient. Secondly, towards the end of the eighteenth century, a large number of European military adventurers operated in India as mercenaries, raising and training their own private contingents which they then offered to employers who could offer the best terms. The Company too used the contingents of these adventurers (referred to as 'irregulars' to distinguish them from the regular units of the Company's army), and after the Second Anglo-Maratha War managed to ensure that most of them were not available to Indian states to be deployed against the British.

Randolf Cooper has pointed out that during the course of the Second Anglo-Maratha War, a formal scheme for encouraging large-scale defections of European mercenary officers employed in the armies of Maratha chiefs, especially Daulat Rao Sindia, to the English side, was worked out by the EIC. These officers were to be either retired, or granted pensions, or (in a few cases) given employment in the Company's army. Simultaneously, sipahis serving under these officers too were to be incorporated into the Company's army to the extent that their defection could be engineered. In other words, the Company was seeking 'to buy out the human resources of the

Maratha armies'.[6] Two public proclamations to this effect were issued in the name of Governor General Richard Wellesley in August 1803.

The East India Company's military organization evolved into three distinct formations—the Bengal Army, the Madras Army, and the Bombay Army (the Bombay Presidency additionally maintained a small naval fleet, known as the Bombay Marine, to patrol the west coast). Each had its own traditions, reflected particularly in their differing recruitment practices. Of the three, the Bombay Army displayed the greatest diversity in terms of the social origins of its sipahis, while the Bengal Army at the other extreme was mostly upper caste and limited its recruitment to a relatively small and compact area. By the beginning of the nineteenth century, recruitment in the Bengal Army was by and large confined to Brahmins, Rajputs, and Pathans from Bhojpur and Awadh (central and eastern Uttar Pradesh; western Bihar). Eric Stokes has pointed out, in the context of Rajputs in the Doab, that with the shrinking size of landholdings of many clans, soldiering in the Company's army became attractive as it was regarded as conforming to their caste status. This would also have been true for other dominant landed groups.[7] At the time of the outbreak of the mutiny in the Bengal Army, its regular infantry contingents consisted of about 84,000 Indian soldiers: roughly 28,000 Rajputs, 27,000 Brahmins, and 13,000 Muslims, while 16,000 belonged to the 'middle castes'.[8]

The Bengal Army was to emerge as the most formidable fighting force in the British Indian empire by the second quarter of the nineteenth century. It was equipped with advanced military technology and over a period acquired vast combat experience. Nevertheless, it became an exclusively high caste

[6]Cooper, *The Anglo-Maratha Campaigns*, pp. 235, 319–21.
[7]Cf. Eric Stokes, *The Peasant Armed: The Indian Rebellion of 1857*, edited by C. A. Bayly, Oxford: Clarendon Press, 1986, p. 51.
[8]Kaushik Roy, 'Combat, Combat Motivation and the Construction of Identities: A Case Study', *Mutiny at the Margins*, IV, p. 25.

army (Muslim soldiers too were recruited from among the elite social groups, the ashráf, of the Doab region). Besides, there was some recruitment from a few middle castes. On the other hand, the Bombay Army was more inclusive. It regularly recruited from among lower castes that had been traditionally associated with Maratha military formations. Of these the Mahars and Mangs were prominent. Patterns of recruitment had far-reaching social and ideological implications even though these were not immediately apparent. It needs to be underlined that whereas Indians were recruited as ordinary troopers (sipahis), the officer ranks were monopolized by Europeans. Some sipahis could be promoted as 'native' officers after several years of service. However, commissioned officers, lieutenants, and above were exclusively British, and were products of the East India Company's Military Seminary located at Addiscombe near London. Admission to the institution was mainly through a recommendation from a member of the court of directors. Obviously, no Indian could hope for such a recommendation. Officer-level positions were thus effectively closed to Indians.

SIX

FURTHER CONQUESTS

The Charter Act of 1813 brought to an end the EIC's monopoly on (British) trade with India, a privilege it had enjoyed for over two centuries through the royal charter granted to it by the English crown, initially in 1600 and renewed periodically. From 1814 onwards any British subject could engage in trade with the East Indies, i.e. lands lying east of the Cape of Good Hope—with the exception of China (and the trade in tea). The abolition of the EIC's monopoly coincided with two developments. The first was the conclusion of the Napoleonic Wars in 1814–15. Napoleon abdicated in 1814, and was finally defeated at the Battle of Waterloo in 1815. Henceforth, France, which had posed a serious challenge to British colonial supremacy, was no longer a major threat. Britain was to remain the dominant naval power for the next hundred years till the end of the nineteenth century. This secured its position as the leading imperialist power for the rest of the century. Secondly, in Britain itself, the free-trade lobby became increasingly powerful, aggressively pushing for the opening of new markets and territorial aggrandizement. The first phase of the Industrial Revolution was well underway by this time. In this phase, cotton textiles produced in the mechanized factories of Lancashire (where the industrial city of Manchester was the main production centre) were the most important commodities. The Lancashire cotton manufacturers had built up a campaign for putting an end to the Company's monopoly. Following their success in 1813, which was completed in 1833 when the China and tea monopolies too came to an end, they mounted pressure for expanding the empire. More territories, it was argued, meant more markets for Lancashire cotton.

The four decades or so following the end of the East India Company's monopoly of trade with India witnessed large-scale territorial expansion. Though the Company had lost its monopoly over trade, it continued to govern the Indian empire down to 1858. Between 1814 and 1852, the Company inflicted a series of bloody wars on the Indian subcontinent to extend its direct territorial control over a vast area: western Maharashtra, Sind, Punjab, Assam, and Burma (Myanmar); other political entities were subjugated and reduced to the status of indirectly ruled 'native states' in Gujarat, Rajasthan, Malwa, Kashmir, Manipur, Tripura, and Bundelkhand. The Awadh state was annexed in 1856.

◆

Within a year of assuming office in India, Lord Hastings, also known as earl of Moira (governor general, 1813–23), launched an offensive against the kingdom of Nepal. The kingdom had emerged as a distinct political entity in the latter half of the eighteenth century. The several chieftaincies in this largely mountainous region had been unified under Prithvi Narayan Shah (d. 1775), the ruler of Gorkha. Gorkha is located to the northwest of Kathmandu. By the end of the 1770s, Prithvi Narayan had brought much of the western part of present-day Nepal, including the Kathmandu Valley, under his control. This was a military state in which the military leadership constituted the nobility. The leading courtier clans were the Thapa, the Pande, and the Basnyat. Moreover, enlisting in the army became attractive for the people of the middle hills due to the possibility of acquiring cultivable land through conquest. This has been referred to as the 'land–military complex' by Ludwig Stiller.[1]

[1]Ludwig Stiller, *Rise of the House of Gorkha*, New Delhi: Manjusri Publishing House, 1973.

The state was based upon the relentless exploitation of the peasantry.

Since Gorkha was the seat of Prithvi Narayan Shah's authority, the kingdom established by him was generally known as the 'Gorkha kingdom'; later it came to be called Nepal (derived from the Newar people, the main ethnic group of the Kathmandu Valley at that time). The kingdom continued to expand under the successors of Prithvi Narayan: in the east in the direction of Sikkim; in the west up to the river Sutlej (Garhwal, Kumaun, the Dun Valley, and portions of the Himachal hills including Shimla); and to the southwest in the tarai lowland region at the foothills of the Himalayas. Forays into Tibet, to the north, were checked by China. In 1792, following reverses in a military conflict with Tibet, Nepal became a tributary of China. However, as the authority of the Qing rulers of China was itself being undermined in the early nineteenth century, the status of Nepal as a tributary of China was a nominal one at the time of the EIC's offensive against the kingdom. China played no role in the encounter.

In the latter half of the eighteenth century, the Company had occasionally tried to meddle in the affairs of Nepal, siding with the opponents of Prithvi Narayan and of his successors. An official of the Company, Colonel William Kirkpatrick, was sent on an intelligence-gathering mission to Kathmandu in 1793 against the backdrop of the war between China and Nepal, ostensibly to mediate between the two states. On his return he published a volume on the basis of the information collected during the mission (*An Account of the Kingdom of Nepaul*, 1811).[2] This information was to prove useful for planning the Company's war against Nepal. From around the turn of the century, the kingdom was making fresh conquests, especially

---

[2]William Kirkpatrick, *An Account of the Kingdom of Nepaul: Being the Substance of Observations Made During a Mission to that Country in the Year 1793*, London: William Miller, 1811.

in the west. The de facto ruler of Nepal, Bhimsen Thapa (who held the position of mukhtiyar, from 1806 to 1837), vigorously expanded the kingdom's territorial control in this period. In view of the setback in the tussle with China, expansion was now mainly possible in areas lying in the northwest and southwest of Nepal, which in turn threatened to disrupt the Company's territorial consolidation in the tarai, and hilly tracts north of Saharanpur and the Dun Valley. The Company had recently, in 1805, organized its acquisitions in the region (territories that Awadh had been forced to cede to it in 1801, and Sindia-controlled tracts annexed in 1803) as the Ceded and Conquered Provinces. As Nepal kept pushing forward its frontier in the vicinity of the newly constituted Provinces, as well as Gorakhpur, north Bihar, and north Bengal, it came into direct conflict with the Company, which too was seeking to expand its territorial control along the extensive border with the kingdom. The truncated kingdom of Awadh, which shared a long border with Nepal, was sandwiched between the Ceded and Conquered Provinces in the northwest, and Gorakhpur in the east.

Moira began his tenure in India with the Anglo-Nepalese War of 1814–16. From 1813 onwards border tensions had already become a regular affair. The Company demanded cession of some of the portions of the tarai that Nepal had recently occupied; the Kathmandu durbar refused to comply with these demands. The British declared war against Nepal in October 1814. The war was fought on two fronts: in the east the front extended from Gorakhpur to the river Bagmati in north Bihar; in the west, the Dun Valley and the hilly region lying east of Ludhiana. The Dun Valley witnessed some of the fiercest fighting. The valley was the entrance to Kumaun and Garhwal, both of which had been annexed by Nepal, and thence to Tibet. From the point of view of Nepal, control over the Dun Valley was crucial as, apart from the possibilities of agriculture in the Dun, it gave access to the fertile tarai region.

It did not take very long for colonial military officials to realize that it was no easy matter conducting military operations in a harsh mountainous terrain. Even though the number of British troops was as much as three times that of the Nepalese army, the first phase of the campaign of 1814–15 nearly ended in disaster for the British. Heavy casualties were inflicted on them by the Nepalese troops and one of their very illustrious commanders, Robert Gillespie, was killed right at the outset of the campaign at the battle of Nalapani. The fort at Khalanga near Nalapani (close to Dehradun) was to become a symbol of Nepali heroism in the war. After the death of Gillespie, the fort was besieged for more than a month by the Company's troops. The Nepali force was led by Balbhadra Kunwar. After Balbhadra evacuated the fort, the British, upon entering it, found a large number of dead bodies: most of the casualties had been caused by the lack of drinking water as the enemy had cut off the water supply. Whereas the Company's army faced reverses in the several theatres of war, one of the contingents in the west commanded by David Ochterlony made some progress. By the end of 1815, fighting came to an end and a compromise was rushed through. In December 1815, a treaty was agreed upon by the two sides (Treaty of Sagauli), though as a result of the unwillingness of the Calcutta authorities to accept some of its provisions (which led to the resumption of fighting), its ratification was delayed. The treaty was finally accepted and ratified by both sides in March 1816.

According to the terms of the Treaty of Sagauli (1816) the kingdom retained its core area, but lost some of its recent conquests. These included Kumaun, Garhwal, and the Dun Valley. It was thus that the British came into the possession of hills on which prominent hill stations, including Shimla, Mussoorie, and Naini Tal, were to come up later in the century. In the east, the acquisitions included the site at which the hill station and summer capital of the Bengal Presidency was developed, i.e., Darjeeling. The treaty also provided for the residence of a British representative (resident) at Kathmandu. It should be noted that Nepal remained formally independent throughout the period of colonial rule in India. In order to keep Nepalese power in check in the east, the British entered into a 'protective' treaty with the raja of Sikkim, thereby subjugating this strategically located territory, parts of which had earlier been annexed by Nepal. A wedge was thereby inserted between Bhutan and the eastern frontier of Nepal, keeping the route from northeast India to Tibet open, as well as blocking the possibility of Nepalese expansion in the area. Finally, the Company could now tap into the reservoir of military labour in Nepal. Given that the kingdom had at its disposal a formidable fighting force consisting of well-trained soldiers with extensive combat experience, it could supply recruits for the Company's army, especially as Nepal was no longer in a position to regularly undertake wars of conquest. The enlistment of soldiers from the hills had commenced in 1815 itself. The sipahis were recruited exclusively from the mountainous region, mainly from among the Magars, Gurungs, Khas, Limbus, and Rais. Soldiers from Nepal came to be designated collectively as Gurkhas. The first contingent of Gurkha sipahis, the Sirmoor Rifles, was a battalion formed out of prisoners of war taken in the Nepal war (the contingent was named after the state of Sirmaur located south of Shimla; the Sirmaur district is in present-day Himachal Pradesh). This constituted the nucleus of the Company's Gurkha troops. Gurkhas were to emerge as a prominent component of the Bengal Army in the post-1857 period.

◆

The Third Anglo-Maratha War (1817–18) finally ended the independence of the Maratha states—Nagpur, Indore, Gwalior, Baroda—and made the EIC a major territorial power in western and central India. The peshwa's nominal authority was terminated, his seat of authority, Pune, formally became part of the Company's territories, and Baji Rao II was exiled to

Bithur near Kanpur. Yet the Sindias (Gwalior), Holkars (Indore), Gaikwads (Baroda), and Bhonsles (Nagpur) still retained large tracts of territory at the end of the war, being incorporated into the British Indian empire as princely states. Among these, the Sindia state retained sufficient reserves of power to challenge the British after 1818, so that a formidable military campaign had to be launched against it as late as 1843 to ensure its final subordination.

The final Anglo-Maratha war overlapped with a large scale campaign against the Pindaris. In fact, the so-called Pindari menace provided the pretext and justification for military mobilization against the Marathas. The years between the end of the Second Anglo-Maratha War and the beginning of the Third Anglo-Maratha War, i.e., c. 1805–17, were marked by large-scale Pindari military and political presence in Malwa. Originally, the Pindaris were one of the numerous people living on the margins of settled agrarian society in Malwa. In the latter half of the eighteenth century many of their bands found a place in the Maratha military organization. By the end of the century they had become a regular part of Maratha campaigns north of the Narmada in Malwa.

In the years preceding the Third Anglo-Maratha War, Karim Khan and Chitu had emerged as the most prominent Pindari chieftains. Of the two, Karim Khan was more important politically, having been on the verge of creating an independent state in the first decade of the nineteenth century. His territories were located mainly in eastern Malwa, on the outskirts of the Bhopal state, which was close to extinction in the 1810s. With their military resources having been curtailed at the end of the Second Anglo-Maratha War, the Sindias and Holkars (the two leading Maratha ruling houses in central India and Malwa), came to look upon the Pindaris as relatively inexpensive military allies. We have already noted that the Maratha armies had customarily employed the Pindaris in their campaigns in central India since the late eighteenth century. They were at that time mainly an informal auxiliary force used to harass and plunder the enemy. After 1805, Daulat Rao Sindia and Yashwant Rao Holkar forged alliances with the leading Pindari chiefs, which in turn led to the Pindaris acquiring a limited share in political power. This provided Pindari bands with an opportunity to enlarge the scope of their activities. Karim Khan and Chitu, among others, were assigned specific territories for the maintenance of their contingents.

It is not surprising that when Hastings embarked upon the final campaign to destroy the power of the Maratha-ruled states he regarded the annihilation of the Pindaris as a matter of urgency. Two armies, with a combined strength of 1,20,000 troops were assembled for the military offensive against the Pindaris. The Southern Army was led by Lieutenant General T. Hislop which carried out the major operations; the Northern Army was commanded personally by Hastings. The sheer military might of the Company resulted in victory. Most of the Pindari bands simply dissolved. There was no direct encounter with them in the field. Chitu retreated to the Vindhya forests where he was killed by a tiger. Karim Khan surrendered in February 1818.

As has already been mentioned, the military operations against the Pindaris were carried out almost simultaneously with the large-scale campaign against the leading Maratha-ruled states. Already in 1802, Peshwa Baji Rao II had come to terms with the British by signing the Treaty of Bassein. The treaty, which compelled the peshwa to accept a subsidiary force, had precipitated the Second Anglo-Maratha War. British victory in the war reinforced the Company's ascendancy at Pune. This was challenged by Trimbakrao Dengle, who had emerged as Baji Rao's leading advisor and minister in the years preceding the Third Anglo-Maratha War. An incident that occurred in 1815, and in which British officials alleged that Trimbakrao had played a key role, became the starting point of developments that eventually led to the war. In July 1815, the Anglophile envoy of the Baroda state, Gangadhar Shastri (who had also for some time had been an employee of the Company) was assassinated at the pilgrimage centre of Pandharpur. He had gone to Pandharpur while on a visit to the Pune court to put forth the case of the Gaikwad ruler of Baroda relating to some residual claims that the peshwa had in Gujarat. The British held Trimbakrao responsible for the assassination. This charge has been repeated in most colonial writings so that even though it remains unsubstantiated it is considered to be an established fact. It is much more likely that a faction at the Baroda court which was opposed to Gangadhar Shastri was behind the murder.

This incident offered the Company with an excuse to intervene in the dispute between Pune and Baroda; the resident at the peshwa's court, Mountstuart Elphinstone, immediately demanded that Trimbakrao be handed over to the Company as it had guaranteed the safety of the Baroda envoy. After some initial hesitation Baji Rao conceded this demand and his minister was incarcerated by the British in Salsette near Bombay. The mysterious killing of Gangadhar Shastri and the suspicion about the complicity of Trimbakrao provided the British with an opportunity for weakening the anti-Company lobby at the Pune court.

A dramatic change in the situation was brought about by Trimbakrao's escape from detention in 1816. The escape was followed by the rallying of forces that were trying to resist the East India Company's attempts to bring western Maharashtra under its control. Meanwhile, in June 1817, Elphinstone forced Baji Rao to sign a revised version of the subsidiary treaty of 1802 which was intended to further subordinate the peshwa. This was the Treaty of Poona (1817); it completely subjugated the peshwa to the British. As payment for the so-called 'protection' of the peshwa's dominions, large chunks of territory in northern Karnataka and Konkan as well as revenues of Gujarat were ceded to the Company. Pune was to give up all its rights in areas lying north of the Narmada and south of the Tungabhadra. The important fort of Ahmadnagar was handed over to the Company. The long-standing dispute with the Gaikwads over various claims was settled with the peshwa agreeing to an annual payment of four lakh rupees from Baroda. Most of the cavalry contingents of the peshwa were disbanded. Pune was to have no direct relations or correspondence with any other political entity in India. Finally, and very unusually for a subsidiary treaty, there was a formal declaration by the peshwa in the treaty itself that Trimbakrao Dengle was guilty of the murder of Gangadhar Shastri.

In the months following the signing of the treaty Baji Rao attempted to renegotiate its terms, drawing the attention of the Company's officials to the severity of these terms. Simultaneously he mobilized for armed opposition to the British, though some of this mobilization might have been spontaneous. By the end of October the Company's officials realized that a military conflict with the peshwa was in the offing. On 1 November, Elphinstone, along with the Company's contingents, moved from Pune to the adjacent village of Kirki. Immediately after this the residency at Pune was plundered and burnt down. On 5 November, a battle was fought at Kirki between the Company's army and the peshwa's forces. This was the first of a series of armed engagements that took place between the two sides, and continued till June 1818.

From Kirki Baji Rao moved southwards to Satara while the British occupied the city of Pune. During the next few weeks, troops loyal to the peshwa were regrouping. Baji Rao proceeded to Pandharpur, and then to Junnar located north of Pune, and southwards again in the direction of Satara. The peshwa had mobilized a large cavalry force by this time. A fierce battle took place between the two opponents on 1 January 1818 at Koregaon near Satara. Trimbakrao was among those who commanded the peshwa's military force at Koregaon. By the beginning of February the Company had formally announced that it had taken over all the territories of the peshwa (barring Satara, residence of the Bhonsle ruler Pratap Singh, nominal overlord of the peshwa being a descendent of Shivaji). The subjugation of the peshwa's domain took several months. Several military campaigns had to be carried out to put down resistance in various parts of western Maharashtra even as the peshwa continued to be on the move. There was yet another battle in the third week of February, the last major encounter between Baji Rao II and the British, at Ashti located northeast of Pune. The peshwa's forces were led by Bapu Gokhale in this contest; Bapu Gokhale was killed in the fighting. This deprived the peshwa of his most capable military officer. Baji Rao nevertheless continued with his resistance for a few more months but was unable to get any support from other Maratha rulers (except for a brief attempt to form a coalition with the Nagpur ruler and Chitu). Eventually he agreed to negotiate with the Company through John Malcolm, one of the leading colonial officials in central India. Baji Rao agreed to formally abdicate. He was sent to Bithur where he lived in exile till his death in 1851. The Company granted him an allowance which was hardly commensurate with the resources that came under British control as a result of the annexation of the peshwa's territories. Interestingly, many senior officials of the Company felt that Malcolm had been too generous in granting to the peshwa an allowance of Rs 8 lakh per annum!

Another major objective of the 1817–18 military campaign against the Maratha-ruled states was the subjugation of the Nagpur state which was ruled by the Bhonsle dynasty. During the Second Anglo-Maratha War the ruler of Nagpur, Raghoji Bhonsle II, had fought unsuccessfully against the British, as a result of which the state had been forced to accept the unfavourable terms of the Treaty of Deogaon signed in 1803. By this treaty, Nagpur had lost a substantial part of its territories (Orissa to the British, some of Berar to the nizam). When Raghoji Bhonsle II died in 1816 the Company's officials posted in Nagpur intensified their attempts to destabilize the state. The main instrument of British interference was the resident, Richard Jenkins. Jenkins prevailed upon Madhoji Bhonsle II (also known as Appa Sahib), successor of Raghoji, to sign a subsidiary treaty which enabled the Company to place troops under the command of British officers in the Nagpur territories. Appa Sahib was a nephew of Raghoji, and initially had been appointed regent for Raghoji's minor son Parsoji. Parsoji was soon assassinated, and Appa Sahib formally became ruler of the state.

At the outbreak of the military conflict between the Company and Baji Rao II in late 1817, Appa Sahib aligned himself with the peshwa. He had already been in touch with Baji Rao who had conferred a robe of honour on him. Towards the end of November 1817 Appa Sahib began to mobilize his forces against the British. The residency and British cantonment located in Nagpur were abandoned on 25 November. The British force stationed in Nagpur took up position at Sitabuldi Fort strategically located on a hillock in the city. On 26 November, hostilities commenced and fierce fighting continued till the next day. Even though Appa Sahib faced a setback in this encounter, he continued to be the ruler of the state. The British had a difficult time overcoming the resistance of a section of the Nagpur troops, and it was only with the arrival of reinforcements in December that Jenkins was able to dictate terms to Appa Sahib. A treaty was signed by which some more territories of Nagpur were surrendered to the British. As Appa Sahib continued to mobilize his troops for another contest, the British deposed him, and held him captive for some time after that.

Since at least March 1818 Appa Sahib had been in contact again with Baji Rao who, Appa Sahib hoped, would bring to Nagpur the troops that still remained with him after the Battle of Ashti. Appa Sahib succeeded in escaping from confinement and proceeded in the direction of Asirgarh, whence Baji Rao was also moving. Coinciding with this was the movement of Chitu, from northern Malwa, in the direction of Asirgarh. Unfortunately the military potential of a possible convergence of Baji Rao, Appa Sahib, and Chitu could not be realized. Chitu was forced to flee to the Vindhya forests as British troops closed in on Asirgarh. His body was subsequently found mauled by a tiger. Baji Rao began his negotiations with Malcolm in May, the outcome of which has been described above. Appa Sahib could not be recaptured by the British and eventually found shelter in Jodhpur. A minor from the Bhonsle family was placed on the gaddi of Nagpur as Raghoji III (d. 1853), with real authority being in the hands of the resident. All the territories of Nagpur lying north of the Narmada were annexed by the British.

As for Sindia and Holkar, there was no direct military engagement with the former and a brief encounter with the latter. Following the death of Yashwant Rao Holkar in 1811, the state was formally ruled by Tulsi Bai as regent for the Holkar ruler Malhar Rao II, then a minor. Actual power was wielded by the army. A major section of the army was hostile to the Company, and had close links with some of the Pindari chiefs. Against the backdrop of the military manoeuvres against the Pindaris, and the resistance put up by the peshwa in Pune and Appa Sahib in Nagpur, the Holkar army resolved to fight against the British. (Tulsi Bai was in favour of negotiations with the Company's officials.) This resulted in a violent clash, culminating in the killing of the regent on 20 December 1817. On the twenty-first, Holkar troops fought a fierce battle against the British force led by Hislop. British casualties in this battle, which was fought at Mahidpur located north of Indore and Ujjain, were very high, amounting to nearly 800. Nevertheless, the Holkar army was defeated. The Treaty of Mandsaur (6 January 1818), which the state was compelled to sign after the battle, substantially reduced the territorial possessions of Indore. The Company annexed parganas (districts) located south of the Satpuras. Some of the

Holkar parganas in Rajasthan were handed over to Zalim Singh, the de facto ruler of Kota. Two new principalities were carved out of the Holkar possessions: Tonk (under Amir Khan) and Jaora (under Abdul Ghafur Khan). The other terms of the treaty severely curtailed the autonomy of the state.

In the case of Gwalior, the Company, through its show of strength, ensured that Daulat Rao disengaged himself from the Pindaris, abandoning their leaders to their fate. Besides, the assurance that had been given by the British to Sindia under the terms of the Treaty of Mustafapur (November 1805) at the end of the Second Anglo-Maratha War, that they would not interfere in matters relating to the Rajasthan states (e.g., Mewar, Marwar) over which the Sindias exercised control, was now withdrawn. This paved the way for the subjugation of the Rajasthan states.

The Third Anglo-Maratha War ended the control of the Marathas over Rajasthan. For over half a century, the Marathas had encroached upon the authority of the rulers of the Rajasthan states, regularly collecting tribute from them. Sindia and Holkar were compelled to give up their claims over these states, leaving them with no option but to accept British dominance. Article VIII of the Treaty of Mustafapur with the Sindia state had stated that 'The Honourable Company engages to enter into no treaty with the Oudepore and Joudepore, and Kotah, or other chiefs, tributaries of Dowlut Rao Sindia, situated in Malwa, Mewar, or Marwar, and in no shape whatever to interfere with the settlement which Sindia may make with those chiefs.' The revised treaty between Daulat Rao and the Company (Treaty of Gwalior, 5 November 1817) abrogated Article VIII of the 1805 treaty. However, Mewar, Marwar, Bundi, Kota, and other Rajasthan states which had tributary obligations towards Sindia were to continue with the payments, though henceforth through the British. At the same time, under the terms of the Treaty of Mandsaur, the Holkar state had to give up its tributary claims over Rajasthan states.

Udaipur, Jodhpur, Jaipur, Jaisalmer, Bikaner, Kota, Jhalawar, Bundi, and the several smaller states of the region now became subordinate allies of the Company. In all, nineteen states signed treaties surrendering their independence. None of them had the resources to engage in a military contest to resist colonial supremacy, making the extension of colonial rule in the area a relatively smooth affair.

Gujarat, much of which was ruled by the Gaikwads, was brought under the Company's control during the first decade of the nineteenth century. In 1802, the Baroda state had become part of the subsidiary alliance system. The Gaikwads helped the Company to consolidate its position in western India which made them, along with the rulers of Hyderabad, the foremost princely rulers of the British Indian empire. The British subsequently concluded separate agreements with the petty chiefs of the Kathiawar peninsula (Saurashtra), most of whom paid tribute to Baroda, thereby establishing their supremacy over this region. Whereas standard colonial accounts portray the acceptance of the Company's authority by the Kathiawar chiefs as a peaceful process, actually many of them were intimidated with threats of the use of force before they submitted. On the eve of the war with Baji Rao II, the Company signed a revised treaty with Baroda (6 November 1817), which increased the strength of the subsidiary force stationed in the state and further subordinated the Gaikwads to the British. The city of Ahmedabad, which had been jointly subject to the peshwa and the Gaikwads since the 1750s with a complicated revenue-sharing arrangement, was formally ceded to the British under the terms of the 1817 treaty with Baroda.

SEVEN

MORE BLOODSHED

As part of its long-term objective of bringing under imperial control the northwestern part of the Indian subcontinent, the East India Company tried to extend its empire to Afghanistan by launching a war against the kingdom in 1839. This war, the First Afghan War, ended in a colossal defeat for the British. They were forced to withdraw from Afghanistan at the beginning of 1842, with all their troops being massacred as they struggled to retreat through the Khyber Pass with almost no survivors. This was perhaps the worst military disaster for the British during their expansionist drive in the first half of the nineteenth century.

What is known as the First Anglo-Afghan War was in fact a much larger affair; it encompassed Punjab, Sind, and Baluchistan as well, culminating in the subjugation of all these regions by the end of the 1840s. We need to go back to the beginning of the century to narrate the story of the Afghan War. At this time, Afghanistan was ruled by Zaman Shah (r. 1793–1800), a grandson of Ahmad Shah Abdali. Zaman Shah was ousted in 1800 and blinded on the orders of his half-brother, Shah Mahmud, who replaced him. Shah Mahmud in turn was overthrown in 1803, and Shah Shuja (Shuja-ul-Mulk), a real brother of Zaman Shah, became the ruler of Afghanistan. The British, engaged as they were in a global war against France, sent a mission led by Mountstuart Elphinstone in 1808 to negotiate a treaty with Shah Shuja mainly with the aim of preventing the Afghan ruler from assisting Napoleon should there be a French invasion of the Indian subcontinent through his kingdom. Within a few weeks of signing the treaty, Shah Shuja was expelled from Afghanistan by Shah Mahmud (1809). From 1815 onwards Shah Shuja resided at Ludhiana which had been occupied by the Company following the 1809 Treaty of Amritsar with the ruler of the vast Punjab kingdom, Ranjit Singh (r. 1801–39). Further upheavals followed in Afghanistan. Dost Mohammad, who belonged to a different clan, came to power in 1826. Meanwhile, Shah Shuja had been trying to mobilize support for a campaign to dislodge Dost Mohammad and regain power. In 1833, he launched an invasion of eastern Afghanistan. He was supported by Ranjit Singh and had obtained the 'best wishes' of the British. However, in the middle of 1834 Shuja was defeated by Dost Mohammad at Kandahar.

Over the next few years the British committed themselves more seriously to the cause of Shah Shuja, making him an instrument of their policy of expansion in Afghanistan. This policy was vigorously pursued by George Eden, also known as the earl of Auckland (governor general, 1836–42). It should be noted that Auckland's failed attempt to make Afghanistan a part of the British empire and the huge military losses that had to be sustained were a great embarrassment for historians who glorified colonial aggression. Many of them have tried to suggest that the Afghan War was a misadventure for which Auckland and some of his advisors were personally responsible. Yet the invasion of the region had the full backing of the board of control headed by John Hobhouse, and the Whig cabinet (Auckland himself was a prominent Whig leader) with Lord Melbourne as prime minister.

Soon after Auckland assumed office there was sustained propaganda in India and Britain suggesting that Russia, which was then penetrating Central Asia, might become a threat to the British Indian empire. Rumours were circulated about Russian intrigues in Afghanistan, and the need to pre-empt any Russian military advance that would bring it close to northwestern India. A servant of the Company named Alexander Burnes, who in the early 1830s had been sent to 'explore' the Indus river, Sind, Afghanistan, and parts of Central Asia so as to gather information about these regions that might be useful for British colonial expansion, was deputed to Kabul in 1837 on a so-called commercial mission. The mission was more in the nature of an espionage operation with the additional aim of ensuring British presence and influence at the court of Dost Mohammad. Burnes was to play a leading role in subsequent events. For the time being, Burnes was unsuccessful in diplomatic negotiations with Dost Mohammad relating to Peshawar. In 1834, Ranjit Singh had formally made Peshawar part of his kingdom. The city and its environs had earlier been under Dost Mohammad. In the negotiations with Burnes, Dost Mohammad had been seeking British support to regain Peshawar as the basis of an alliance between the two. This proposal was decisively turned down by Auckland. It was now decided that Shah Shuja be actively helped to overthrow Dost Mohammad. As a prelude to the implementation of this scheme a treaty was signed between Shah Shuja, Ranjit Singh, and the British (Tripartite Treaty of 1838). The treaty was negotiated by William Macnaghten, a senior civilian official who was entrusted with the implementation of Auckland's Afghan policy. Macnaghten was a strong advocate of the proposal to actively support Shah Shuja.

The Tripartite Treaty was essentially an agreement between Ranjit Singh and Shah Shuja. The British signed the treaty mainly by way of endorsing the agreement. Shuja was not even consulted about the terms of the treaty, which was negotiated by the British with Ranjit Singh. According to the original plan, Ranjit Singh was to render military support to Shah Shuja to enable him to acquire control over Afghanistan. In return, Shuja was to renounce claims over those territories of Afghanistan which had been acquired by the Punjab kingdom, particularly Peshawar.

Eventually, it was decided that British troops would accompany Shuja on his march to Kabul. There was an influential group of colonial officials who were of the view that the plan could only succeed if Shuja was backed by a strong British military force. In his remarkably detailed account of the First Afghan War, John W. Kaye particularly held Auckland's private secretary, John Colvin, responsible for shaping the governor general's aggressive Afghan policy.[1] Besides, it has been suggested that Macnaghten and a relatively junior official, Henry Torrens, too exerted a strong influence on Auckland's policymaking. Together, Colvin, Macnaghten, and Torrens pushed for greater British military involvement in Shuja's expedition. But ultimately it was the governor general who, with the concurrence of the British cabinet, decided to go ahead with a full-fledged invasion of Afghanistan. Burnes, who had not advocated for such a venture as he was not convinced of the hostility of Dost Mohammad towards the British, too fell in line.

Once the plan was finalized, a statement was issued by Auckland on 1 October 1838 (usually referred to as the Simla Manifesto, as it was issued from Simla), in which supposed reasons were set out for the invasion of Afghanistan. This is a document of unabashed imperialist arrogance. It sought to justify the military aggression against Afghanistan in terms of the superior claims of Britain. It stated that Dost Mohammad had to be removed as he was conniving with Iran (Persia) for a military campaign that would bring hostile Iranian armies to the banks of the Indus. This was quite incorrect. Moreover, the British had been openly meddling in Herat, located in western Afghanistan, in a conflict between Iran and the chief of Herat. Iranian forces had besieged Herat since 1837. The Herat chief was assisted informally by the British through a military officer of the EIC, Eldred Pottinger, while the Iranians had the support of Russia. The situation in Herat was also cited as a reason for

[1]John W. Kaye, *History of the War in Afghanistan*, 2 vols., London: Richard Bentley, 1851.

sending British troops into Afghanistan. The Simla Manifesto concealed the fact that the siege had already ended in September. It was later revealed that the British cabinet and senior colonial officials in India, especially Auckland, had resorted to falsehoods in correspondence relating to the Afghan affair placed before parliament in 1839.

In December 1838, Ranjit Singh fell seriously ill, and never fully recovered. He passed away on 27 June 1839. The removal of Ranjit Singh from the scene, and the uncertainties of succession in the Punjab kingdom, made Shuja even more dependent on the British. The Punjab army was to march from Peshawar to Kabul via the Khyber Pass. The Company's contingents, which now constituted the main force—Army of the Indus—was to take a southerly route through Sind and Baluchistan and proceed to Kabul through the Bolan Pass. Macnaghten was the chief political official accompanying the expedition, and was Auckland's representative with Shah Shuja. The Army of the Indus commenced its march through Sind in early 1839. There was considerable resentment in Sind over granting passage to British troops. Auckland brushed aside the objections of the Sind authorities with a display of haughtiness. As we shall see below, the Afghan War led to the subjugation of Sind. The British occupied the strategically located port of Karachi in Sind as a prelude to the annexation of the region. The march through Baluchistan provided an opportunity to begin the process of subordinating the area to colonial rule.

The Army of the Indus was able to occupy Kandahar and Ghazni on its way to Kabul. Dost Mohammad retreated from Kabul as the British army approached the city; the invading force entered on 7 August 1839 and Shah Shuja was proclaimed as the ruler. Auckland had declared that the British would withdraw once the objective of restoring Shuja to power was achieved. It soon became apparent that the new ruler could not maintain his position without continuing British presence. Thus it was decided that the British force would stay on for some time.

Macnaghten and Burnes were the key colonial officials who determined administrative and military policy. Nevertheless, it was clear that a large armed force stationed at a considerable distance from the borders of the Indian empire was an expensive proposition. A prolonged stay in Afghanistan was financially unviable. Another cause of worry was that Punjab was unwilling to allow the British army to march through its territory, so that the return march would have to take place along the more circuitous route through Sind. It is in this context that more pressure began to be exerted on Punjab, and suggestions for annexing the kingdom began to be floated. While on the one hand expenses mounted (apart from the military expenses, Macnaghten had to literally purchase the support of many powerful Afghan chiefs by giving large sums of money to them on a regular basis), on the other hand Dost Mohammad was able to gather sufficient supporters by September 1840 to carry out attacks on Shuja's territories. In one particular campaign against him the British received a setback, but Dost Mohammad decided to negotiate with them since his forces were too small for a sustained offensive. The British authorities agreed to his voluntary exile in India. He was placed under virtual house arrest in Mussoorie. He was to return a few years later as ruler of Afghanistan.

The situation continued to deteriorate despite the exile of Dost Mohammad. By 1841, there was widespread unrest and troops had to be constantly rushed to put down armed rebellions. There was a popular uprising in Kabul itself, in November, leading to the killing of Burnes. British officials seem to have been taken by surprise at this turn of events, and the civilian and military leadership was completely paralysed. Macnaghten was assassinated in December. A confusing sequence of events followed, at the end of which the Army of the Indus commenced its retreat in the first week of January 1842. It met with stiff opposition from local tribal communities on the route linking Kabul with Jalalabad. Jalalabad is located at the Afghanistan-end of the Khyber Pass on the traditional road leading to Peshawar. There was a British garrison stationed at Jalalabad. It should be borne in mind that the march was taking place under the most adverse weather conditions; the winters in the mountain passes of Afghanistan are harsh and severe. Almost the entire British force (which consisted of a large number of Indian sipahis fighting a colonial war), of nearly 16,000 men, was wiped out much before Jalalabad. According to standard accounts there was only one survivor, though actually several more survived, including those who had been taken hostage or made captives. Nevertheless, there were just a handful of survivors. The First Afghan War was the most comprehensive defeat the British faced in their colonial wars during the nineteenth century, and one in which they suffered huge losses. The final catastrophe for the British cause was the assassination of Shah Shuja in April 1842.

In February 1842, Auckland had been succeeded by Edward (Law), Lord Ellenborough as governor general (1842–44). Given the political vacuum that was created with the killing of Shah Shuja, and the limited options available to the British, it was decided that Dost Mohammad be released so that he could return to power in Afghanistan. One might mention that Dost Mohammad's son, Akbar Khan, had played a leading role in organizing armed resistance against the military occupation of Afghanistan by the British and had emerged as the de facto ruler with the assassination of Shuja. Upon his return to Kabul, Dost Mohmammad once again became the ruler of Afghanistan and reigned till his death in 1863. The dynasty founded by him continued to rule the country down to the third quarter of the twentieth century.

In order to salvage British prestige, and avenge the humiliation of the Afghan debacle, Ellenborough formed a so-called Army of Retribution, which indulged in senseless violence in Afghanistan and then returned to India. This allowed Ellenborough to claim that the British army was victorious and therefore invincible! Prior to the operation that was undertaken by the Army of Retribution, British troops had been sent from Peshawar to Jalalabad via the Khyber Pass to strengthen the garrison. Reinforcements had been necessitated due to the threat of a siege of Jalalabad by forces loyal to Akbar Khan. For some time, there was a sharp difference of opinion among army officers commanding Jalalabad. While some favoured evacuation, others were hopeful of withstanding the siege. The matter was settled with the arrival of reinforcements from Peshawar. This coincided with the assassination of Shah Shuja. The situation at Jalalabad was still unstable. In the subsequent operations Akbar Khan was forced to retreat, and the danger to Jalalabad receded. It was then that orders were sent out for the numerically large British contingent stationed at Kandahar to march northwards to Kabul, via Ghazni which is situated on the way. The garrisons at Kandahar and Ghazni had remained in a strong position while British armed forces were being routed in other parts of eastern Afghanistan. Simultaneously, troops were to proceed from Jalalabad to Kabul. This Army of Retribution converged in Kabul in the middle of September 1842. The army was then withdrawn in the second week of October; Ellenborough was satisfied that the Afghans had been punished. Before marching back towards the Khyber Pass, the army destroyed the main marketplace of Kabul and engaged in large-scale loot and plunder in the city, killing a large number of its inhabitants. The violence that was unleashed against villagers, mostly non-combatants, as the Army of Retribution made its way back to Punjab has been ignored in most accounts of the Afghan War.

One more task with which the army was entrusted was of a very sinister nature, intended to sow seeds of religious discord. Ellenborough had issued specific instructions that the force marching from Kandahar to Kabul via Ghazni was to raid the tomb of Sultan Mahmud at Ghazni. The 'Gates of Somnath', erected at the entrance to the tomb, were to be removed and ceremonially brought to India. According to some legend that Ellenborough had chanced upon, these were the wooden doors that had been carried back by Mahmud after his raid of Somnath. The language of the proclamation issued on the occasion leaves one in no doubt about its divisive intent: 'The insult of eight hundred years is at last avenged. The gates of the temple of Somnauth, so long the memorial of your humiliation, are become the proudest record of your national glory, the proof of your superiority in arms over the nations beyond the Indus' (emphasis added).[2] The notion of the medieval period of Indian history as marking 'eight hundred years of slavery' (beginning with Mahmud Ghaznavi's raids, c. 1000), which later became so crucial to communal versions of India's past, is indeed identical to the notion of the 800 years of humiliation that Ellenborough's proclamation spoke of. The gates were discovered to have nothing to do with Somnath and were deposited in the Agra Fort where they can still be seen. A young British officer who accompanied the gates as they were taken around various pilgrim centres in north India for public display stated that this memento elicited no response from the people who saw it. While Ellenborough insisted that they were a valuable prize, in fact they were historically of little value. Later in the century this episode contributed to creating animosities along religious lines. This is how British colonialism extracted retribution for being vanquished in Afghanistan.

◆

The Afghan War had created conditions for the conquest of Sind. The process which finally led to the annexation of the region was set in motion just as British forces retreated from Afghanistan. In the early nineteenth century Sind was ruled by chiefs or amirs of the Talpur clan which had brought various

[2]Cited in Edward Thompson and G. T. Garratt, *Rise and Fulfilment of British Rule in India,* London: Macmillan, 1935, p. 353.

parts of the region under their control during the last quarter of the eighteenth century. The political entity constituted by the Talpur amirs comprised territories lying on the two sides of the Indus River and extending to Baluchistan in the west and included large portions of the Thar Desert in the east; with Punjab in the north, and bounded by the Arabian Sea towards the south. In a sense, it was under the Talpur rulers that modern Sind came into existence. The peculiarity of their political system, based on sharing of power, was that various members of the clan administered separately the several administrative units of Sind. Hyderabad (the reference in the discussion that follows is to the city of Hyderabad located in Sind), was the common capital. Apart from Hyderabad, where the senior amir had his seat, the two other important centres of Talpur power were Mirpur and Khairpur. This arrangement had its origins in a division of Sind among four brothers of the ruling Talpur family at the turn of the century.

As has been mentioned earlier, it was in the early 1830s that the British began to systematically gather information about Sind. Burnes's espionage mission of 1831 was the first major attempt to explore the lower Indus. It is no coincidence that Alexander Burnes's brother James visited Hyderabad in the late 1820s and published an account of his stay at the court of Hyderabad.

The colonial penetration of Sind dates back to 1809. During the Napoleonic Wars, a treaty was signed with the amirs under which they agreed not to allow the French into the region. This was followed up by another treaty in 1820 intended to exclude all Europeans (and Americans) from Sind. A more substantial treaty was concluded in 1832 which compelled the amirs to open up their territories, the river Indus particularly, to commerce. This marked the beginning of regular British intervention in the affairs of the Sind. A resident, the usual instrument for such meddling, was posted at the court of Hyderabad from 1838 onwards, Henry Pottinger being the first incumbent. Murad

Ali (r. 1828–33) was the chief of Hyderabad at the time when Pottinger negotiated the 1832 treaty. He was averse to admitting the Company's resident to his court. His son, and successor as the senior amir, Nur Muhammad (r. 1833–41), too resisted the British demand to post a resident in Sind, but had to eventually give in. As is obvious from even a cursory perusal of the very extensive documentation published officially by the Company in 1843, *Correspondence Relating to Sinde, 1836-1843*, Pottinger, who was in Sind for several years as the Company's agent prior to his appointment as resident, played a prominent role in the 1830s in undermining the authority of the Sind amirs.[3]

The southward expansion of the Punjab kingdom in the direction of northern Sind lent urgency to British manoeuvres. In 1836, Ranjit Singh was reported to be planning to occupy the city of Shikarpur in northern Sind. Shikarpur was a major commercial centre. The Punjab ruler claimed that the tribute that the amirs had earlier given to the ruler of Afghanistan was now due to him as he had taken over the territories of the Afghan rulers in the northwestern part of the Indian subcontinent. The threat to occupy Shikarpur was meant to pressurize the amirs to pay the tribute.

At this point, the British intervened and offered their 'protection' to the amirs, forcing another treaty on them (April 1838). It was this treaty that led to the appointment of a resident at Hyderabad. This did not prevent constant demands being made upon the amirs during the invasion of Afghanistan. They were humiliated, threatened with annexation, coerced into providing funds to Shah Shuja for the Kabul expedition, and had to allow British troops to march through their territories. Karachi was occupied in February 1839, following which another treaty was signed with the amirs under which they were forced to accept a subsidiary force and pay Rs 3 lakhs per annum towards its expenses.

---

[3]*Correspondence Relating to Sinde, 1838-1843*, London: T. R. Harrison, 1843.

Shortly after Ellenborough took over as governor general, Charles Napier, a senior British military officer, was appointed the Company's supreme military commander in Sind and given wide-ranging political authority. Napier was a veteran of the Napoleonic Wars and had no experience of India. His appointment was a clear signal that the British intended to militarily subjugate Sind at the earliest. Within six months of his arrival in September 1842, Sind had been conquered. Obviously, annexation had already been decided upon by Ellenborough when Napier was sent out to the region. Napier was first asked to enquire into allegations that during the Afghan War the amirs had conspired against the British. This was followed by the farce of Napier examining the relevant correspondence without any knowledge of the language. He declared that the amirs were indeed guilty of misconduct. This became the pretext for imposing a new treaty on them. The conditions were so unreasonable that the amirs were unwilling to comply. The terms included virtual surrender of sovereignty, demands for territory, resources, and money. At the same time the British made use of a factional tussle at Khairpur, where Rustam Ali (r. 1811–42) was the amir, to further their interests. They assisted Rustam Ali's half-brother, Ali Murad, in dislodging Rustam Ali and then promptly accorded recognition to Ali Murad.

Meanwhile, by the second week of February the other chiefs had reluctantly signed the new treaty at Hyderabad. As news of what had happened at Khairpur spread, there was a spontaneous mobilization for resistance against the British. A major objective of this mobilization was the reinstatement of Rustam Ali. More generally this was a last-ditch effort at preventing the British from taking over Sind. Troops loyal to the amirs gathered at Hyderabad, where the residency was stormed. Napier had already been marching with his troops towards Hyderabad. On 17 February 1843, a battle took place between the two armies at Miani, on the outskirts of Hyderabad, and the Sind forces were defeated. The victorious British troops thereupon let loose violence against the inhabitants of Hyderabad, engaging in large-scale loot and plunder. Napier's official share ('prize') of this loot was £50,000. Most of the amirs, including the amir of Hyderabad, Muhammad Nasir Khan (r. 1841–43), were taken as prisoners of war and exiled. One of the amirs, Sher Muhammad, the chief of Mirpur, still held out. Many of the contingents that had fought at Miani now joined Sher Muhammad. An engagement took place between British troops led by Napier and the forces of the Mirpur chief at Dubbo (Dabba), near Hyderabad, on 24 March 1843. Sher Muhammad's contingents were defeated in the battle, though the British suffered heavy casualties. Even after Dubbo, Sher Muhammad continued to put up resistance. The British found it difficult to capture him due to the popular support he enjoyed. There was one final clash between British forces and Sher Muhammad's supporters. The British again won in this encounter (Shahdadpur, 14 June); Sher Muhammad retreated to Afghanistan where he lived in voluntary exile until his death in 1874.

Ali Murad was rewarded for his support by being acknowledged ruler of the principality of Khairpur (Khairpur and some of the adjoining districts). Khairpur was incorporated into the British Indian empire as a princely state ruled by Ali Murad and his descendants. The rest of Sind was annexed by the British. Napier was made governor of the province, a position he held till 1847. In 1847, Sind was attached to Bombay Presidency and placed under a commissioner as its chief administrator. There was severe criticism of the annexation of Sind by officials in India and Britain. Political opinion in Britain was sympathetic to the amirs, who it was felt were treated in a shameful manner. James Outram, a key official posted in Sind, was a fierce critic of Napier's policies and was instrumental in mobilizing opinion in England against annexation. Largely due to the campaign carried out by Outram, the court of directors of the EIC censured Ellenborough. The British cabinet too unanimously disapproved of the annexation. However, it did not publicly disown the annexation, so that ultimately Sind continued to be a part of the empire.

◆

The annexation of Sind, preceded by the setback of the First Anglo-Afghan War, marked the limits of British colonial expansion in northwestern India till the late 1840s when Punjab was conquered. The empire however continued to expand in the northeast and Burma (Myanmar). The whole of Burma was conquered over nearly six decades, between 1826 and 1885. Three major wars were fought between the British and the kingdom of Burma in this period. The conflict commenced in the 1820s when the EIC was attempting to extend its control over the Brahmaputra Valley, approaching it from the west, while Burma was engaged in consolidating its position in Manipur, Jaintia Hills, Cachar, and Assam. Burma was at this time ruled by the Kongbaung dynasty. The founder of the dynasty, Alaungpaya (r. 1752–60) had unified most of what is present-day Burma, bringing these territories under the Kongbaung state. He had also begun the process of penetrating Manipur and the Brahmaputra Valley in the northwest. The Brahmaputra Valley was the core area of the Ahom kings; Ahom rule in the region dated back to the thirteenth century. Manipur had emerged during the course of the eighteenth century as a cohesive political entity, especially due to the endeavours of its ruler Bhagya Chandra (r. 1759–98). By the beginning of the nineteenth century, the Kongbaung rulers of Burma claimed jurisdiction over Manipur, Assam, Jaintia Hills, and Cachar. They had succeeded in establishing their authority over some of these territories but were still attempting to stabilize their position when they came into conflict with the British during the 1820s. The eastern border of Bengal between Burma and British India (the Chittagong area) too was a zone of conflict.

As the EIC tried to expand its sphere of influence eastwards, beyond Bengal, it encountered resistance from the Burmese, resulting in the First Anglo-Burmese War (1824–26). In this war, the Burmese forces were led by Maha Bandula, a brilliant military strategist who created a precarious situation for the British by launching a two-pronged attack on Bengal—from Cachar and Jaintia Hills in the north and Chittagong in the south—with the objective of converging on Calcutta from two directions. The plan however did not succeed and the Burmese were defeated, though at the cost of enormous casualties on the British side. The war ended with the signing of the Treaty of Yandabo (1826). Under the provisions of the treaty, the Burmese had to pay a massive indemnity to the British and had to give up their claims over Manipur, Assam, Cachar, and Jaintia Hills. They also had to cede some of their territory (located in the southern part of the kingdom) to the British. These were administrative units named Arakan and Tenasserim lying on either side of the delta of the Irrawaddy River. The Irrawaddy delta still remained part of the kingdom of Burma with its capital at Ava in north Burma.

The treaty became the basis of the British conquest of the northeastern part of the Indian subcontinent, as well as of Burma. The Second Anglo-Burmese War (1852), fought during the time of Dalhousie, brought to the British control over the rich Irrawaddy delta (in which Rangoon/Yangon is located). The Third Anglo-Burmese War (1885) resulted in the annexation of northern Burma, thus completing the subjugation of all of Burma. The last king of the Kongbaung dynasty, Thibaw (r. 1878–85) was captured and exiled to Ratnagiri in Maharashtra where he passed away in 1916.

◆

The conquest of Sind in 1843 was followed by a major expansionist thrust in northwestern India: the conquest of the Punjab kingdom. Punjab was conquered through two fiercely fought wars in the latter half of the 1840s. The kingdom, with its capital at Lahore, extended (at the time of the two Punjab wars) from the southern bank of the river Sutlej in the east to the approaches to the Khyber Pass in the west. It included the Jammu region, Kashmir, Hazara, and Peshawar. As we have already noted, in the 1830s Ranjit Singh had been trying to extend its southern borders by encroaching upon the territories of northern Sind. We need to briefly recapitulate the history of the East India Company's penetration of Punjab during the reign of Ranjit Singh to make sense of the developments of the 1840s.

The occupation of Delhi in 1803 had provided the EIC with a frontier outpost for collecting information about, and developing contacts in, Punjab. Shortly after the occupation of Delhi, the Company began interfering in the affairs of the smaller Punjab states (Patiala, Faridkot, Jind, Nabha, Kapurthala, etc.), located between Delhi and the eastern boundaries of Ranjit Singh's kingdom, in order to convert them into a base for acquiring control over the whole of Punjab. This had to be a long term project as Ranjit Singh was too powerful a ruler to be easily subordinated. Further, the Company at this stage had inadequate knowledge of the geography and politics of Punjab and the northwestern portions of the Indian subcontinent.

In 1809, the Treaty of Amritsar was signed between Ranjit Singh and the Company whereby the British sphere of influence in Punjab was confined to the political entities situated east of the river Sutlej—the Cis-Sutlej states—which were brought under so-called British protection. Patiala was the most prominent among these states and territorially the largest. It would appear that Ranjit Singh did not wish to get bogged down in a military tussle with the British for ascendancy over these states. He was now able to concentrate his energies on expanding his kingdom towards the west and the north where the decline of Afghan power had left a vacuum. In the next two decades, Peshawar, Hazara, and Kashmir were incorporated into Ranjit Singh's kingdom. His major concern was stabilizing his rule over these territories rather than dealing with the British. Although there was no open confrontation between the British and Ranjit Singh down to his death in 1839, their relations were not entirely cordial. There were tensions over issues such as the attempt by the Company to assert its authority over the Talpur amirs.

Punjab was conquered within ten years of Ranjit Singh's death. Ever since the Treaty of Amritsar, the Company had been gradually infiltrating the state apparatus of the Punjab kingdom through espionage and diplomacy so that Punjab had already become vulnerable to its manoeuvres by 1839. Following Ranjit Singh's death, dissensions were encouraged at the Lahore court, allowing the British to easily undermine the authority of the ruling elite. Nevertheless, they faced stiff resistance, especially from the army, in the endeavour to bring Punjab under their sway. Two difficult wars had to be fought before the kingdom could be overwhelmed.

Ranjit Singh had been succeeded by his eldest son Kharak Singh. He had the support of three powerful Dogra chiefs of Jammu who were influential at Ranjit Singh's court: Gulab Singh, Dhyan Singh, and Suchet Singh. They were brothers and had been given the Jammu region as a jagir for services they had rendered to Ranjit Singh. Of the three, Dhyan Singh was the key figure at the Lahore court. There was another group of prominent chiefs, including the Attariwala family, related to Ranjit Singh which put forth the claims of Kharak Singh's son Nau Nihal Singh as the successor. By the end of 1839, Kharak Singh had been divested of his authority and Nau Nihal Singh became the de facto ruler. Kharak Singh died on 5 November 1840; Nau Nihal Singh died on the same day when a gateway, likely accidentally, fell on him.

The influence of Dhyan Singh had steadily increased in the previous months. He now mobilized support for Sher Singh, a half-brother of Kharak Singh, to succeed as the maharaja. Sher Singh became the new ruler in 1841. He in turn was assassinated in 1843, and Dhyan Singh too was killed. It has been suggested by some scholars that the British had a hand in the killing of Sher Singh. Here it should be noted that he was quite hostile to the Company. In fact, ever since the death of Ranjit Singh, British officials in Punjab had been involved in the disputes over succession. They were constantly seeking to strengthen the position of pro-Company elements in the kingdom. After all, the struggle for power in Punjab was taking place against the backdrop of the Afghan War. The beginning of Sher Singh's reign coincided with the retreat of British forces from Kabul. For the British, it was necessary to have a friendly regime in Punjab.

Of the two remaining Dogra brothers, Suchet Singh was killed in 1844 while Gulab Singh departed for Jammu along with most of his armed contingents so as not to be directly involved in the violent conflicts at Lahore. For a few months following the assassination of Suchet Singh, Dhyan Singh's son Hira Singh became an important figure at the court (Ranjit Singh had been very fond of him). In December 1844, Hira Singh too was killed.

Following the death of Ranjit Singh, the formidable army of the Lahore kingdom had become the main player in the struggle for power. The soldiers and their commanders tended mostly to act independently. The Lahore durbar no longer had any effective control over the troops, whose support was vital for being in power. These troops had constituted regimental councils (panchayats) through which they asserted themselves collectively. The army now supported the claim of Dalip Singh, the youngest son of Ranjit Singh, to be the maharaja. Dalip Singh was a minor, barely five years old at this time. He was the son of Rani Jindan (Jind Kaur). In September 1843, Dalip Singh was formally proclaimed ruler of Punjab, as the successor of Sher Singh. Rani Jindan became regent for the minor maharaja. The strong support of the army ensured the ascendancy of Rani Jindan in the years between the accession of Dalip Singh and the First Punjab War. Her brother Jawahir Singh became the new prime minister (vazir) after the assassination of Hira Singh in 1844. In 1845, Jawahir Singh too was killed. Lal Singh, who enjoyed the confidence of Rani Jindan, became the vazir.

It was reported, in the latter half of 1845, that the British were making preparations to launch a war against Punjab. By this time, the Company had consolidated its position in Sind so that it was possible to mobilize troops on a large scale for the invasion of the Lahore kingdom. Meanwhile, Lal Singh and the commander of the army, Tej Singh, had been secretly engaged in negotiations with the British. Through them the British had information about the resources and plans of the Punjab army. The governor general, Henry Hardinge, who had succeeded Ellenborough in 1844, declared war on 13 December 1845. The First Punjab War dragged on for nearly two months.

The war was a clear case of unprovoked aggression, as whatever the internal problems of Punjab, the British did not have the slightest pretext for launching a war against the kingdom. There is enough evidence to show that the British had already made up their mind to annex Punjab when they began their military preparations. Ever since the arrival of Hardinge there had been a build-up of forces on the Punjab border, at Ferozepur, as well as at the neighbouring cantonment of Ambala. As soon as war was declared British forces commenced moving from Ambala to Ferozepur. The first confrontation between the two sides took place at Mudki, south of the Sutlej (18 December). British forces were led by Hugh Gough. The battle of Mudki resulted in heavy losses for the British, amounting to nearly 900, including a prominent officer of the rank of major general—Robert Sale who had commanded the garrison at Jalalabad during the Afghan War.

The fighting now shifted to the neighbouring village of Feroze Shah. Here, a battle raged continuously from 21 to 22 December. Lal Singh, who was commanding the Punjab troops, retired from the field resulting in confusion. Fighting resumed with the arrival of reinforcements. British casualties amounted to nearly 700 men. The Lahore army retreated to the right bank of the Sutlej, commencing a march in the direction of Ludhiana. Before it could reach Ludhiana it was intercepted by the British at Aliwal where a battle took place on 28 January. The final battle of the war was fought at Sobraon, not far from Aliwal, on the banks of the Sutlej. In this battle the British decisively defeated the Punjab army. It needs to be emphasized that apart from Lal Singh, Tej Singh also assisted the British side in the war. The soldiery fought on its own, putting up a tough fight. At Sobraon, the British lost 2,400 men, an unusually high figure for their forces. Given the kind of resistance that it encountered, the Company gave up the idea of immediately annexing Punjab. This would have involved prolonged fighting for which the British lacked the strength for the time being. Consequently, Hardinge decided to use the victory to weaken the kingdom politically. He set up camp on the outskirts of Lahore to work out the details of an agreement with the durbar through Gulab Singh who had been entrusted with the task of negotiating with the British. His nomination was endorsed by the Punjab army as well.

The deal worked out between Hardinge and Gulab Singh was incorporated in the Treaty of Lahore (9 March 1846). Under the terms of the treaty, the Punjab kingdom was to cede the strip of territory it had on the left bank of the Sutlej. More importantly, it was to cede the fertile Jalandhar Doab lying between the Sutlej and Beas. Further, the British were to be indemnified with Rs 1.5 crores for the expenses of the war. Article IV of the treaty contained a significant provision, with far-reaching consequences. Having already ascertained that the Lahore durbar was not in a position to pay such a huge sum, a devious stipulation was made in this article which stated: '...the Lahore Government being unable to pay the whole of this sum at this time...the Maharajah [Dalip Singh] cedes to the Honourable Company, in perpetual sovereignty, as equivalent for one crore of Rupees, all his forts, territories, rights and interests in the hill countries, which are situated between the

Rivers Beas and Indus, including the Provinces of Cashmere and Hazarah'. Thus Kashmir was handed over to the British, who then by a separate treaty (Treaty of Amritsar, 16 March 1846) gave it to Gulab Singh in return for a sum of Rs 75 lakhs. At the same time another article (Article XII), equally devious, was inserted in the treaty, which stated that as an acknowledgement of the 'services rendered' by Gulab Singh to the Punjab kingdom, especially 'towards procuring the restoration of the relations of amity between the Lahore and British Governments' he was to be recognized as the sovereign ruler of Jammu. In other words, these two treaties together made Gulab Singh independent of Punjab. He was now the ruler of the princely state of Jammu and Kashmir, his reward for the assistance he had given to the British.

Under the terms of the Treaty of Lahore the strength of the Punjab army was reduced to 20,000 infantry and 12,000 cavalry (at the time of the death of Ranjit Singh the total strength of the army was 85,000; it had actually increased subsequently). It was decided that British forces would continue to remain in Punjab till the end of 1846. Due to the complications that had arisen in Afghanistan as a result of an extended military occupation, Hardinge was reluctant to allow the army to stay on in the kingdom for too long.

Tensions soon surfaced between the resident at Lahore, Henry Lawrence, and the regent, Rani Jindan. A new treaty was signed in December 1846 to strengthen the position of the resident and simultaneously marginalize Rani Jindan. A council of regency was constituted, comprising eight Punjab chiefs. The council was to function under the supervision of the resident. British troops were to remain in Punjab, for whose maintenance Rs 22 lakhs had to be paid annually. The treaty envisaged that this arrangement would continue till 1854 when Dalip Singh came of age. Rani Jindan, as might have been expected, continued to be very hostile to the Company's officials. The Punjab army too had not yet reconciled to British presence in the kingdom. In August 1847, Rani Jindan was compelled to leave Lahore so as to curtail her influence.

Mounting opposition to the regime that had been put in place after the treaty of December 1846, which made the resident the de facto ruler, culminated in the outbreak of armed insurrections by 1848. There had been a change of personnel: Lord Dalhousie, a ruthless colonial administrator, had taken over as governor general in January 1848 (he was to remain governor general till 1856); Henry Lawrence had gone to England on leave and was replaced by Frederick Currie as resident at Lahore. The situation in several areas of Punjab was unstable, and often the Lahore authorities had to rely on the Company's apparatus to deal with problems. This was inevitable since the durbar lacked sufficient authority under the new administrative arrangements created by the December 1848 treaty. In April, Multan emerged as a major trouble spot. Here, there was a dispute between the durbar and the governor of Multan, Mulraj, over the share of revenue to be paid into the Lahore treasury. Two relatively junior British officials were sent to Multan with an armed escort to sort out the problem. Their intervention led to an armed uprising by Mulraj. Operations were launched against him and in September 1848 Multan was besieged. Currie despatched troops from Lahore under the command of a prominent chief, and member of the council of regency, Sher Singh Attariwala. Sher Singh went over to the side of the rebels along with his troops. Several other chiefs who were opposed to the Company organized themselves with their supporters under the leadership of Sher Singh. Sher Singh entered into negotiations with Dost Mohammad and secured his support. Sher Singh's father Chattar Singh Attariwala, who was posted as governor of Hazara, joined the rebels. A large number of the dismissed soldiers of the Punjab army flocked to the rebel forces. The extensive support that the rebels had been able to gather made the situation in Punjab critical for the British and their collaborators. The commander-in-chief of the

British forces, Hugh Gough, was reluctant to launch operations to suppress the insurrection during the monsoon; moreover he wanted some time to make adequate preparations for a full-fledged military offensive in Punjab. The siege of Multan lingered on. Rani Jindan, who had allegedly been encouraging soldiers of the Lahore army to support the cause of the rebels, was exiled to Banaras.

Once the preparations for the invasion were completed, British forces under Gough crossed into Punjab in November 1848. This marked the beginning of the war, even though no formal declaration of war was made. The first major battle of the Second Punjab War took place at Chillianwala on the banks of the Jhelum on 13 January 1849. Sher Singh Attariwala played a crucial role in this battle. The British were utterly defeated at Chillianwala. In colonial historiography, the battle is often shown to have been indecisive, which is entirely incorrect. The British were routed. There was fierce criticism of Gough and the manner in which he had handled the operation. It was decided to replace Gough with Charles Napier. After all, British casualties had been colossal, amounting to nearly 3,000 men.

The Punjab army could not take the victory at Chillianwala to its logical conclusion due to the lack of sufficient officers. It should be remembered that it was essentially the rebel army that was engaged in the fighting. Most of the experienced officers had already betrayed the soldiers. It was mainly the soldiers who fought this war, just as they had taken the lead in the First Punjab War. The Battle of Chillianwala coincided with the final phase of the British offensive against Mulraj at Multan. This should be seen as another theatre of the war. For three weeks, from 2 January 1849 onwards, fierce fighting was taking place at Multan. Mulraj surrendered on 22 January. The capture of Multan was accompanied by the indiscriminate slaughter of the civilian population of the city. The city itself was almost destroyed. Its recovery and rehabilitation took a long time.

Before Napier could take over as the commander-in-chief, another engagement took place between the Punjab troops and the British. This was the battle that decided the fate of Punjab. It was fought at Gujrat, close to the Chenab River, on 22 February. Ceasefire was finally agreed to on 12 March. On 29 March, a proclamation was issued by Dalhousie that Punjab had been annexed. A board of administration, comprising three members, was constituted to administer Punjab as a province of the Company's Indian empire. An important reason for this administrative arrangement was that Dalhousie wished to marginalize Henry Lawrence, who had returned from leave and had been made president of the board of administration. Lawrence had no overriding powers over the other two members, one of whom was his brother John. Whereas John's views regarding the traditional elites of Punjab were similar to those of the governor general who wanted to divest them of their power, Henry and Dalhousie differed sharply on this question. Henry was of the opinion that these elites should not be eliminated. This would allow the Company to stabilize its rule in Punjab. Eventually, Henry Lawrence was shunted out of Punjab. The board of administration was dissolved in 1852 and John became the chief commissioner of the province with wide-ranging powers.

◆

The Second Anglo-Burmese War, referred to above, marked the second phase of the conquest of Burma. Globally, British colonialism had become increasingly aggressive by the mid-nineteenth century. In the Indian subcontinent, with the conquest of Sind and Punjab, an arrogant Company engaged in further territorial expansion through various means: outright war, intimidation, coercion, disdain for treaties, and deception. The conquest of Lower Burma was carried out through military invasion of the region in the manner of a piratical expedition. It began with a demand for a huge sum of money with the threat that if it was not paid, the country would be attacked.

The war had its supposed origin in a petty dispute (June–August 1851) wherein acting on complaints made by sailors of two British merchant ships against their respective captains (the sailors were subjects of the Indian empire), the governor of Rangoon imposed fines amounting to about £170 in all. The captains approached the Calcutta authorities, urging them to intervene in the matter and demand a compensation of £1,920 from the Burmese. Interestingly, this amount was found to be excessive, and the Calcutta authorities reduced it to £920. Two naval ships were then sent from Calcutta, under the command of Commodore George Lambert, to convey to the governor of Rangoon the demand for this compensation. Lambert was explicitly instructed not to behave in a hostile manner. However, on his arrival he immediately began to vitiate the atmosphere so that soon conditions were created for war.

Upon reaching Rangoon towards the end of November 1851, Lambert encouraged local merchants, mostly from British India, to present to him their grievances against the Burmese government. They were asked to submit these complaints in writing by 28 November. One day before this deadline he wrote to the Calcutta authorities that he was withholding the original demand until he had forwarded the complaints to the governor general. All this information, usually suppressed in colonial historiography, was set forth lucidly in a booklet published in 1853, entitled *How Wars Are Got Up in India*.[4] The author of the booklet, Richard Cobden, was a radical and a strong advocate of peace and disarmament; the booklet was a forceful condemnation of the war. It was based upon papers laid before the British Parliament which were put together by the government in such a way that the events leading up to the war were not easily comprehensible. The so-called complaints of

[4]Richard Cobden, *How Wars Are Got Up in India: The Origin of the Burmese War*, London: Richard Barrett, 1853.

merchants, which are often referred to in colonial writings on the war, can hardly be taken seriously as being a factor. Many of them relate to fines imposed by the Rangoon administration in matters relating to petty domestic quarrels. Others, as Cobden notes, were absurd. No dates or other relevant details of these grievances were provided in the parliamentary Blue Book in which they were reproduced. Moreover, there was no verification of the complaints.

Nevertheless, Lambert sent a letter to the Ava court seeking action against the governor of Rangoon. The governor was removed and another appointed in his place. The new governor (special commissioner) assumed charge on 4 January 1852. On 6 January, Lambert sent a communication to the governor through a clerk of the British establishment. A brief delay in receiving this communication was perceived as an insult. Within six hours of this minor episode Lambert declared Rangoon and its entire coastline under blockade. A royal ship belonging to the king, the *Yenanyin*, was forcibly seized. British subjects (i.e., mainly Indians resident in Rangoon) were asked to evacuate the city. Bombardment by British warships caused nearly 300 deaths. Despite these serious provocations which amounted to aggression against the kingdom's territories, the Burmese authorities were conciliatory. Notwithstanding the lack of hostility on the part of Burma, an ultimatum was issued to the court of Ava in February, demanding a compensation of £100,000. This was over a hundred times the original demand to pay £920 to the captains of British ships! The ruler was threatened with war in case the sum was not paid. While the British awaited a reply from Ava, hectic preparations began to be made for war. Nearly 6,000 troops, mainly of the Madras Army, had reached Burma by the first week of April 1852.

Operations commenced in the second week of April, focused initially on the Gulf of Martaban. It should be kept in mind that the coast lying southeast of Rangoon in Tenasserim was under British control. The port town of Martaban, located close to Moulmein (Mawlamyine) at the northern end of Tenasserim was the first to be captured. Moulmein was the administrative capital of Tenasserim. A few days later, a massive assault was made on Rangoon. By 14 April, Rangoon had been occupied. Bassein lying southeast of Rangoon was the next strategically located town to be captured (19 May). Pegu (Bago) was occupied in June; fighting was resumed at Pegu in November, and eventually the British occupied the town. By this time another Burmese city, Prome, lying north of Rangoon along the Irrawaddy, had also been taken. In December 1852, Dalhousie declared that Pegu had been annexed. A ceasefire was agreed to between the British and the commander of the Burmese forces, General Dabayin (son of the legendary Maha Bandula referred to earlier) but the court of Ava refused to sign a formal treaty. Neither did it recognize the cession of Pegu. Dalhousie, on the instructions of the London authorities, insisted on a treaty being formalized. He threatened the king with an invasion of northern Burma if this demand was not accepted. This plan had to be abandoned due to the fierce resistance that the British continued to encounter. Some of the powerful chiefs who controlled the areas lying along the Irrawaddy, north of Rangoon, such as Myat Toon and Shwe Ban, launched a guerrilla war after the annexation of Pegu. They were opposed to attempts by a section of royal officials to negotiate with the British. Operations against armed troops loyal to Myat Toon continued during the first half of 1853 and involved fierce fighting in the jungle. A force under Colonel John Cheape was sent into the interior to stamp out the resistance of Myat Toon. Cheape was able to dislodge Myat Toon after a bloody struggle lasting several days in February–March 1853 in which howitzers had to be used by the British. Myat Toon remained powerful in northern Burma till his death in 1878.

Burmese defeat in the Second Burma War led to sharp differences at Ava over the question of appropriate policy for dealing with the British menace. This culminated in a struggle for power in which the ruling king Pagan Min (r. 1846–53) abdicated the throne and his half-brother Mindon Min (r. 1853–78) became the new ruler. Though Mindon Min was in favour of concluding peace with the British, he too declined to sign a formal treaty. A formal ceasefire was declared in June 1853. Pegu was placed under a commissioner, Arthur Phayre being the first incumbent. In 1862, the commissionership of Pegu was combined with the two other commissionerships of British Burma, Arakan, and Tenasserim, to constitute the province of Lower Burma under a chief commissioner. Phayre was chief commissioner from 1862 to 1867. Rangoon was made the administrative capital of Lower Burma.

In several accounts of the war, Lambert has been singled out as the person responsible for perpetrating it. It is likely that initially Dalhousie might not have considered the compensation issue as being serious enough to justify an invasion of the Burmese kingdom and Lambert might have been acting mostly on the basis of his personal understanding of how British authority was to be asserted. At the same time, the confidence with which he ignored written instructions enjoining him not to be aggressive would suggest that he had the tacit support of the governor general, who in turn seems to have been sure of support from the British government. This is borne out by the promptness with which preparations were made for war at the beginning of 1852, within a few weeks of the arrival of Lambert in Burma. At no stage were his actions disowned. As a matter of fact, he received a series of promotions after the war, retiring in 1864 with the rank of vice admiral.

The kingdom of Burma had been deprived of its entire coastal area, of access to the sea, and of the rich Irrawaddy delta. This substantially reduced its resources. Further, from Lower Burma the British steadily penetrated northern Burma, preying upon its resources, particularly the extensive forests of high-quality teak. From the 1860s there was intense pressure, in the name of free trade, to 'open' up independent Burma to British commerce. This led to large-scale plunder of its resources. Apart from high-quality teak, Burma was a major source of rubies and tin. In the latter half of the nineteenth century, it emerged as a leading producer of rice for the world market. Unfree migrant labour was brought from the Indian subcontinent, under the indenture system, for the cultivation of rice. Credit for rice cultivation was provided by Chettiar moneylenders of Tamil Nadu. These developments transformed the Burmese economy significantly in the decades following the Second Anglo-Burmese War. Colonial subjugation intensified the appropriation of the resources of the country. The Bombay Burmah Trading Corporation (BBTC), a British company, acquired a virtual monopoly over the timber resources of Burma, including large stretches of forest in Upper Burma. The massive scale of the plunder carried out by the BBTC was to lead to serious tensions in the 1870s when the royal government attempted to curtail the activities of this company. This led to an orchestrated campaign by chambers of commerce in Britain which created the political conditions for the annexation of the kingdom of Burma. This, as has already been noted, was achieved through the Third Anglo-Burmese War of 1885–86.

◆

The First Opium War (1839–42), waged by the British against China, was closely linked to colonial interests in India. Along with the implications that it had for the 'imperialism of free trade' in the context of China, the war should also be viewed as an extension of aggressive empire building in the Indian subcontinent. For nearly three quarters of a century, since the late 1760s, the British had steadily increased their commercial activities in China, mainly for procuring Chinese tea for the British market. As noted earlier, the Charter Act of 1813 had ended the Company's monopoly on (British) trade with India; the Company retained its monopoly of trade with China until 1833–34. This monopoly was important for the commercial interests of the Company as there had been a rapid growth in the demand for tea in Britain from the 1780s onwards, particularly with the massive reduction in duties on the import of tea in 1784 (Commutation Act of 1784). By the early decades of the nineteenth century, tea had become an article of mass consumption: tea and sugar could provide cheap calories to industrial workers and their families, becoming a popular everyday beverage for the English working class. However, large quantities of precious metal had to be carried to China for the purchase of tea (and Chinese silk), something that was considered undesirable for the British economy, and was becoming difficult towards the end of the eighteenth century as a considerable amount of bullion had to be diverted for financing the costly wars of conquest in India. The solution to this problem was provided by opium.

Following the conquest of Bengal and Bihar, the Company had established control over the opium produce of the Ganga region. Most of this opium was produced in Bihar. Subsequently, another important opium producing tract, Banaras–Ghazipur, was taken over by the Company (1795). By the 1790s, the production of and trade in opium had become a direct monopoly of the Company. The poppy plant, which yields opium in its raw state, could only be cultivated by obtaining a licence from the Company, and all the opium extracted from poppies had to be handed over to local offices of opium agencies established for the purpose. The opium agencies processed the raw liquid received from cultivators. Processing mainly involved desiccation, and packing large balls of the drug in wooden chests. Opium in bulk was reckoned in 'chests': one 'chest' of 'Bengal opium' (as the Company's monopoly opium was called), weighed 160 lbs avoirdupois, net.[5] Packaged opium was taken to Calcutta where it was sold to private traders through public auction. The opium

---

[5]Avoirdupois is a system of weights, based on pounds and ounces, wherein 1 lb=16 oz (160 lbs=72.575 kg).

auctioned at Calcutta was intended entirely for export, for the most part to China. At the turn of the century, 4,000–5,000 chests of Bengal opium were being sold at the Calcutta auctions. At this stage, the Company, as a matter of policy, restricted the number of chests put up for sale to this figure.

The Qing imperial authorities had imposed a ban on the import of opium into China in 1729. Consequently, the Company preferred to let private traders run the risk of selling the drug at the China-end, rather than carrying opium in its own ships. This was a smuggling venture in China. Nevertheless, this smuggling venture became possible due to the protection that was provided by the East India Company, and the British government. When the Qing authorities threatened to extinguish smuggling of the commodity in the 1830s, by which time it had become a large-scale undertaking, the British promptly sent in military forces to prevent them from doing so, and thereby uphold the principles of 'free trade'. This is what led to armed conflict and to the First Opium War.

Opium was smuggled into China via Canton and the maritime zone lying south of it. This zone consists of several islands which could be used to temporarily store the drug and carry out illicit transactions without easy detection. The topography of the area, with its numerous waterways, including the Pearl River estuary, was peculiarly suited to clandestine transportation. The drug would be offloaded from ships at some distance from Canton and carried in small boats to outlying islands to be conveyed to the interior. Business transactions relating to the sale and purchase of opium chests, between the importers and Chinese wholesale dealers, were undertaken at Canton. The imperial authorities had confined foreign trade to Canton since 1760. European and American merchants were allowed to establish 'factories', i.e. offices and godowns, on a small strip of land on the waterfront. The various foreign companies were allocated separate areas for their respective nations (British, French, Dutch, Spanish, American, Austrian,

Swedish, and Danish). It may be mentioned that the Portuguese had their own establishment in neighbouring Macao, which had been leased from the Chinese. All business dealings between the European and American traders at Canton were conducted through a small group of Chinese merchants authorized by the Qing government, collectively known as the 'Cohong'.

Once the opium that was consigned to China had been sold, the earnings would be usually deposited in the Company's treasury at Canton. The Company used this money to finance its own purchases of tea (and silk). Bills of exchange were issued to the opium dealers, equivalent to the silver specie received from them. These bills of exchange could be encashed either in Calcutta or London. The London bills, which were in great demand in India, were important for transferring private British earnings to the metropolis. This pattern of 'trade' allowed the East India Company to dispense with shipping of precious metal to China for its purchases. Export of silver to China by the Company had ceased by 1800. Another development at the beginning of the nineteenth century was the expansion of private European and American commerce at Canton. The Company had to tolerate the presence of private British firms in China as these firms (along with some American firms) handled the opium cargoes shipped from India.

In the first two decades of the nineteenth century there had been a steady increase in sea-borne opium exports from India to China, particularly due to the influx of the drug from the west coast of India. This was opium produced in the Malwa region (present-day western Madhya Pradesh), hence called Malwa opium, to distinguish it from Bengal opium. Unlike the opium produce of eastern India, the Company exercised no control over the production of, or wholesale trade in, Malwa opium. This opium was produced entirely in princely states, and even though the British tried hard during the 1820s to regulate the opium economy of Malwa, it failed to do so. Ultimately, in 1830, the Company decided to levy a duty on

Malwa opium brought to Bombay for shipment to China. The opium trade of western India was thus wholly in the hands of private merchants, both Indian and British.

Among the private British firms in China engaged in opium smuggling the two most prominent were Jardine & Matheson and Dent & Co. By the 1820s a substantial portion of the drug sent out from Calcutta and Bombay was consigned to them. Of the two, Jardine & Matheson was the bigger of the two enterprises and pushed its business more aggressively. The two partners of the firm, William Jardine and James Matheson, became the spokespersons for private British opium dealers at Canton in the endeavour to prevail upon the British government to use military force, if necessary, in order to compel the Qing emperor to 'open' China to free trade. Their lobbying was critical to orchestrating a campaign in Britain during the 1830s for armed intervention in China, mainly to safeguard the interests of opium smugglers—all in the name of free trade.

The abolition of the East India Company's monopoly of trade with China led to an increase in the number of private traders operating in the South China Sea from 1834 onwards. At the same time there was a substantial rise in the number of opium chests shipped to China. According to figures worked out by Michael Greenberg, the leading historian of the crucial formative phase of the colonial opium venture in China and of the role played by the drug in unleashing the Opium War, exports of Bengal and Malwa opium roughly doubled between 1834/35 and 1838/39, from 21,885 chests to 40,200 chests.[6] This situation led to a crisis. Opium smugglers insisted on their right to sell increased quantities of the commodity. For the Qing authorities it was now essential to initiate drastic measures to put an end to the opium commerce, which in any case had been illegal since the early eighteenth century. The opium

[6]Michael Greenberg, *British Trade and the Opening of China, 1800-1842*, Cambridge: Cambridge University Press, 1951, Appendix I.

trade embargo was to be strictly implemented; connivance of local officials in smuggling was to be punished severely; opium stocks were to be confiscated; and opium consumers were to be imprisoned so as to discourage consumption of the drug.

The British had already adopted an aggressive posture towards China since the early 1830s. Soon after the Company's monopoly came to an end, the government appointed superintendents of trade to look after the commercial interests of British traders at Canton. William Napier was named chief superintendent in 1834. Upon his arrival in China, he travelled to Canton without the permission of imperial officials. As he had not been issued a passport he was ordered to leave Canton. When he refused to do so the premises occupied by British firms were blockaded. Trade with these firms was officially suspended and all British residents of Canton were asked to leave the city. Napier responded by sending armed vessels to fire on Canton, to which the Chinese retaliated. This marked the beginning of a minor armed conflict. Eventually, Napier was forced to retreat to Macao where he passed away in October 1834. Following this incident, the Chinese were demonized and hysteria was whipped up in Britain over the supposedly unreasonable stance of the Qing authorities towards foreign traders. The attempt to put an end to the opium trade came to be seen as an attack on legitimate commerce. By 1839, colonial policymakers had committed themselves to a major military campaign against the Qing empire. The resolve of the emperor to annihilate opium smuggling, and the relentless drive that was initiated to achieve this objective, provided the pretext for a full-scale war against the Chinese.

Towards the end of 1838, the Daoguang emperor (r. 1820–50) appointed Lin Zexu, a senior Chinese official, as imperial commissioner for Canton with wide-ranging powers to eradicate opium smuggling. Lin Zexu arrived in Canton in March 1839. Lin Zexu had consistently advocated strong measures to stamp out the drug trade. By the end of the month, he sent orders to foreign traders to stop their opium transactions and surrender their existing stocks of the drug, and declared that those found dealing in the commodity would be executed. As the smugglers delayed handing over their opium chests, the Chinese authorities encircled the factories and placed the traders in confinement. The waterfront was blockaded so that the traders could not flee from Canton. Chinese servants employed in the factories were ordered to vacate the area. The blockade lasted for forty-seven days, from 24 March to 21 May.

Given the seriousness of the situation, the main British representative in China, Charles Elliot, who had occupied the position of chief superintendent of trade at Canton since 1836, intervened to prevent a total collapse of business. After all, British traders were the principal target of Lin Zexu's measures. Elliot persuaded the British merchants to hand over to the Chinese authorities their stocks of opium, a little over 20,000 chests. Further, he assured the traders that the British government would reimburse the full value of the opium surrendered by them. This amounted to £2.4 million. Scholars have pointed out that Elliot's guarantee that the British government would be answerable for the value of the opium given up to Chinese officials and the huge sum involved, in effect transformed a private matter into a dispute between Britain and China.

The chests confiscated by Lin Zexu were ordered to be destroyed. In May 1839, massive quantities were dumped into the river and eventually flushed out into the sea. In the following months, the situation became increasingly tense due to continuing violations of Chinese regulations by British traders. Another provocation was the killing of a local villager by British sailors and the refusal to give up the culprits to the Chinese authorities for punishment. By August, the British had been forced to shift to Hong Kong harbour and their supplies of food and fresh water were cut off. Hostilities commenced in September 1839, though at this stage the fighting was on a very small scale. These early encounters near Canton continued till November.

Meanwhile, the British government decided to send a naval force to China. Arriving in the South China Sea in June 1840, this naval force established a blockade at Canton. Simultaneously, another fleet of warships was sent up the coast and captured Chusan (Zhoushan), lying south of Shanghai, in July. British ships then proceeded further north towards Beijing, and entered the Peiho River on the way to Beijing. A letter from the British foreign secretary Lord Palmerston was handed over to Chinese officials for transmission to the emperor. The letter was an imperialist assertion of the right of Britain to use force to compel China to engage in trade on terms laid down by the British. By this time, Lin Zexu had been replaced by another official, Qishan. Qishan was amenable to a compromise with the British and was willing to abandon the inflexible policy of Lin Zexu. He asked the British to return to Canton for negotiations. However, it was difficult for the Chinese to accept the unreasonable proposals of the British and after terms for a treaty that had been worked out between Qishan and Elliot were rejected by the emperor the war began in earnest. Canton was the main focus of the campaign launched by the British, although there were several other theatres of war. Fighting on both land and sea continued from February 1841 to August 1842. Hugh Gough was sent out from India, along with contingents of the Company's army, as commander-in-chief of the land forces. Gough led the offensive launched for the capture of Canton. Elliot was replaced by Henry Pottinger as chief superintendent of trade, with the authority to conduct negotiations with Chinese imperial officials. On the Chinese side, Qishan had been removed from his position in disgrace, and replaced by Yishan.

The Chinese found it difficult to withstand the massive military onslaught of the British. The British mobilized force on a large scale, unleashing the firepower of their advanced warships, of which the most formidable was the iron-clad steam-propelled frigate *Nemesis*. The *Nemesis* wreaked havoc on Canton; the city was the worst affected in the fighting. Finally, in August 1842, terms for a ceasefire were worked out. This led to the signing of the Treaty of Nanking (Nanjing) on 29 August. The treaty was ratified by the emperor in September. According to the key provisions of the treaty, China was compelled to pay to Britain indemnity of 21 million ounces of silver and had to cede Hong Kong to the British. Further, five ports had to be opened to international trade (Canton, Amoy, Fuzhou, Ningbo, and Shanghai).

EIGHT

'INDIRECT RULE' AND THE DALHOUSIE ERA

The decade of the 1850s witnessed several crucial changes in the mechanism for governing the Indian empire. These reflected shifts in policy, both before and after the revolt of 1857. Some of these shifts may be discerned in the late 1840s, especially during the era of Lord Dalhousie, who was governor general for eight years, from 1848 to 1856. The most significant change took place towards the end of 1858 when the British crown directly assumed charge of the Government of India. This was preceded by the Charter Act of 1853, the last occasion on which the East India Company received a charter.

When the Company's charter came up for renewal in 1853, the parliament asserted, much more explicitly than it had done earlier, its right to determine the manner in which India was to be governed. The long-standing demand of free traders to put an end to the system of governing India through the mechanism of the Company could not be resisted for much longer. They had recently won an important victory with the repeal of the Corn Laws in 1846. The Corn Laws were intended to protect landed interests in Britain from international competition, by imposing very high import duties on foodgrains. Yet the Company could still muster sufficient political support to be able to continue with its hold over the Indian empire, even though this hold was considerably weakened by the 1853 Act.

The Charter Act of 1853 subjected the EIC's empire in India to much tighter control by the British government than had been attempted by legislation of the earlier part of the nineteenth century. A decisive measure was the provision for reconstituting the court of directors such that one-third of its members were now to be nominees of the British government. The strength of the court of directors was brought down from the existing twenty-four to eighteen: six members of the court were henceforth to be nominees of the government. The government could thus have a direct say, 1853–54 onwards, in this all-powerful organ of the colonial state. Unlike the previous charters, the Charter Act of 1853 did not specify the duration for which it would be valid. In other words, the British government reserved the right to directly take into its own hands the administration of the Indian empire whenever it chose to do so. The Act declared that the Company held its Indian territories 'in trust' for the British crown.

Furthermore, members of the court of directors were, by the Charter Act of 1853, deprived of the privilege of nominating candidates for appointment to superior posts in the civil service. The selection of covenanted civil servants was now to be on the basis of an open competition. A committee was constituted by the board of control to work out the modalities of the competition. Public examinations commenced in 1855.

As noted earlier, the Charter Act of 1833 had added a law member to the governor general's council whose presence was essential when the council took up legislative matters. The law member was now made a full member of the council (earlier he could only attend meetings of the council when legislative matters were on the agenda). More importantly, the Charter Act of 1853 substantially modified the composition of the governor general's council when it met for legislative purposes. The 1833 Act had, it was felt, led to excessive centralization in matters of legislation as the presidencies and provinces no longer had any authority to enact laws or regulations. In order to have adequate inputs from the several presidencies and provinces, as well as from the judiciary, six more members were added to the council when it met to deliberate upon legislative matters. These additional members were the chief justice and a judge of the Supreme Court of Calcutta; and one member each from the three presidencies of Bengal, Madras, and Bombay, and from the North-Western Provinces. The idea of a distinct 'legislative council', which was already conceptually present in the Charter Act of 1833, was now developed further. This was now a body of twelve members comprising the governor general, four 'ordinary members' (including the law member), the commander-in-chief, and six 'additional members'. The additional members did not sit when the council met to discuss matters pertaining to the executive functioning of the government. The Act also provided for the appointment of a separate governor for the Bengal Presidency. This was intended to reduce the routine administrative tasks relating to the presidency which had to be attended to by the governor general (who, it may be mentioned, was simultaneously governor of Bengal Presidency). In 1854, a lieutenant governor was appointed for Bengal, instead of a full-fledged governor.

Whereas the board of control monitored, on behalf of parliament, the Company's political and military functions, the Company's own establishment remained vital for the entire decision-making process. John Dickinson, a prominent critic of the EIC whose writings were among the sources used by Karl Marx for his articles on the EIC, and who was strongly opposed to the renewal of the Company's charter in 1853, underlined in his writings the extent to which the British government was dependent on the Company's apparatus for determining policy relating to the Indian empire. The huge volume of paperwork made the Company's vast clerical establishment, with its almost exclusive access to detailed information, indispensible to policymakers in London. The Company was, after all, the main repository of knowledge about the colony in the metropole. Marx, writing in 1853, perceptively remarked that, 'When the East India Company was only a commercial association, they, of course, requested a most detailed report on every item from the managers of their Indian factories, as is done by every trading concern. When the factories grew into an Empire, [and] the commercial items into ship loads of correspondence and documents, the Leadenhall clerks went on in their system, which made the Directors and the Board their dependents; and they succeeded in transforming the Indian Government into one immense writing-machine.'[1]

A few years later, when the parliament was debating the abolition of the Company's rule over the Indian empire against the backdrop of the revolt of 1857, access by the Company to specialized knowledge about India was put forth as the key argument by ideologues who were opposed to crown rule. These included John Stuart Mill, one of the leading political thinkers of the time. This argument, as we shall see, did not prevent parliament from legislating in August 1858 for the crown to directly take over the governance of the Indian empire.

◆

The aspect of the Dalhousie era which has received the most attention in historical writings is his policy towards princely states, the infamous 'doctrine of lapse', which is often considered to be one of the major factors responsible for the revolt of 1857. This doctrine was enunciated with the objective of justifying the formal annexation of the territories of several princely states in the late 1840s and early 1850s. Two major states annexed by Dalhousie were those of Awadh and Nagpur.

During Dalhousie's lengthy tenure there was a distinct alteration in colonial policy towards princely states. Whereas in the period following the Third Anglo-Maratha War there had been a tendency to leave the territories of these states untouched, Dalhousie strongly advocated decreasing the areas under indirect rule and bringing them under direct British administration. This trend might have continued beyond his tenure had not the revolt intervened. The revolt of 1857 altered

[1]Karl Marx, 'The Government of India', *New York Daily Tribune*, 20 July 1853.

the attitude of the British towards princely states: after the revolt their collaboration was actively sought and they came to be considered vital for the stability of the empire.

By the middle of the century, nearly two-fifths of the area of the Indian empire was under numerous princely rulers who ruled over political entities referred to as 'native states' (princely states). These ranged in size from tiny territorial units comprising just a few villages, to very large states encompassing extensive portions of the subcontinent. Hyderabad was the largest state, followed (in terms of area) by Kashmir. Mysore, which for most of the nineteenth century was actually administered by the British, too was a major princely state. There were roughly over 500 states on the eve of the revolt of 1857. During the course of the nineteenth century, the British attempted to arrange the princely states in a hierarchy. At the top were Hyderabad, Mysore, and Baroda (to these were added in the early twentieth century Gwalior and Kashmir). In all, there were about 120 entities which had the status of full-fledged 'native' states, as indicated by their rulers being formally entitled to gun salutes. The remaining states were essentially large (at times not so large) zamindaris with pretensions to royal status. To refer to them as princely states is somewhat misleading.

In the south, the state of Travancore (southern Kerala) was the only other prominent princely state apart from Mysore and Hyderabad. There were no princely states located in the Tamil Nadu region, with one exception—Pudukottai, though there were some princely rulers without any territory (e.g., the nawab of Arcot). The central part of the Indian subcontinent had a large concentration of states. In fact, there was a continuous zone of princely rule extending diagonally from the non-coastal areas of Orissa in the southeast, to coastal Gujarat in the west. This is also a major tribal belt, a large portion of which comprised dense forests or difficult hilly terrain. There was a tendency, in the colonial period, to avoid administering such tracts directly, but this was not always the case. The Chhota

Nagpur plateau was dotted by several minor states, as were the adjoining Baghelkhand and Bundelkhand regions.

The fertile Malwa plateau (lying in present-day western Madhya Pradesh, north of the Narmada) was entirely under princely states, predominantly ruled by Maratha and Rajput dynasties. The leading states were Gwalior (ruled by the Sindias) and Indore (under the Holkars). Besides, there was the Bhopal state whose Pathan lineage had several women rulers in the colonial era. Almost all of Gujarat was controlled by the British through princely states. There were nearly four hundred princely states in this region alone, the overwhelming majority of which were tiny principalities. There were also some very large states in the region, as for instance Baroda (ruled by the Maratha Gaikwad dynasty) and Junagarh. Neighbouring Rajasthan too was almost completely under princely rule, Udaipur, Jodhpur, Jaipur, Jaisalmer, and Bikaner being some of the major states. As the states of Rajasthan were ruled largely by Rajput dynasties, the British designated the region as Rajputana, privileging this caste over other castes of the area.

At the northwestern extremity of the Indian empire was the state of Kalat in Baluchistan, and a couple of petty tribal chiefdoms in the northwestern frontier area. Most of Punjab (extending from the Sutlej in the east to the borders of Afghanistan in the west) was directly administered. There were, however, a few princely states in eastern Punjab, Patiala being the foremost among them. Some princely states were located in the hills of what is now Himachal Pradesh. Kashmir was territorially a vast state lying between Afghanistan and Tibet.

The only state of some consequence in what is now Uttar Pradesh was the relatively small principality of Rampur. In eastern India, Bihar did not have any princely states, though there was the very prominent zamindari of Darbhanga which, while it was not formally recognized as a princely state, was certainly more important politically and economically than most of the petty principalities of Gujarat. In Bengal there was just one princely state, Cooch-Behar (or Koch Behar), besides several zamindari estates such as Burdwan. In the northeast there was Tripura, and the very extensive princely state of Manipur. Sikkim too was part of the British Indian empire.

The colonial relationship with princely states was evolving throughout the early century through constant negotiation and renegotiation. The incorporation of a subjugated political entity in the Indian subcontinent into the British Indian empire as a princely state was a historical process whereby the state was allowed some amount of autonomy while acknowledging the supremacy of the British. The extent of autonomy varied from state to state and depended upon the historical conditions in which the state had been subjugated. The question of sovereignty, the extent to which princely rulers could be regarded as sovereign, remained a grey area in the early part of the nineteenth century. It was only after the revolt that the British crown asserted its sovereign status and attempts were made to theorize about the constitutional status of the states vis-à-vis the crown.

Unlike the presidencies and provinces of British India, which were administered directly by the Company through its own personnel, princely states were administered by personnel of the respective states. However, they were subject to surveillance and monitoring by the Company's officials. Residents or else political agents headed the British supervisory mechanism in the princely states. Residents were usually posted in the more important states, while smaller or less important states would usually be grouped together in an 'agency' (e.g., Central India Agency), and placed under a political agent. Residents and political agents often wielded enormous authority, and constituted parallel centres of power, as for instance in Awadh. The branch of the Company's government which handled matters pertaining to princely states was known as the foreign department, political branch. Rulers of princely states had no authority in matters pertaining to defence, communications, and foreign relations. Foreign relations included relations with other princely states.

Several colonial officials posted in princely states emerged as prominent ideologues, shaping the understanding that the respective states had about their past. The most well-known figure is James Tod (political agent, Mewar and Western Rajputana, 1818–22), who profoundly influenced modern historical narratives of the medieval period of Rajasthan. His *Annals and Antiquities of Rajasthan* (1832) was to provide ample material for those historiographical trends that attempted to present, from the late nineteenth century onwards, the conflict between Mewar and the Mughals in terms of a religious conflict.

Whereas the British frequently claimed that they were not interested in interfering in the internal affairs of princely states, in practice they attempted to steadily erode their autonomy. The relationship with Mysore, which otherwise ranked just next to Hyderabad in the hierarchy of princely states, is illustrative of British policy in the first half of the nineteenth century. Mysore derived its symbolic importance in the colonial imperial scheme from the fact that it had been the Company's most formidable opponent in the early phase of its expansion. Four major wars had to be waged against the kingdom of Mysore before it could be subjugated. Following the final defeat, and death in battle, of Tipu Sultan (1799), a substantial portion of his territories was annexed by the British and a truncated Mysore was constituted as a princely state under Krishnaraja Wodeyar III (r. 1799–1868). Krishnaraja was invested with full powers in 1810. The state had to pay a huge sum, initially Rs 25 lakhs, as tribute to the Company (the amount was temporarily enhanced during the Second and Third Anglo-Maratha Wars). Besides, it had to contribute towards the cost of the armed contingents imposed upon it. These contingents, commanded by Europeans, had their headquarters at Bangalore, situated at a short distance from Mysore. Bangalore became the largest British cantonment in south India in the nineteenth century.

While the city of Bangalore itself was under the Mysore ruler, the cantonment was under British rule.

The huge financial burden placed on the state resulted in greater exploitation of the peasantry. The tribute levied on Mysore represented more than half the total estimated revenue of the state. The brutally oppressive measures adopted against peasants by revenue officials of the state seriously aggravated agrarian distress by the 1820s, precipitating an insurrection. In 1830, a rural uprising against the Mysore government broke out in the northern areas of the state, rapidly spreading to other parts. The British had to intervene militarily to suppress the uprising. It was against this backdrop that the British decided to take over the administration of the state in 1831. The Company would have preferred to annex Mysore, but was prevented from doing so by an adverse judicial ruling in England on this move. For the next fifty years the state was administered by colonial officials headed by a commissioner who had extensive powers. The first commissioner, Mark Cubbon, held the office for nearly three decades. His uninterrupted tenure which lasted till 1861 virtually made him the ruler of the state, facilitating the smooth implementation of colonial policies. Bangalore with its huge cantonment was also the seat of government. Mysore, where the ruler resided, was marginalized as an urban centre and the maharaja was reduced to being a ceremonial figure.

Two prominent states, Nagpur and Awadh, and some relatively small states in various parts of the empire, were annexed in the late 1840s and early 1850s. Besides these, the Company acquired a portion of the territory of the Hyderabad state, a longstanding ally of the Company. One of the instruments of policy used frequently by Dalhousie for annexing princely states was the so-called doctrine of lapse (or doctrine of the right of lapse). Under this, the British claimed that they had the prerogative of taking over a state in the event of an unsatisfactory succession. The British had a long history of intervening in matters of succession in princely states.

Every succession was an occasion for asserting the authority of the colonial state over the respective princely states. No succession was considered valid without the recognition of the Company. This meant that the Company arbitrated in disputes over succession, usually promoting disputes to extend the scope of its power. It also claimed the right to determine whether an heir was legitimate or not; or whether the adoption of an heir was acceptable. The accession of a new ruler was often used as an opportunity to extract tribute, demand cession of territory and/or amend existing treaties and agreements in a manner that further subordinated these states.

There were two significant cases of annexation under the doctrine of lapse. The first was the small principality of Satara. In fact, it was the question of the Satara succession, which had some complications, that provided the immediate context for developing an elaborate argument about the prerogative of the colonial power to seize a princely state. The doctrine was expounded in a minute penned by Dalhousie in August 1848. The state of Satara, as we have noted in the previous chapter, though not very large in terms of territory, had considerable symbolic importance as the ruler of the state was a descendant of Shivaji, and as chhatrapati had been the nominal overlord of the peshwa. In the closing phase of the Third Anglo-Maratha War, the British had considered it necessary to keep the state intact so as to legitimize their occupation of the peshwa's territories by claiming the support of the ruler of Satara. It may be recalled that after the Third Anglo-Maratha War, Pratap Singh was recognized as the ruler of Satara. In 1839 he was forced to abdicate and was exiled to Banaras. The British alleged that he had been conspiring against them, hence his removal was necessary. Pratap Singh's brother, Shahji (better known as Appa Sahib; not to be confused with Appa Sahib, the former ruler of Nagpur), succeeded him as the raja of Satara. Appa Sahib died in April 1848. Pratap Singh had passed away the previous year. Neither of them had natural male heirs. Pratap Singh's family continued to agitate for their right to the state (in the name of an adopted heir), and one of their loyal officials, Rango Bapuji, was to play a prominent part in mobilizing for an uprising in western Maharashtra in 1857.

Appa Sahib of Satara had adopted a son shortly before his death, who was nominated his successor. Dalhousie refused to recognize this succession, and then put forth his detailed note on the desirability of denying princely rulers the right to have adopted heirs as successors. Instead, in such circumstances the said state would lapse to the British. In his minute on the doctrine of lapse, he made a distinction between what he called 'independent' states and 'subordinate states'. Independent states were those which, before the Company established its supremacy, had not acknowledged any suzerain; subordinate states were those that had derived their authority from an overlord. It was assumed that the British as successors to the overlords of the subordinate states had inherited their prerogatives, one of these being that of resuming the territories of the state. The distinction between independent states and subordinate states was quite arbitrary, and in practice meaningless. Moreover, according to Dalhousie's understanding, those states which owed their existence or survival to the British fell in the category of subordinate states. Thus, Satara, which from the point of view of colonial officialdom, had been resurrected at the end of the Third Anglo-Maratha War, was actually a British creation. Therefore, the state could justifiably, according to the British, be treated as having lapsed in the absence of a natural heir and in 1848 it was declared to have been annexed.

Another petty principality ruled by a Maratha dynasty, the state of Jhansi located in the Bundelkhand region, was also annexed under similar circumstances. Jhansi had first come under British 'protection' during the Second Anglo-Maratha War, in 1804. After the Third Anglo-Maratha War it no longer owed nominal allegiance to the peshwa, acknowledging the supremacy of the Company. Jhansi was incorporated into the

Indian empire as a 'native' state. When its ruler Gangadhar Rao (r. 1838–53) died in 1853 without any natural heir, the British refused to sanction the succession of his adopted son, Damodar Rao. The state was declared to have lapsed to the Company. This decision was contested by the widow of Gangadhar Rao, Rani Lakshmi Bai, who went on to play an important role in the revolt of 1857. Following the death of Gangadhar Rao, Lakshmi Bai had a long dispute with the Company over the annexation of the state. It may be mentioned here, especially in the context of the revolt, that when Baji Rao II died in 1851, the British declined to accept the claim of Baji Rao's adopted son Nana Sahib to the title of peshwa and to the allowances to which Baji Rao had been entitled. Nana Sahib too emerged as a prominent leader of the anti-colonial struggle of 1857.

The case of Nagpur was more or less identical to that of Satara and Jhansi, though less complicated. We have noted that by the time the Third Anglo-Maratha War came to an end, the Nagpur state with its much-reduced territories had been completely subordinated by the Company. Given the resistance they had encountered during the conflict with Appa Sahib, the British were reluctant to immediately annex the kingdom. It was therefore reduced to the status of a princely state, with the resident as the de facto ruler. The new ruler, Raghoji III, was a minor and for the next ten years, till 1827, Jenkins held the position of resident (he had been appointed in 1810, and before that had officiated as resident since 1807).

In 1826, when Raghoji attained the age of majority, it was decided to formally hand over the charge of the administration to him. Simultaneously, a new treaty was negotiated with him and signed in December 1826. According to the terms of this treaty the Nagpur state was to be ruled by Raghoji without the direct involvement of the resident. Nevertheless, the British retained control over the military establishment. The Nagpur troops continued to be commanded by British officers. Besides, Raghoji was to cede territories yielding revenue of Rs 17 lakhs for the maintenance of the armed contingents. There were sharp differences among colonial policymakers both in India and Britain over the extent of autonomy that was to be conceded to the Nagpur state. Jenkins was strongly in favour of restricting the authority of the ruler. In England, Ellenborough, who held the position of president of the board of control—virtually minister for India—from 1828 to 1830 (the first of his four terms, which continued with gaps till 1858) too was opposed to giving up in any significant way the power exercised by the resident. Incidentally, it was in the context of the Nagpur question that Ellenborough first articulated the view that the British Indian government should actively try to extend its control over princely states. At this stage the court of directors was in favour of maintaining the status quo, preferring not to make any substantial changes in the existing arrangements in the matter of princely states.

In 1829, the terms of the 1826 treaty with Nagpur were modified by signing another treaty. The new treaty reflected the position of Bentinck on the question of princely states. According to the provisions of the revised treaty, the ruler was to have a much greater say in administering the state. More importantly, the military establishment (the scale of which was reduced) was no longer under the Company and European officers were withdrawn. The provision in the 1826 treaty pertaining to cession of territory was annulled. Instead, the state was to pay to the British a tribute of Rs 8 lakh annually. Ellenborough was extremely critical of this treaty and would have liked Bentinck to abrogate it. The understanding formulated by Ellenborough vis-à-vis princely states was to become dominant in the next two decades and provided the basis for Dalhousie's policy.

Raghoji died suddenly in 1853. He had no surviving male heir, and had adopted no successor. Consequently, Dalhousie immediately proceeded to annex the state, in pursuance of the doctrine of lapse. From the official correspondence it is quite clear that a major factor that led to the annexation was that Nagpur was a major producer of raw cotton. The British were keen to take over the cotton producing districts of the state. Further, this was the time when proposals for the construction of railway lines linking Calcutta with Bombay through central India were being finalized. These would pass through large stretches of territory located in Nagpur. Therefore, it was vital that the opportunity provided by the death of Raghoji be immediately seized upon.

It is no coincidence that it was at the same time that Dalhousie decided to seize the cotton-rich Berar districts of the state of Hyderabad. The protests of the nizam were ignored, as was the long history of cordial relations with the state. The districts were to be taken over in settlement of arrears relating to payment for the large subsidiary force (henceforth called the Hyderabad Contingent) that had been imposed on Hyderabad since the late eighteenth century. Arrears had steadily accumulated as the state did not have sufficient resources to pay for the maintenance of the subsidiary force. This constituted a huge financial burden, which the Hyderabad state had been unable to bear. Through a treaty signed in 1853, Berar, along with Naldurg (Osmanabad) and Raichur, were taken over by the Company in lieu of the arrears and to provide for subsequent payments for the contingent. The estimated gross revenue of these tracts was Rs 50 lakhs. The two latter areas were later restored to Hyderabad after the 1857 revolt.

Berar was one of the regions that emerged in the mid-nineteenth century as a source of raw cotton for the English textile industry (and, in the latter half of the century, for the cotton mills of Bombay). In 1853, Berar was taken over 'in trust' by the Company. The possession was confirmed by a treaty signed in 1860 according to which all surplus revenue, after deducting the expenses incurred for the upkeep of the military force and for administrative functions, was to be remitted to the nizam. Hyderabad received virtually no share of the revenues of Berar and over a period of time the districts ceased to have any real connection with the state.

Politically, the most significant acquisition of territory, without resorting to outright war, during Dalhousie's tenure, was the annexation of the kingdom of Awadh. This was to have serious repercussions. The annexation of Awadh has been regarded as a major factor responsible for the 'mutiny' of the sipahis of the Bengal Army in 1857. The area of the kingdom had already been substantially reduced during the first half of the nineteenth century. In 1801, the Company had annexed nearly half the territories of the state in return for the support it had given to Saadat Ali (r. 1798–1814) to become the ruler of Awadh. The annexed districts included the low-lying region of present-day Uttarakhand; Bareilly and tracts around it; and large portions of western, central, and eastern Uttar Pradesh (present boundaries).

Saadat Ali died in 1814 and was succeeded by his son, Ghaziuddin Haidar (r. 1814–27). During the last years of Saadat Ali's reign, constant interference in the affairs of the state by the resident, John Baillie, resulted in tensions between the Awadh court and the Company. Saadat Ali resented the aggressive manner in which Baillie tried to impose his views about administering the state. The earl of Moira, the then governor general, was not inclined to disturb the status quo, and instructed Baillie to desist from too much interference. These instructions were largely ignored by the resident. Initially, after the accession of Ghaziuddin, the resident was able augment his own influence and succeeded in persuading him to give to the British a sum of Rs 1 crore out of the large accumulated treasure left behind by Saadat Ali (estimated to have been £18 million). This was treated as a loan for financing the Nepal War. Shortly thereafter relations between Ghaziuddin and Baillie deteriorated. Baillie, whose manner of dealing with the Awadh ruler was not endorsed by the governor general, was removed from the position of resident in 1815.

One particularly cynical move by the Company, as part of its Awadh policy, might be mentioned here. Ghaziuddin was prompted by the British to adorn the title of 'king' in order to announce his formal renunciation of subservience to the Mughal emperor, hitherto nominal overlord of the rulers of Awadh. The subedar of Awadh was generally known by the title of nawab-vazir by the end of the eighteenth century. Since the time of Shuja-ud-daula, the Awadh subedars had nominally been hereditary vazirs of the Mughal emperor. In 1819, Ghaziuddin Haidar declared himself 'badshah' of Awadh, thereby declaring that he was a sovereign ruler owing no allegiance to any superior authority, i.e., that he did not derive his right to rule over Awadh from the Mughal emperor. Henceforth, he was styled as 'King of Oudh' by the British.

While on the one hand the Company recognized the sovereign status of Ghaziduddin as badshah, on the other hand he and his successors had to constantly face the threat of annexation on grounds of 'misrule'. Colonial officials posted in the capital of Lucknow regularly sent back reports of misrule, justifying their interference in the administration of Awadh on the grounds that the rulers were incapable of governing the state. In 1834, the Company's court of directors sent instructions to Governor General William Bentinck authorizing, if necessary, the take over of the administration of Awadh by the British, reducing the 'King of Oudh' to a titular sovereign. The then resident at Lucknow, John Low, was somewhat reluctant to go ahead with this proposal which would have fundamentally altered the Company's relationship with Awadh. Before any decisive measures could be initiated for assuming the administration of the state, the reigning king, Nasiruddin Haidar (r. 1827–37) died of suspected poisoning. There was a brief dispute over succession, and Low managed to ensure that the Company's nominee was enthroned. The new king of Awadh, Muhammad Ali (r. 1837–42) an uncle of Nasiruddin Haidar, was presented with the draft of a revised treaty as the price of his accession.

There was a provision in the treaty which allowed the transfer to the British, indefinitely, of any part of Awadh on grounds of 'misrule'. Further, an additional subsidiary force was to be imposed on the state, for which Awadh was to pay Rs 16 lakh per annum. This treaty was signed in 1837. However, the court of directors rejected the treaty in its entirety, and Governor General Auckland was ordered to abrogate it. Even though the treaty was abrogated, Muhammad Ali was deceitfully informed in 1839 that only the provision pertaining to the additional subsidiary force had been annulled. The provision relating to assuming the administration of any portion of Awadh on grounds of misrule was to be invoked in Dalhousie's time to provide a supposedly legal basis for the annexation of the state.

It was during Dalhousie's tenure that decisive steps were taken to do away with whatever little freedom was left to Awadh. A prominent colonial official, William Sleeman, was appointed as resident at Lucknow, to prepare the ground for taking over the state. He assumed charge in January 1849 and within a few months had prepared a report on conditions in the kingdom, intended to substantiate the Company's contention that the existing administration was completely inept. Sleeman was in favour of assuming the government of Awadh, but did not recommend outright annexation. The British were to act as 'trustees' for the royal family, and the state was to be administered by Awadh personnel, supervised by the Company's officials. In order to provide more detailed information for establishing allegations of misrule, Sleeman undertook an extensive tour of the Awadh countryside from December 1849 to February 1850. His lengthy account of the tour, which is partly in the form of a diary, supplemented by a large amount of additional information and anecdotes, was printed in 1852 under the title *Journey Through the Kingdom of Oude*, and was initially circulated only among senior officials of the Company in India and England. The account became publicly available when it was published in 1858 against the backdrop of the 1857 revolt and its suppression.[2] The diary provided the relevant material for justifying the annexation of Awadh on grounds of misrule. Sleeman's term as resident ended in 1854 and he was succeeded by James Outram; Sleeman passed away in 1856. Outram shared Sleeman's perception that the state was misgoverned, and that this gave to the British the right to intervene.

The British government had by this time decided to annex Awadh, for which purpose Dalhousie was asked to urge the ruler, Wajid Ali (r. 1847–56), to sign a new treaty which would facilitate annexation. Wajid Ali declined to sign the treaty. The kingdom was seized and he was exiled to Calcutta. This political act of the Company had far-reaching military consequences since Awadh was a major recruiting area for the Bengal Army. On the eve of the revolt nearly one-third of the sipahis in the Bengal Army came from Awadh. The result was that widespread discontent against colonial exploitation in the countryside (as well as in the cities, to which a large section of the rural poor flocked) could seek expression in military rebellion initiated by the Awadh 'peasants in uniform'.

The policies pursued from the late 1840s till the outbreak of the revolt had to be urgently reconsidered in 1858. The consensus which emerged among colonial policymakers was that the cooperation of the princely rulers had to be enlisted for restoring the authority of the colonial state. Considering that a large number of princely rulers had actively assisted the British in the suppression of the revolt, it was felt that their support was vital for stabilizing the Indian empire on a long-term basis. Moreover, given that that most of the princely rulers and the ruling classes of princely states were politically and socially conservative, they were unlikely to encourage elements that might disturb the status quo. They would therefore be

[2]W. H. Sleeman, *A Journey Through the Kingdom of Oude in 1849-50*, 2 vols., London: Richard Bentley, 1858.

useful in keeping discontent in check. For this reason, when the crown directly assumed control over the Indian empire in 1858, Queen Victoria issued a proclamation (1 November 1858) guaranteeing to the princely rulers their autonomy and assuring them that they would not be divested of their territories. This amounted to publicly disowning the policy of annexation which had been so vigorously implemented during Dalhousie's term as governor general, although as we have seen such a policy had been advocated since the 1820s. The following chapter outlines the history of the revolt of 1857 which did much to determine the manner in which the Indian empire was governed, its brutal suppression notwithstanding.

NINE

THE GREAT REVOLT

It is generally recognized that the revolt of 1857 was the most widespread and violent struggle against colonial rule in India during the nineteenth century. It lasted for more than two years and encompassed large parts of northern, central, and eastern India. Several hundred thousand Indians, a significant proportion of whom were non-combatants, were killed during the upheaval and immediately after it had been ruthlessly crushed. The revolt was not an isolated event. It was part of a long tradition of anti-colonial resistance throughout the Indian empire and must be seen as a momentous phase in this continuous struggle against colonial oppression.

The events of 1857 have been the subject of an intense debate, essentially between those who seek to belittle the significance of this great anti-colonial struggle and those who highlight the historical importance of the revolt as a glorious chapter in the history of the fight against imperialist oppression and exploitation. The immense output of published material on the revolt during the latter half of the nineteenth century, exclusively from the perspective of the triumphant British, ensured the dominance of the colonial version of the event. Accounts of the revolt began to appear as early as 1857 itself. From 1857 onwards there was a flood of books, pamphlets, sermons, newspaper reports, and articles about the revolt in the metropolis. The publication of tracts or pamphlets on the uprising became something of a cottage industry in Britain. Yet, till as late as the beginning of the twentieth century there was virtually nothing in the public domain from the point of view of the subjugated. The one notable contemporary exception was the series of articles on the revolt written by Karl Marx and Frederick Engels. These were published in the *New-York Daily Tribune*. This was a progressive newspaper, well known for its forceful opposition to slavery in America. During the 1850s, Marx and Engels contributed several articles to it on various current events. The articles on the revolt began appearing in mid-July 1857. About twenty-five articles were published on the progress of the revolt and its suppression. The last article, which appeared in the issue dated 1 October, is signed by Engels. Some of the articles are unsigned, and it is only recently that their authorship has been established. Not many people knew about Marx's writings on the revolt for nearly a hundred years after they were initially published. Most of these articles were reprinted in a compilation which came out in 1959. Together with a few more articles, which were retrieved subsequently, and some related correspondence, a substantial contemporary commentary by Marx and Engels on the revolt is now accessible. The two closely followed the military endeavours of the anti-colonial resistance, reporting them in detail in their articles. They constantly, till as late as the middle of 1858, expressed the hope that the revolt would lead to the overthrow or at least the undermining of British rule in India and were disappointed that this did not happen.

In the last article of the series, Engels concluded with the following comment: '...for the present, the British have reconquered India. The great rebellion, stirred up by the mutiny of the Bengal Army, is indeed, it appears, dying out. But this second conquest has not increased England's hold upon the mind of the Indian people. The cruelty of the retribution dealt out by the British troops, goaded on by exaggerated and false reports of the atrocities attributed to the natives, and the attempt at confiscating the Kingdom of Oude...have not created any particular fondness for the victors'.[1]

◆

The revolt commenced with a mutiny by sipahis of the Bengal Army stationed in Meerut, on 10 May 1857. Meerut had been developed as a major military station of the Bengal Army and had one of the largest cantonments in north India. Official news of the mutiny at Meerut and subsequent developments reached Britain more than a month after the events of 10 May. The governor general, Lord Canning (1856–62) had been reluctant to speed up the transmission of the news to London, even declining the offer of the governor of Bombay to despatch a special steamer for the purpose. For its part, the British cabinet headed by Lord Palmerston was inclined to underplay the seriousness of the developments in India. The Whigs had just returned to power under the leadership of Palmerston following the general election of April 1857. It has been suggested that since the Whigs had been in power for long spells since the 1830s, they were keen to ensure that the rebellion did not become an occasion for criticizing their policies relating to India. The revolt coincided with major realignments and shifts in British parliamentary politics during the 1850s, including the emergence of the Liberal Party.

Palmerston had become prime minister in 1855 following the resignation of Lord Aberdeen during the Crimean War (1853–56). Aberdeen had led a coalition government in which the Whigs had been part of the alliance; the 1855 Palmerston ministry was predominantly Whig. The Crimean War was still in progress when the new government was formed. The war drew to a close in early 1856. The Palmerston regime then unleashed a war against China in October that year, the Second Opium War. The Second Opium War (1856–60)

[1] Frederick Engels, 'The Revolt in India', New-York Daily Tribune, 1 October 1858, available at <www.marxists.org/archive/marx/works/1858/10/01.htm>.

overlapped with the revolt in India. As details of the military campaigns in China became available in Britain, there was strong criticism of Palmerston's aggressive policy, leading to a censure motion against his ministry in March 1857. Elections were then announced, and Palmerston returned to power with a Whig majority. Due to differences with colleagues over some legislative measures, he had to resign in February 1858. A minority Tory ministry was then formed with Lord Derby as prime minister. The Tories, or Conservatives (as they came to be known), constituted the other major political formation, besides the Whigs, at this time. Derby's government lasted till June 1859. Simultaneously, towards the end of the 1850s, the Whigs and their allies in parliament had come together to form the Liberal Party. The Liberals, led by Palmerston, went on to win a decisive victory in the 1859 election which took place following the fall of Derby's government. Palmerston remained in office till his death in 1865. He died shortly after the general election of 1865 in which the Liberal Party (now contesting formally with that label), won an even larger majority. In other words, the revolt and its suppression occurred in the Palmerston era. However, during the crucial final phase of military operations there was a Tory government in power, and it is Derby who oversaw the transition from company rule to crown rule. There was nevertheless considerable continuity in the policies pursued by Palmerston and Derby ministries with regard to the Indian empire.

The Whigs and their supporters, including the pro-government *London Times*, were emphatic that the revolt was essentially a military mutiny. There were two variants of this argument, one that saw the military mutiny as the result of long-term policies of military recruitment and organization, and the other which saw the mutiny as an episode caused by opposition to the introduction of greased cartridges. The greased cartridge explanation, which was to figure prominently in most of the subsequent discussions on the causes of the revolt, represented the narrowest understanding of 1857.

However, the Tories also characterized the revolt as an uprising involving large sections of Indian society. When the debate on Indian affairs began on 27 July 1857, Disraeli, who led the Tories in the House of Commons, and had demanded a discussion on the issue in the house, declared that, 'The decline of empires are not affairs of greased cartridges. Such results are occasioned by adequate causes and by an accumulation of adequate causes.'[2] Disraeli, himself an enthusiastic supporter of imperial expansion, analysed in his lengthy speech the policies which had led to discontent and eventually the outbreak of the rebellion, which according to him amounted to a full-fledged revolution. The revolution argument was based on a comprehensive critique of the manner in which the Indian empire had been governed. The policies pursued by successive regimes during the previous half century or so were analysed to establish that these had led to widespread social, religious, and political discontent. These were perceptions that were shared by a large section of political opinion ranging from missionaries at one end (who found the military mutiny argument inadequate), to Irish nationalists and Chartists at the other. The EIC was a major target of attack. In fact, governing the empire through a body of merchants was itself seen as a problem since the people of India were unable to reconcile themselves to this kind of a peculiar ruler.

Another line of reasoning about the outbreak of the revolt was that this was a conspiracy hatched by princely rulers and chiefs, who had lost their territories, privileges, and power. These rulers had come together and entered into a conspiracy to overthrow British rule. Of course, those who adhered to the conspiracy theory had to reluctantly admit that there was also

[2]Hansard, House of Common Debates, Vol. 147, Col. 475, 27 July 1857, available at <api.parliament.uk/historic-hansard/commons/1857/jul/27/motion-for-papers>.

large-scale popular participation in the rebellion so that the conspiracy eventually culminated in civil rebellion. A specific variant of this argument was that the revolt was a Muslim conspiracy led by fanatic religious elements, or by erstwhile Muslim rulers. This explanation was to have significant consequences after the revolt and continues to be put forth even in some recent writings.

The dominance of the colonial narrative was in a large measure established by the sheer volume of published material that told the story of the revolt exclusively from the point of view of the British. Colonial writings on the revolt carried detailed descriptions of the supposed barbarities perpetrated by the 'rebels'. Heart-rending accounts of the slaughter of white women and children, and of rape, were presented in writings on events at Kanpur, Lucknow, and Delhi. Of course, the incidents were grossly exaggerated, and the allegations of rape were actually false. But it was exceedingly difficult to challenge this narrative in the atmosphere of fear and terror that prevailed in the immediate post-1857 period or to rewrite this history at an individual level. Such a task could only have been undertaken in conjunction with another major anti-colonial struggle. Thus, conditions for evolving an alternative understanding of the history of the revolt became favourable as the national movement gathered momentum at the beginning of the twentieth century.

The foundations of colonial historiography on the revolt were laid by the immensely influential work of John W. Kaye, *A History of the Sepoy War in India, 1857-1858*. Kaye was a colonial official and a military historian. During the writing of the history of the revolt he received considerable support from the ruling establishment which placed a huge amount of official documentation at his disposal. Kaye also made use of the accounts of British officials, both military and civilian, who were involved in the campaign to crush the uprising. The first volume of *History of the Sepoy War* was published in

1864; two subsequent volumes were published in 1870 and 1876 respectively. Kaye passed away in 1876 by which time he had only completed the story of the revolt in Delhi, and had provided details about the early phase of developments in Awadh, including Lucknow. It may be mentioned here that the first volume was entirely devoted to a lengthy discussion on the historical background to the revolt, beginning with the mid-1840s. Following Kaye's death, another colonial official, who was an amateur historian as well (with several books to his credit), George B. Malleson, published a three-volume history of the revolt entitled *History of the Indian Mutiny, commencing from the close of the second volume of Sir John Kaye's History of the Sepoy War* (1878–80). Simultaneously a comprehensive index of the two histories (Kaye's and Malleson's), compiled by Frederic Pincott, was issued in 1880, thereby firmly linking these separate works. Later, the histories of Kaye and Malleson, together with a revised version of the Pincott index, were all brought together as a six-volume set ('Cabinet edition') with the title *Kaye's and Malleson's History of the Indian Mutiny* (1889). Most probably this was done at the instance of the publisher, W. H. Allen (London), who had undertaken the publication of all these works. In the process, the third volume of Kaye's *History of the Sepoy War* was dropped. The six-volume Kaye–Malleson account immediately became the authorized version of the history of that tumultuous phase of British rule in India, holding sway with its numerous editions, reprints, and abridgements, till 1947 and even beyond. The two original works, by Kaye and by Malleson, continued to be published separately as well. Several editions of Kaye's *History of the Sepoy War* were published after his death and continued to be much in demand.

Whereas Kaye's work is relatively more nuanced than that of Malleson, his is ultimately a powerful colonial narrative. Shahid Amin has perceptively remarked that 'Kaye's *History* is not so much about the Black Man's rising as about the White Man's suppression of that uprising.'[3] For Kaye it was the historical destiny of Britain to emancipate India. British rule had put India on the path of civilization, thereby arousing the hatred of forces of darkness and superstition. These sinister forces were responsible for fomenting the insurrection. In heroically putting down the rebellion the British had salvaged Indians from backwardness and ignorance. They had ensured that Britain was allowed to fulfil its historical destiny of civilizing India. In the words of Kaye, 'The story of the Indian rebellion of 1857 is, perhaps the most signal illustration of our character yet recorded in the annals of our country. It was the vehement self-assertion of the Englishman that produced this conflagration; it was the same vehement self-assertion that enabled him...to trample it out.'[4] History textbooks written by Indians during the late nineteenth century, in Urdu and Bengali for instance, largely reproduced colonial narratives of the revolt.

It has been argued that the revolt was a reaction against endeavours by the British to introduce changes in Indian society and thereby bring to it some of the achievements of modern western civilization. This is a view that assumes that Indian society was eternally backward and would have been unable to progress without British rule. A recent version of this argument is to be found in the work of Niall Ferguson, a prominent apologist for empire. According to Ferguson the revolt was primarily a reaction 'against a succession of British interferences with Indian culture which seemed to—and in many ways actually did—add up to a plot to Christianize India'.[5] This understanding, which is firmly part of the colonial

[3]Shahid Amin, 'English Dominance and Indian Subordination: A reading of John Kaye's classic *History of the Sepoy War in India,* 3 volumes, London, 1864-76', *Biblio,* July–August 1997, p. 36.
[4]John William Kaye, *A History of the Sepoy War in India, 1857-1858,* Vol. 1, London: W. H. Allen, ninth edition, 1880 (first published, 1864), p. xii.
[5]Niall Ferguson, *Empire: The Rise and Demise of the British World Order and the Lessons for Global Power,* New York: Basic Books, 2004, p. 122.

narrative, goes back to writings on the revolt which began to be published from the end of the 1850s. In Kaye's influential *History of the Sepoy War*, the valour of the British lay not merely in individual acts of courage, but in the justness of the cause for which they fought. British rule had put India on the path of progress and had the 'mutiny' been successful it would have relapsed into ignorance, superstition, and obscurantism. The 'mutiny' represented the opposition of regressive forces to improvements brought about by the Company.

The abolition of the practices of sati and female infanticide, removal of restrictions on widow remarriage, and the coming of advanced modes of communication and transport such as the telegraph and railways were perceived, according to such interpretations, as being disruptive of the traditional way of life. The proselytizing activities of missionaries from 1813–14 onwards (the Charter Act of 1813 had made it possible for evangelicals from Britain to officially undertake missionary activity in the Indian empire, the outcome of which has been much exaggerated) were viewed with alarm and suspicion. The aggressive propaganda of some of the Christian missionaries added to growing resentment against the Company's policies. It was in this context that Hindu and Muslim orthodoxy in north India allegedly began mobilizing for the revolt. Besides, disgruntled sections of the old aristocracy joined in the conspiracy to overthrow British rule. These were the forces of darkness from which the British heroically rescued the Indian people.

Rumours about the use of grease procured from the fat of animals that were taboo, were the work of these forces. Through the circulation of chapattis (a phenomenon repeatedly referred to in most writings, though based entirely on hearsay), they added to the sense of panic and fear which preceded the revolt. The defeat of the rebels, through the superhuman sacrifice of white warriors, had ensured that India would continue to remain on the path of progress. In this narrative, the suppression of the revolt was projected as being moral, while the revolt itself was portrayed as immoral. Nevertheless, it does seem that many of the conservative sections of Indian society had come to regard the Company's 'raj' as amounting to a serious interference in social and religious customs. This rendered them inimical to British rule for which reason they sided with the rebels in 1857–58, and in many areas actually led the uprising.

◆

The first major full-length account which challenged the colonial perspective was V. D. Savarkar's *The Indian War of Independence, 1857*, published in 1909. Savarkar, who was pursuing his studies in London at that time, began writing his book (originally in Marathi) in 1907 by way of commemorating the fiftieth anniversary of the revolt, giving it the title *Atthharahasau Sattavanche Swatantrya Samar* (*The War of Independence of 1857*). His massive volume is based entirely on standard colonial histories of the revolt. Savarkar, however, provided a fresh interpretation of the uprising, during the course of which he put forward the thesis that the revolt was the result of a prior conspiracy of which the leaders were, among others, Nana Sahib, the adopted son and heir of Peshwa Baji Rao II; Rani Lakshmi Bai of Jhansi; and Emperor Bahadur Shah II. Its outbreak was supposed to coincide with the centenary of the Battle of Plassey (23 June 1757). In their impatience to overthrow British rule some of the sipahis of the East India Company's Bengal Army mutinied prematurely so that the uprising commenced earlier than had been planned. Savarkar presented no new evidence to substantiate his argument. Nevertheless, his main purpose was not to write a work of history but a political manifesto. The text was intended to inspire its readers to engage in a united struggle against British rule in the manner of the 'rebels' of 1857. A major theme of Savarkar's book, as Jyotirmaya Sharma has recently argued, is the purificatory role of violence.[6]

The prominent freedom fighter and Gandhian, Pandit Sunderlal, provided a well-researched revisionist account of the revolt in his voluminous history of British rule in India, *Bharat Mein Angrezi Raj* published in 1929.[7] It should be borne in mind that the colonial version of the history of the revolt, disseminated and popularized through writings published on a massive scale for over seventy years, had made it virtually impossible to challenge this version. *Bharat Mein Angrezi Raj* challenged and sought to undermine, very forcefully, the colonial narrative. The political significance of the book was immediately grasped by the colonial state which promptly imposed a ban on it. Though the British did not delay taking action in this matter, nevertheless 1,700 of the 2,000 copies which had been printed were already in circulation by the time the book was proscribed. This ensured that several hundred copies circulated underground, and the political message of the book reached a large audience.

However, it was not until after Independence that a distinct historiographical shift took place in writings on the revolt. The year 1957, marking the centenary of the uprising, was a particularly productive year. Most of the works published in that year were written by academics. An officially commissioned history of the revolt, authored by a respected historian Surendranath Sen (*Eighteen Fifty-seven*) was produced under the auspices of the Government of India. The distortions of colonial historiography were so extensive that the newly independent nation state considered the project of rewriting the history of this crucial phase of the anti-colonial struggle as an important responsibility. Hence its decision to sponsor the publication

---

[6]Jyotirmaya Sharma, 'History as Revenge and Retaliation: Rereading Savarkar's *The War of Independence of 1857*', *Economic and Political Weekly*, 12 May 2007, pp. 1717–19.

[7]Sunderlal, *Bharat Mein Angrezi Raj* (Hindi), Allahabad: Omkar Press, 1938 (first published, 1929).

of a new, nationalist account of the revolt authored by an academic. In his lengthy foreword to the volume the then education minister, Abul Kalam Azad, stated that, 'In January 1955 I decided that the work of preparing a new history of the Indian struggle of 1857 should be immediately taken in hand.... I decided to invite Dr. S. N. Sen, a well-known Indian historian, to undertake this task and made an announcement to this effect during the annual meeting of the Indian Historical Records Commission. All records on the subject were placed at his disposal...'.[8] Although Sen presented a more balanced version of the events of 1857–59—this remains till date the only comprehensive work on the revolt written from a non-colonial perspective—he relied too heavily and at times uncritically on official records of the colonial state. As a result, *Eighteen Fifty-seven* too, at times, reproduced accounts that portrayed events from the point of view of the British.

A collection of essays written within the Marxist historical framework was also published in 1957. Edited by P. C. Joshi (who had been the general secretary of the Communist Party of India during the final phase of the freedom movement), the collection was entitled *Rebellion 1857: A Symposium*. Some of the other significant works on the revolt published in its centenary year were: S. B. Chaudhuri's *Civil Rebellion in the Indian Mutinies*; R. C. Majumdar's *The Sepoy Mutiny and the Revolt of 1857*, and Syed Mahdi Husain's *Bahadur Shah Zafar and the War of 1857 in Delhi* (1958).

◆

Of the three armies of the EIC, the Bengal Army was at the time of the outbreak of the revolt the most formidable fighting force in the British Indian empire. It was equipped with advanced military technology and had vast combat experience.

[8]Surendra Nath Sen, *Eighteen Fifty-seven*, third reprint, Delhi: Publications Division, 1995 (first published, 1957), p. xxviii.

The cartridge issue, i.e. the resentment among sipahis over new cartridges, the paper wrappers of which were greased with animal fat that was taboo for many of them, was the outcome of the introduction of the state-of-art Enfield Pattern 1853 (P53) rifle. This rifle occupies an important place in the history of combat weapons in the mid-nineteenth century, something which has typically not received any attention in writings on the revolt. An improved version was used extensively in the American Civil War.

The Bengal Army was regularly used by the British in their imperialist wars both in the Indian subcontinent and outside. In the four decades preceding the revolt the Bengal Army had been constantly engaged in military campaigns. Between the 1810s and 1857 it had fought in Nepal, Afghanistan, China, Burma, Punjab, and Sind. These campaigns had been exhausting for the sipahis who had shouldered the main burden of fighting. The casualties in the Afghan War were massive; and deployment in China during the First Opium War, and then in the Second Opium War from 1856 onwards, had meant fighting under very difficult conditions in theatres of war located at a great distance from India.

Further, even though the Indian soldiers had to bear the main burden of fighting, they were routinely humiliated by their British officers. Besides, they had few avenues of promotion. As has already been mentioned, Indians could not be officers in the Company's armies. At best a few sipahis could, after long years of service rise to the position of subedar (in this context a military rank), a handful of whom could then get the rank of subedar-major, the highest rank open to Indian soldiers.

The adverse conditions under which sipahis had to undertake military campaigns in distant lands led to considerable discontent. This could at times result in acts of defiance. In 1824, at the time of the First Burmese War, soldiers of the Bengal Army were not inclined to proceed to Lower Burma by sea, preferring the land route via Chittagong. However, when arrangements for travelling from the important cantonment of Barrackpore to Chittagong, where they were to embark on vessels to take them by the sea route to Rangoon, were found to be grossly inadequate, a mutiny broke out. This is regarded as the first major mutiny in the Bengal Army. It may be recalled that the Madras Army had mutinied in 1806. The 1806 mutiny at Vellore was the earliest large-scale mutiny in the EIC's armed forces.

The 1824 Barrackpore mutiny began on 1 November when the 47th Bengal Native Infantry refused to commence their march unless proper arrangements were made for carrying their knapsacks, each weighing over 10 kilograms. The sipahis had to pay for the carriages to transport their individual equipment; due to an acute shortage, the rates at which the carriages were available were exorbitant. Consequently, the soldiers were in no mood to obey orders unless provision was made to facilitate the transportation of their knapsacks. The 47th Bengal Native Infantry was joined by several sipahis of the 26th and 62nd native regiments. On the next day, the mutineers were asked to lay down their arms, which they refused. Reinforcements had been sent to Barrackpore under the commander-in-chief, Edward Paget. The troops led by Paget launched an offensive against the rebel sipahis, killing nearly 200 Indian soldiers. Many others were captured and court-martialled. Binda, the sipahi who had led the mutiny, was brutally tortured and executed. The 47th Bengal Native Infantry was disbanded, and its name removed from the army list.

The deployment of the Bengal Army in wars of conquest in Sind, Afghanistan, and Punjab for over a decade—from the late 1830s to the end of the 1840s—was strongly resented by the sipahis. They had to traverse unfamiliar ground, march through very difficult terrain, and engage in fighting for an extended period of time at a great distance from their areas of recruitment in the Doab. As the regions, particularly the territories lying west of the Indus, were perceived to be 'foreign' lands and were located outside the usual zone of the Bengal Army's operations, the soldiers insisted on getting an extra allowance for campaigns in Sind and Afghanistan. The issue of the extra allowance or bhatta for service in distant areas was to remain a constant cause of tension between the sipahis and the Company right till the outbreak of the revolt of 1857. The demand for bhatta was related to the low pay that the sipahis received and their expenses. From the 1790s down to 1857 the pay of an ordinary soldier remained fixed at Rs 7 per month. Out of this they had to spend more than half on food and other necessities. Expenses could be much higher in areas where supplies were difficult to procure. Therefore, the bhatta was a matter of vital concern to the soldiers.

In 1838, on the eve of the Afghan War, there were reports that some of the units, as for example the 44th Bengal Native Infantry, might defy orders to march if their demand for bhatta was not conceded. The problem was temporarily resolved by an assurance that the extra allowance would be given for serving in territories located across the Indus. The allowance continued to be given till the conclusion of the Sind campaign. It was then stopped on the grounds that Sind was now part of the Company's territories, and not a 'foreign' area. As a result, a number of sipahi contingents expressed their unwillingness to be stationed in Sind. One of these was the 64th Bengal Native Infantry. The regiment defied orders when it learnt that it was not to receive the promised bhatta, upon which the leaders of the mutiny were executed. Besides, thirty-two sipahis were sentenced to imprisonment. A more serious mutiny broke out in the 34th Bengal Native Infantry in 1844. Severe punishment was inflicted on the mutineers and the entire regiment was disbanded. It was found necessary to bring in contingents of the Madras Army to reinforce the troops stationed in Sind. The Madras Army sipahis for their part were also averse to serving in such a distant area and there were several instances of insubordination while they were en route to the northwestern part of the subcontinent. As we have seen, the British met with fierce resistance in their attempt to subjugate the region. This required a prolonged military occupation of Sind. The administration of Sind too remained under Charles Napier who had commanded the British armed forces during the campaign to conquer the kingdom.

Similar incidents occurred at the conclusion of the Second Punjab War. During the military campaigns in Punjab the sipahis were entitled to the extra allowance for serving in the region. However, the bhatta was discontinued at the end of the Second Punjab War. A huge proportion of the Bengal Army was stationed in Punjab between 1849 and 1857, as high as 45 per cent of its Indian soldiers. It has been estimated that there was one sipahi to every 120 persons in Punjab when the revolt broke out in 1857. This was an army of occupation. From the point of view of the purabiya (easterner) sipahis this was 'foreign' territory, i.e. beyond the Company's immediate boundaries. The withdrawal of the bhatta caused widespread anger among the sipahis. Quite a few of them resisted orders to proceed to Punjab. The incidents of insubordination culminated in the mutiny of the 66th Bengal Native Infantry in January 1850. The regiment was stationed at Gobindgarh, Amritsar. The sipahis launched an attack on Gobindgarh Fort. As there were no British troops at this location, the commanding officer, Lieutenant Colonel Bradford, had to rely on the 1st Native Cavalry to suppress the mutiny. The 66th Bengal Native Infantry was disbanded and its name erased from the army list. Gurkha troops were brought in to replace the Bengal Army contingents. This punishment was intended to send out a strong message to rebellious purabiya troops in Punjab. Nevertheless, the British were rather wary of recruiting sipahis in Punjab due to the general hostility of the erstwhile military contingents. Even though some of the soldiers of the disbanded army of the Lahore kingdom began to be recruited from 1850 onwards, the Company proceeded with caution. As a matter of policy sipahi regiments were not to have more than a fifth of its soldiers coming from the province. Usually, the number of sipahis from Punjab fell below this figure. This situation continued till 1857. During the revolt the British were compelled to rely on recruits from the region. However, they initially found it extremely difficult to get sufficient recruits except from the areas lying east of the Sutlej which were under princely rule.

The discontinuance of the bhatta added to the grievances of the sipahis of the Bengal Army, becoming a contributory factor in the disaffection that was building up in the years preceding the revolt. At the same time, the British were suspicious of the soldiery enlisted in Punjab, and could not entirely rely on their loyalty. The sipahis of the region, including those belonging to the Sikh community (contrary to what colonial narratives of the revolt state), joined their comrades from the Ganga–Jamuna Doab in the mutinies that took place in 1857 in several cantonments situated between the Sutlej and Indus.

The long and almost uninterrupted exposure to fighting, with the enormous risk and sheer physical toil this involved, combined with the daily experience of having their dignity trampled upon, made the sipahis discontented with the conditions of their service. The absence of adequate opportunities of promotion added to their despair. The imposition of the new Enfield P53 rifle appears to have been seen as further worsening the already adverse service conditions of the sipahis. Opposition to the rifle was articulated in religious terms, the tabooed animal fat used as grease for the cartridges of the rifle being particularly objectionable. There were several incidents at the beginning of 1857 in which soldiers of the Bengal Army declined to use the cartridge. This soon became an emotive issue around which sipahis could be rallied. From January 1857 onwards senior military officers of the Bengal Army were getting worried over reports about the growing indignation among sipahis on the issue of the cartridges. The cantonment at Barrackpore, located a short distance from Calcutta, was the centre of protests by sipahis against the introduction of the new rifle. The disquiet spread to other cantonments in Bengal and in the last week of February 1857, troops of the 19th Native Infantry stationed at Berhampore cantonment (Baharampur, district Murshidabad) mutinied. The defiant soldiers were brought under control by British officers and the regiment was ordered to march to Barrackpore. Here the contingent was disbanded on 31 March. Meanwhile, at Barrackpore itself a serious act of defiance had occurred on 29 March. Mangal Pandey, a sipahi in the 34th Bengal Native Infantry, attacked one of the British officers of the regiment. This prompted many other sipahis to disobey orders. It was obvious that they were hostile to the officers, and that their sympathies were with Mangal Pandey. Mangal Pandey was executed on 8 April. Subsequently, following an enquiry, the 34th Native Infantry was disbanded on 6 May (some of the 'loyal' companies, and a few 'loyal' Indian soldiers and officers were retained). This punishment was meted out to the regiment shortly before the outbreak of the mutiny at Meerut on 10 May 1857, which marked the beginning of the revolt. Both the 19th Native Infantry and the 34th Native Infantry had been stationed in Awadh when it was annexed. Their first-hand experience of the manner in which the British had treated the kingdom might have added to their anger. All these incidents, which were a reflection of the almost complete alienation of Indian soldiers from the Company 'raj', formed the prelude to the revolt.

◆

In the last week of April, eighty-five sawars belonging to the 3rd Regiment of the Light Cavalry posted at Meerut refused to take part in a practice drill that was intended to teach them how to load the new rifle. After a preliminary enquiry they were put on trial and on 8 May were sentenced to rigorous imprisonment for ten years. This harsh sentence aggravated an already tense situation, culminating in a violent uprising on

10 May. The British were taken completely by surprise. J. A. B. Palmer's study, *The Mutiny Outbreak at Meerut*, argues quite convincingly that British officers at Meerut had absolutely no inkling of the intensity of the anger which the humiliation of the sipahis had provoked among their comrades.[9] Palmer has pieced together most of the vital available evidence relating to the events of 10 May: his work focuses almost exclusively on the occurrences of that particular day in the town, paying close attention to the layout and topography of the cantonment, regimental bazars, and adjacent localities. Whereas the actions of the sipahis might not have been entirely spontaneous, they do not appear to have been planned much in advance. The immediate objective of the mutinous soldiers was the release of the imprisoned sipahis, in which they were successful. The upheaval began in the evening, a few hours before dusk, and within a short time British authority collapsed both in the cantonment and the city. Widespread violence broke out at several places. The sipahis then marched to Delhi, where they arrived the next morning. Almost all the mutinous soldiers had departed from Meerut before midnight. It was assumed by the European officers, most of whom still remained in the cantonment, that the sipahis would disperse to the countryside and gradually make their way towards their homes. They were unaware of their movement in the direction of Delhi. Consequently, Company officials in Delhi had no prior warning about the impending confrontation.

The rebel soldiers began arriving in the city shortly after dawn. Within a few hours they had put an end to the EIC's administration in Delhi and assumed control of Shahjahanabad and its immediate outskirts. The Mughal emperor, Bahadur Shah (II) Zafar (r. 1837–57) was urged by the sipahis to bless their cause, which he did. The appeal to the Mughal emperor

---

[9] J. A. B. Palmer, *The Mutiny Outbreak at Meerut in 1857,* Cambridge: Cambridge University Press, 1966.

was an indication of the symbolic importance of the Mughals as the legitimate sovereigns of most of the EIC territories. The Company too had reluctantly recognized the de jure authority of the Mughals. Through this gesture the sipahis were seeking to delegitimize the colonial state; by associating the name of the Mughal emperor with their cause they proclaimed that the Company's rule was no longer legitimate. At the same time, they were attempting to gain the widest possible acceptance for their regime.

After the 'rebel' soldiers had established their control over the city, they set up a new administrative apparatus. A large section of the local police force had gone over to the sipahis immediately after the liberation of Delhi. This constituted the nucleus of the sipahi regime's organizational structure for managing the day-to-day governance of the city. Apart from having the responsibility of maintaining law and order, the police personnel were required to arrange for supplies and labour for the military operations of the sipahis, and ensure that civic services continued to function normally. A large quantity of police records belonging to that period are available—an indication of the attention that the police establishment paid to keeping its records in order even in such an emergency—and they show that the work of constables and thanedars increased manifold after 11 May. What is also clear from these records is that the sipahi regime attempted to ensure that a mechanism was in place for administering the city efficiently, something that is remarkable considering that it was operating in a war situation. This is quite contrary to the picture of utter chaos that is presented in colonial accounts.

Till the end of June 1857, the main person who coordinated all these efforts (including the major task of defending the city) was Mirza Mughal, the eldest surviving son of Bahadur Shah. Subsequently, the leadership of the 'rebels', and of the administration of Delhi, was taken over by Bakht Khan. Bakht Khan, a subedar in the artillery unit of the Bengal Army, arrived in Delhi with a large force at the beginning of July. He was to emerge as one of the most prominent figures of the revolt. The sipahi regime had to defend the city, arrange for supplies, raise finances, and make administrative arrangements. When the soldiers had entered Delhi on 11 May, the Company's administration had completely vanished within a few hours of their arrival. This had resulted in a vacuum that had to be urgently filled. We have already noted that the defection of the constabulary to the 'rebel' side had placed at the disposal of the sipahis a readymade infrastructure for governing the city. At the same time, with the disappearance of the Company's authority a new constitutional edifice had to be designed. For this purpose, a Court of Administration was established by the sipahis. All executive, judicial, and revenue authority was vested in the court. The court was organized essentially on democratic principles, although formally Bahadur Shah was the head of the state. It consisted of ten members: six from the three branches of the army (infantry, cavalry, artillery), and four civilians. The latter were elected by majority from among people who were regarded as 'intelligent, wise, and capable'.[10] The members of the court elected a president (sadr-e-jalsa) from among themselves, and a vice-president (naib sadr-e-jalsa). The president had two votes. The court held daily sessions. Bahadur Shah had the right to be present at all sessions, but the court took the actual decisions. His approval would then be sought, and his seal would be put on documents recording these decisions.

The sipahi regime found it increasingly difficult to function because it had hardly any access to resources. Wealthier sections of the city were unwilling to give money to it as they did not have sufficient confidence in the rebel leaders. Soon, differences surfaced between Mirza Mughal and Bakht Khan, leading to the

---

[10]Six page 'constitution' of the Court of Administration, translation in Sen, *Eighteen Fifty-seven*, p. 72.

emergence of two rival centres of power. This was unfortunate as the pressure of the British forces had grown considerably by August. The defence of the city had acquired much greater urgency. The British had launched a counter-offensive in the first week of June. On 8 June 1857, they had defeated a large force of the rebels at Badli-ki-Sarai, a short distance from Delhi. They then succeeded in taking over the ridge, a hilly area located north of Shahjahanabad. This gave them a great advantage as they were located at a height.

The British force numbered around 6,500, but it had superior strategy and tactics. It was better organized and had access to more effective weapons. Throughout the summer months the British force remained stationed on the ridge. Then in mid-September 1857 they carried out a major assault to capture the city. From the ridge, the British troops moved in the direction of the Kashmere Gate of Shahjahanabad. The gate was stormed and taken. The attack was led by John Nicholson who was wounded and died shortly afterwards. By 20 September 1857, the entire city had been reconquered. Then began a period of vicious large-scale massacres of the 'rebels' and of the ordinary people of Delhi; a large number of those killed were non-combatants. Bahadur Shah, who, along with several members of his family, had taken shelter on the outskirts of the city, was taken captive by Captain William Hodson. Hodson killed several members of the royal family, including three of Bahadur Shah's sons in cold blood. Later, the British conducted a mock trial of the last Mughal emperor and exiled him to Rangoon where he died in 1862.

Following the 10 May uprising at Meerut and the liberation of Delhi, there were mutinies at several places in north India in quick succession: Aligarh (20 May), Bulandshahr (21 May), Mainpuri (22 May), Etawah (23 May), Bareilly and Shahjahanpur (31 May), and Saharanpur (3 June). This suggests that there might have been some prior consultation among sipahis stationed in the Ganga–Yamuna Doab. The mutinies in this region prompted sections of local elites to join the sipahis, which in turn resulted in putting an end to the Company's rule in large portions of what is now Uttar Pradesh. Some of the liberated areas remained free for nearly a whole year before they could be reconquered by the British. For instance, the new regime that took over Bareilly with the success of the uprising of 31 May in the city, survived for nearly one whole year. On the other hand, Kanpur, located on the banks of the Ganga and along the Grand Trunk Road, was held by the 'rebels' for just a few weeks, although this prominent centre of the revolt witnessed some of the fiercest fighting in the Doab in the first few months of the struggle.

Kanpur emerged as a major centre of the revolt in the first week of June. Indian troops belonging to contingents of the Bengal Army quartered in the city's cantonment joined the struggle against the British on 4 June. Soon afterwards charge of the liberated city was handed over by the sipahis to Nana Sahib, who resided at Bithur near Kanpur. British troops, commanded by Hugh Wheeler, were immediately besieged by the sipahis and soon forced into submission. The large European population of the city (most of them civilians) too had taken refuge at the location where the British force was encamped. Towards the end of June, Wheeler agreed to surrender on the condition that the British were assured a safe passage to Allahabad. However, in a confusing sequence of events that has been much distorted in colonial accounts, the sipahis began shooting and set the boats on fire. It is not clear whether the shooting was unprovoked. Of the approximately 450 evacuees 130 survived, of whom twenty were able to get away.[11] Survivors, mainly women and children, were then encircled and interned in a building close to the banks of the Ganga. This building is referred to in colonial accounts as Bibighar.

[11]Rudrangshu Mukherjee, '"Satan Let Loose Upon Earth": The Kanpur Massacres in India in the Revolt of 1857', *Past & Present*, No. 128, August 1990, p. 99.

Meanwhile, the Calcutta authorities had been trying desperately to organize an armed force that could restore the Company's control over the Grand Trunk Road connecting the imperial capital with Delhi and Punjab, and carry out the reconquest of Awadh. They eventually chose a ruthless officer from the Madras Army, James Neill, who was summoned to Calcutta to lead a force comprising European troops and 'loyal' remnants of the Bengal Army. On 11 June, Neill reached Allahabad where he, along with the death squads that he had formed, carried out large-scale massacres in the city and the neighbouring countryside. Inhabitants of villages suspected to have supported the 'rebels' were killed, irrespective of their age or gender. The troops (led by another military officer, Henry Havelock, after 30 June) then marched towards Kanpur, destroying entire villages along the way and slaughtering their residents. The rebel army fiercely resisted the British attempt to capture the city, though it had to eventually retreat and Havelock was able to occupy Kanpur on 17 July. Massive violence, the kind which was perhaps not witnessed in any other centre of the revolt, was unleashed against the local population. The unprecedented nature of the violence at Kanpur was justified as being retribution for the carnage at Bibighar that had preceded the British assault on the city. On 15 July, European women and children held in custody in Bibighar were put to death. It is unlikely that the history of this tragic incident can ever be recovered since all that we have are highly prejudiced, often hysterical, colonial narratives. Any narrative that undermined the colonial construction of the incident was systematically suppressed. There is no way, in the present state of our knowledge, to find out what caused this incident or who the persons responsible for it actually were. It has been suggested that as news of the atrocities of Neill reached Kanpur, there was such enormous outrage over the mass killings he had perpetrated that the massacre of the inmates of Bibighar was a way of dramatically avenging those deaths. Yet it is not really possible to determine the motives and objectives of the perpetrators of the Bibighar massacre. In a reappraisal of this issue, Rudrangshu Mukherjee has observed that ultimately the 'rebels' were replicating the violence that the British had used to establish their sway over the Indian subcontinent: 'They "borrowed" from the British and replicated the violence. The terms of their violence were thus derived from that very structure of power against which they had revolted.'[12] Subsequently, the brutal suppression of the revolt was sought to be legitimized by constantly referring to the Bibighar massacre. In the British imagination, Kanpur became a metaphor for the entire revolt. An elaborate memorial built over a well situated close to the site of the massacre, into which the bodies of the European victims were allegedly thrown, became one of the most-visited monuments by British travellers touring India.

The 'rebels' renewed their effort to liberate Kanpur towards the end of the year. The fresh offensive was led by Ramchandra Tope, popularly called Tatya Tope, who was a confidante of Nana Sahib. By about mid-November 1857, Tatya Tope's troops had brought the countryside surrounding Kanpur under their control. In the last week of November, a major military engagement took place between the rebel sipahis and the British on the outskirts of the city. The British force initially suffered a severe setback and was forced to retreat. The fight for Kanpur continued for several days till eventually Tatya Tope's position became untenable and he had to withdraw along with his troops. Tope then joined hands with Lakshmi Bai who was spearheading the struggle in Bundelkhand. The insurrection was widespread in the Bundelkhand region, to the south and southwest of Kanpur. Here Jhansi, the capital of a small Maratha-ruled principality that had been annexed by the EIC in 1854 during the aggressive expansionist drive under Dalhousie, had become the main seat of sipahi authority.

[12]Ibid., p. 112.

Sipahis of the Bengal Army stationed at Jhansi overthrew their European officers on 6 June 1857 and placed themselves under the leadership of Lakshmi Bai. British rule in the area soon came to an end. It has been suggested that Lakshmi Bai agreed to head the new government rather reluctantly even though she had reason to be hostile to the Company due to the annexation of her state. What is significant, however, is that once she had made her choice she led the struggle with great perseverance and courage. As Tapti Roy has shown, the insurrection spread rapidly throughout Bundelkhand with both local elites and peasants combining to fight the British; the entire countryside was in a state of upheaval.[13] Villagers spontaneously organized themselves to oust the British and their Indian collaborators, arming themselves with anything they could lay their hands on—spears, lathis, and wooden rods to which sickles or knives had been tied. Tahsil offices and police stations were attacked and official records burnt. It was firmly believed by the people that the colonial rulers had fled, never to return again. Much of Bundelkhand remained a liberated zone till the beginning of 1858. A British force sent to recapture Jhansi launched an offensive against the city in March. Lakshmi Bai coordinated the efforts to resist this military onslaught. It was with great difficulty that the British were able to force their way into Jhansi by 3 April amidst heavy fighting. Lakshmi Bai was able to escape to neighbouring Kalpi where she joined Tatya Tope who had been on his way to Jhansi to assist the rebels. The two of them, as we shall see, later proceeded in the direction of Gwalior. An impoverished priest who was undertaking a journey from his village near Pune, to Mathura, happened to be in Jhansi during the siege. In his account of the ordeals he had to undergo while the fighting was in progress we get a vivid first-hand portrayal of the valour displayed by Lakshmi

[13]Tapti Roy, *The Politics of a Popular Uprising: Bundelkhand in 1857,* New Delhi: Oxford University Press, 1994.

Bai in defending the city. There is also a detailed description in this account of the violence and plunder indulged in by the besiegers who, after the city had been occupied 'took away whatever they could remove: the bolts from the doors, wood, chairs, fruit from the trees'.[14]

While these developments were taking place in Bundelkhand, something very significant was happening in the Awadh region, especially in the capital of the erstwhile kingdom, Lucknow. The most important action here was the epic siege of the Lucknow residency, seat of the colonial regime in the province. The truncated kingdom of Awadh had been annexed by the British in February 1856. The territories of the annexed kingdom were constituted as the province of 'Oudh' and made part of the Bengal Presidency.

On 30 May, several sipahi contingents stationed at Lucknow rebelled. The British authorities were able to rapidly bring the situation under control and the sipahis dispersed to the countryside, especially to the Sitapur area. Simultaneously, a mass uprising by the inhabitants of Lucknow occurred, but was quickly put down. Large scale preventive arrests were made and the situation remained relatively quiet during June. Meanwhile, the Awadh countryside was up in arms. While many of the rebels in the districts surrounding Lucknow converged on the capital, mobilization for a fresh offensive against the colonial authorities had been underway for some time within Lucknow. On 30 June, a decisive battle between the 'rebels' and the British took place at Chinhat on the outskirts of the city, in which the former won a resounding victory. They were now in a position to take over the capital of the province. British troops and civilian officials retreated to the complex of the former residency (headquarters of the British resident prior to the annexation of the kingdom) and were besieged. Other

---

[14]Vishnu Bhatt Godshe Versaikar, *1857: The Real Story of a Great Uprising*, tr. Mrinal Pande, New Delhi: Harper Perennial, 2011, p. 118.

European inhabitants of the city also rushed to seek shelter in the residency. In all, there were about 3,000 persons within the residency complex (apart from the residency itself the compound included several neighbouring buildings). The long siege of the Lucknow residency commenced on 1 July 1857.

The rebels set up a new government of their own as the legitimate government of Lucknow—in fact of the whole of Awadh—thereby proclaiming the end of the EIC's government. They recognized the authority of Begum Hazrat Mahal who remained their foremost leader throughout the duration of the siege. Hazrat Mahal was a former wife of Wajid Ali Shah. She continued living in Lucknow after Wajid Ali was exiled. When the uprising began she declared her minor son Birjis Qadr as the ruler of Awadh. Birjis Qadr was accepted as the nominal head of government by the rebels. On 5 July, he was installed as ruler in a formal ceremony. Hazrat Mahal was the regent for her son. Henceforth, all official orders were issued in the name of Birjis Qadr. Recognition for Birjis Qadr was also sought from the Mughal emperor. The sipahi regime in Delhi acknowledged him as the governor (subedar) of Awadh. All these arrangements underlined the legitimacy of the Lucknow regime, enabling it to gain widespread support in the region.

The rebels concentrated their military strength around the residency. The siege of the residency compound had an important political significance. This was the seat of the Company's hated administration in Awadh after the annexation of 1856. It is estimated that initially the strength of the rebel forces surrounding the residency was about 6,000. The British were led by Henry Lawrence, who had assumed the office of 'Chief Commissioner of Oudh' in March 1857, i.e. shortly before the outbreak of the revolt. Lawrence was killed in the first few days of the siege, on 4 July.

Military command of the rebels was in the hands of Raja Jai Lal Singh, who had been the názim or administrator of Azamgarh prior to the annexation of Awadh. He was a close confidante of Hazrat Mahal, and as a key member of the military council was entrusted with taking major decisions (the structure of this council resembled that of the Court of Administration at Delhi). Jai Lal Singh was also the main spokesperson for the troops in their dealings with the court of Hazrat Mahal. He was instrumental in mobilizing military support from the districts around Lucknow. Another outstanding leader of the rebels was Maulvi Ahmadullah Shah. It would appear that he enjoyed considerable grassroots support among the urban poor. Although Ahmadullah Shah cooperated with Hazrat Mahal, there were occasionally sharp differences between the two of them. Further, Hazrat Mahal maintained close contact with Nana Sahib.

As the uprising progressed and British administration in the entire province of Awadh collapsed, a large section of the landed aristocracy, namely the talluqdars, came over to the rebel cause. This is indicated by the figures worked out by Rudrangshu Mukherjee in his important study of the revolt in Awadh. According to Mukherjee, the rebels received large-scale reinforcements around the middle of November 1857 when British forces led by Commander-in-Chief Colin Campbell (Lord Clyde) launched a major offensive to recapture the city. At this stage there were over 53,000 rebel combatants in the city, of which roughly 32,000 were listed as 'tallukdar's men'. In the words of Mukherjee, this 'clearly shows that the rebellion in Awadh had transcended a purely sepoy base. For one thing, the fighting force was quite large and for another, more than 60 per cent of the fighting force was drawn from the general rural populace. It is more than probable, given the ties of loyalty that existed in the rural world of Awadh, that the thousands of men supplied by the talluqdars were not all just their retainers but also drawn from tenants, peasants, and clansmen who lived on their land.'[15]

[15]Rudrangshu Mukherjee, *Awadh in Revolt, 1857-1858: A Study of Popular*

It may be mentioned that the Company had adopted an anti-talluqdar policy since the annexation of Awadh. This was an extension of the policy it had pursued in the adjoining North-Western Provinces. The land revenue settlement introduced in the territories which came to be designated from the mid-1830s as the North-Western Provinces, over a period of time led to the impoverishment of the peasantry. The system of assessment and collection was known as Mahalwari settlement. A substantial portion of the territories comprising the North-Western Provinces were areas forcibly acquired from Awadh from 1801 onwards. The North-Western Provinces included Gorakhpur in the east, Etawah in the Doab, and Rohilkhand. There were complex traditional arrangements in these areas for the sharing of agrarian produce and payment of revenue. There was now a tendency to curtail the role of the talluqdars in the collection of revenue. Under James Thomason, who was lieutenant governor of the Provinces for a decade from 1843 to 1853, the policy of reducing the authority of the talluqdars received a fresh impetus.

However, talluqdars were not necessarily owners of big estates in a personal capacity. Many of them were nominal chiefs of dominant clans which had established superior rights over land. These were usually upper caste clans, often Rajput but Brahmin as well; besides there were Pathan and to a lesser extent Sheikh clans. Such talluqdars would mostly be heads of the senior family of the clan. In such cases, the superior rights would be held collectively by the brotherhood, or pattidars. The British pursued a policy of holding the brotherhood responsible for the payment of revenue. This implied that even those who had individually contributed their full share of the total revenue demand had to pay the amount due from defaulters or lose their rights in the village.

Moreover, the revenue settlement generally ignored the claims of talluqdars, thereby eliminating them altogether or else reducing

Resistance, New Delhi: Oxford University Press, 2001 (first published, 1984), p. 95.

them to the status of mere revenue collectors. In the process, the traditional ties of the village were disrupted. This had a cascading effect on holders of subordinate rights, and on tillers of the soil. Further, there was a steady increase in the revenue realized, of as much as 80 per cent in the fifty years preceding the revolt. Obviously, the main burden was borne by the peasants. At the same time, the shares of other sections of society in the agrarian produce were substantially reduced all around.

Of course, village society was not egalitarian and the relationship between the talluqdar and the peasant was based on exploitation. Nevertheless, the bonds that sustained the poor in times of severe adversity (famine, drought) disappeared as rural society underwent rapid disintegration under the impact of the Company's revenue policies. This was all the more so due to the frequent revisions that were carried out under the Mahalwari settlement, every twenty to thirty years or at even shorter intervals. It is not surprising that a very high proportion of holdings changed hands between the 1830s and 1850s. All this had an unsettling effect on peasants, building up a mood of intense hostility towards the Company in the countryside. It is hardly surprising that the revolt was so widespread in the Mahalwari areas. These happened to be areas which had been subjected to severe colonial exploitation for more than half a century. These were also areas from which the Company recruited the bulk of the sipahis of the Bengal Army. A large number of the rebel sipahis came from villages that had been facing acute hardship for more than five decades under British rule. The soldiers were bound by ties of kinship with peasants in the North-Western Provinces. This explains the extensive support that the rebels received in the Doab during the revolt.

In Awadh too, the Company pursued an anti-talluqdar policy following the annexation of the kingdom in February 1856. This was an extension of the policy it had pursued in the adjoining North-Western Provinces. Initially, the newly appointed chief commissioner, James Outram, had moved a little cautiously in the matter of dispossessing the talluqdars. When, however, Outram proceeded on leave in May 1856, his successor C. Coverley Jackson embarked on a harsher policy, taking away the intermediary rights of the talluqdars, assuming their land, and containing their political and administrative power. This gave rise to discontent among the powerful landowning classes in the newly annexed province. Colonial officials were aware of the hostility that Jackson's measures had caused, and for this reason he was replaced by Henry Lawrence. Lawrence was brought in as chief commissioner because he was perceived to be somewhat more sympathetic to the landed elite. But by the time Lawrence assumed office in March 1857 things had already gone too far. Within a few months the revolt broke out and Lucknow came under the control of the rebels. Although the talluqdars were initially reluctant to join the rebels, once the Company's rule disappeared in Awadh a large number of them shifted their allegiance. The British were somewhat surprised that even the peasants whom the talluqdars oppressed should have joined the rebel cause under the leadership of their respective talluqdars. Colonial officials seem to have assumed that the peasants would appreciate the Company's anti-talluqdari measures, since it was claimed that these were supposed to be in the interests of the peasants. The structure of traditional rural society, in which ties of the village and the personal bond between the talluqdar and/ or his retinue and the peasant had an important place, became the basis of solidarity in the struggle against the Company. An instinctive comprehension of the exploitative nature of the colonial regime, which ultimately targeted the surplus produced by the peasant, brought the talluqdars and peasants of Awadh together in the fight against British rule.

◆

As the monsoon season came to an end in 1857, the British made a concerted attempt to regain Lucknow. By this time they had already brought the area between Banaras and Kanpur under their control. Delhi too had fallen by the third week of September. British troops commanded by Havelock attempted to break through the siege. Havelock was accompanied by Outram who had returned from leave and was now asked to assume charge of the province of Awadh. On 25 September 1857, Havelock and Outram, along with a small contingent, managed to reach the residency, but they in turn were besieged. The siege of the residency continued.

Then in November 1857 another attempt was made to lift the siege. We have already referred to this offensive that was led by Campbell. Campbell's military action on this occasion was only a partial success. What Campbell was able to do was to evacuate the besieged inhabitants of the residency. However, Lucknow itself still remained under rebel control. Eventually, a massive offensive was launched in March 1858. The recapture of Lucknow was a matter of urgency; without control over Lucknow, British rule could not be re-established in Awadh. After ferocious fighting, Campbell's contingents occupied Lucknow on 21 March 1858.

With this setback to the 'rebel' cause, Begum Hazrat Mahal shifted her base to the fort of Baundi (district Bahraich), where she continued her struggle till she was forced to evacuate the fort in December 1858. Ahmadullah Shah too continued the struggle in the western parts of Awadh and died fighting in June 1858. From Baundi, Hazrat Mahal moved to the dense jungles of the tarai area. British troops pursued her, but she managed to escape capture. Later, she was offered refuge in Nepal.

Large parts of central India, especially the area lying between the rivers Chambal and Narmada, too were drawn into the massive struggle against colonial rule. There was, in fact, a continuous zone of intense fighting extending from Gwalior to Bundelkhand, linking up with Kanpur and Lucknow, in which the Company's authority ceased to exist in the latter half of 1857. Further, Tatya Tope carried out a series of military campaigns in central India during the latter half of 1858 and early 1859 before he was betrayed, captured, and executed in April 1859. The developments in the Sindia state, territorially the largest princely state in central India, reveal both the possibilities and limitations of the struggle in this zone. In June 1857, sipahis of the Gwalior Contingent of the Sindia princely state rebelled. The contingent was officered by Europeans, and was subject to the overall control of the Company. The sipahis had been growing restive since the last week of May. As news of events at Meerut and Delhi as well as other centres of rebellion reached Gwalior, the capital of the state, the troops geared themselves for an offensive against the Company. By 14 June, British officers had been overthrown. Several Europeans were killed or had to flee the city. There were elements among the Gwalior 'rebels' who favoured a general massacre of the English, but were restrained from adopting this course by the sipahi leadership. The full potential of the strategic advantage gained by the Gwalior soldiers was never realized. They were pre-empted by the ruler Jiyaji Rao (r. 1843–86) who announced that henceforth the troops would serve directly under him. The maharaja undertook to pay their salaries regularly and 'never declined in clear terms to lead them against the British'. This robbed the troops of their autonomy and gave the beleaguered British some breathing space. In the words of Sen, 'Sindhia had rendered a great service to his friends. A formidable body of well-trained and well-armed rebels, whose intervention could at different times decide the fate of Agra, Delhi, and Kanpur, sat idle in their lines at Morar [the military cantonment area of Gwalior] when the British were slowly restoring their authority over North India.'[16] For a whole year after the uprising of 14 June 1857, the Gwalior Contingent did not actively participate as a body in the campaigns of the rebels. It was only after the fall of Jhansi and Kalpi in 1858 that Gwalior became the base of rebel leaders. At the end of May (1858), Tatya Tope and

[16]Sen, *Eighteen Fifty-seven*, p. 289.

Lakshmi Bai, accompanied by Nana Sahib's nephew Rao Sahib and Nawab Ali Bahadur of Banda (another prominent centre of the revolt in Bundelkhand), assumed leadership of the Gwalior troops. Jiyaji Sindia fled to the protection of the British. In mid-June, the British army launched a major operation to capture Gwalior. In the intense fighting that ensued, Rani Lakshmi Bai died in the thick of battle. On 20 June 1858, Jiyaji was escorted back to his capital by British troops.

In the east, a rebellion had broken out in Bihar as early as July 1857. There was an uprising in the city of Patna on 3 July 1857, which was swiftly crushed. Then on 25 July, British troops stationed at Danapur cantonment near Patna mutinied. Subsequently, a bigger mass struggle emerged under the leadership of the famous Kunwar Singh, a landed aristocrat of Jagdishpur in the Bhojpur area of western Bihar. Incidentally, Kunwar Singh himself was a very old man at this time, but he actively led the rebellion in Bihar. He continued to do so right till his death, of a serious wound, in April 1858. It is worth mentioning that Kunwar Singh undertook a long march from Jagdishpur in the western part of Bihar into Jharkhand, then moved via Baghelkhand towards Malwa, Gwalior, and Jhansi. He then marched to Lucknow, Faizabad, and returned to Jagdishpur via Ghazipur. All along this route, he tried to inspire people, encouraging them to join the revolt. Obviously, these people must have had sympathy for his cause since it is not really possible to march with a large body of soldiers unless there is some assurance of supplies and shelter. Eventually by the time Kunwar Singh got back to Jagdishpur, he was severely injured and had to amputate his arm so as to prevent it from getting infected. After Kunwar Singh's death, his brother, Amar Singh, continued to lead the struggle. In the case of Bihar, the period from April 1858 till about the end of 1858 is a period of intense struggle and resistance. Amar Singh launched a guerrilla offensive which the British found difficult to contain. He constantly engaged in launching surprise attacks. The most crucial phase of this guerrilla armed struggle was the period following the death of Kunwar Singh in April, right up to the end of the monsoon in 1858, when the British launched a major counter-offensive which destroyed the resistance.

It is usually assumed that Punjab was unaffected by the uprising. Colonial writings on the subject invariably depict the province as being steadfastly 'loyal'. This is not really correct. British Punjab was a huge province stretching from the Sutlej to the borders of Afghanistan and included large parts of present-day Haryana and Himachal Pradesh. It had come under colonial rule just a few years before the outbreak of the revolt. This explains why the bulk of the Bengal Army was concentrated in the province at the beginning of 1857. Moreover, the proportion of European troops relative to Indian sipahis was much higher in Punjab compared to anywhere else in the subcontinent. It should be borne in mind that this was an army of occupation, intended to stabilize British control over this vast area. The presence of such a large military force meant that insurrections could be suppressed with greater speed than elsewhere. This is something that has not been sufficiently appreciated in historical accounts about the revolt in Punjab. On the other hand, it was precisely because sipahis of the Bengal Army were stationed in the province in such large numbers that there were mutinies at several cantonments, from Ambala in the east to Peshawar in the west. These mutinies created conditions for popular uprisings.

The uprising at Ambala began on the morning of 10 May, a few hours before the mutiny at Meerut.[17] It may be mentioned that the distance between Ambala and Meerut is less than 200 kilometres. The Ambala mutiny was quickly crushed and over a hundred 'rebel' sipahis were executed. But this did not prevent the outbreak of mutinies at other places in the province, for instance at Lahore, Sialkot, Ferozepur, Jalandhar,

---

[17] K. C. Yadav, *The Revolt of Eighteen Fifty-Seven in Haryana,* New Delhi: Manohar, 1977.

and Peshawar. Freshly recruited soldiers from Punjab joined the struggle along with sipahis belonging to the Awadh and Bhojpur contingents. Whereas colonial historiography created the myth of the 'loyal Sikh', it is noteworthy that one of the prominent 'rebel' leaders to be hanged in Punjab right at the beginning of the revolt, Sardar Mohar Singh of Ropar, belonged to the Sikh community. The uprising in the province was sufficiently serious for the British to suppress it with immense violence, much of which was directed against the common people whose participation posed a grave threat to the Company's authority. In the small princely state of Nabha, the inhabitants of the village of Dabri were massacred and the entire village burnt in a manner reminiscent of the reprisals of Neill in the Allahabad countryside. The most gruesome recorded incident in Punjab was the mass killing of civilians and rebel sipahis (these sipahis, stationed near Lahore, had repudiated their allegiance to the Company's army) at Ajnala, near Amritsar, on the orders of Frederic Cooper who was then the main colonial official of the district. Bodies of those killed were thrown into a well, popularly known as 'kalyan-da-khuh', which in local memory is still associated with the incident. A great deal of information about what happened at Ajnala was provided by Cooper himself in his published reminiscences in which he spoke with great pride about his role in the Ajnala incident.

The revolt had an all-India spread even though the struggle was the most intense in northern and central India. In the Madras Presidency there were disturbances in Chengalpattu and Salem. According to an official report, over a thousand sipahis of the Madras Army were court-martialled for attempting to stir up trouble against the Company's government.[18] The northeastern areas of the subcontinent too were affected. It may

---

[18]N. Rajendran, 'The Revolt of 1857: Rebellious Prelude and Nationalist Response in Tamil Nadu', Sabyasachi Bhattacharya, ed., *Rethinking 1857*, New Delhi: Orient Longman, 2007, p. 193.

be recalled that the British were in the process of consolidating their position in Assam, Manipur, Cachar, and Chittagong from the late 1820s onwards, following their conquest of the region in the wake of the wars against Burma. It is not surprising therefore that all these areas (barring Burma) should have witnessed upheavals in 1857. In the Brahmaputra valley, where the Ahom rulers had been deposed, Maniram Dewan organized a struggle on behalf of the Ahom princes for the overthrow of colonial rule in the region. There is evidence of popular support for this struggle, especially among tea garden workers.[19] Maniram was eventually captured, and executed in February 1858. At Chittagong, marking the southeastern extremity of Bengal, sipahis mutinied in November 1857. The sipahis then marched northwards to Cachar via Sylhet and Tripura. They were able to enlist the support of some of the princes of the Manipur royal house, who had been living in Cachar since the 1830s.[20] The British were able to contain the Cachar insurrection by January 1858.

The official colonial view of the uprising of 1857–58 was that it was essentially a mutiny of the sipahis, who were joined by mobs of ruffians ('badmashes') and a handful of disgruntled princely rulers and/or their dependents. However, there can be little doubt that this was a major anti-colonial struggle. Within a few weeks of the initial outbreak at Meerut, the EIC's authority ceased to exist in large parts of the Indian subcontinent. Even in those areas where the scale of the upheaval was not as extensive as it was in northern and central India attempts were made to overthrow British rule. What is even more significant is that almost all social classes, with the exception of commercial classes that had benefited from colonial rule, participated in the struggle. However, it is equally certain that

[19]David R. Syiemlieh, 'Historiography of Literature and Sources on the Uprising of 1857 in North East India', Bhattacharya, ed., Rethinking 1857, p. 213.
[20]Ibid., p. 215.

substantial sections of every social class stayed aloof from the revolt or else actively assisted the British. This is particularly true of princely rulers, feudal elites, and landed aristocrats. It is with the assistance of these sections that the British were eventually able to restore their rule. Nevertheless, it is the united front of various classes which the 'rebels' successfully created that gave to the revolt its historical importance. This united front included princely rulers, landlords, peasants, artisans, the intelligentsia, and the urban poor. S. B. Chaudhuri in his *Civil Rebellion in the Indian Mutinies* highlighted the crucial role of 'civil rebellion' in his assessment of the revolt. While the 'military mutiny' was important, particularly because it struck the initial blow, the sipahis by themselves could not have gone very far. Once 'civil elements' became part of the resistance they transformed its character. In many cases, civilians took over the leadership and determined the course of the struggle which henceforth became a people's uprising.[21] Subsequent research (for instance the writings of Mukherjee and Roy referred to earlier) has confirmed, and strengthened Chaudhuri's conclusions. In recent years, historical scholarship on the revolt has tried to deepen our understanding of popular participation in the revolt by focusing on the participation of marginalized sections of society: women, Dalits, and tribal communities, among others. This history, which though it has survived in folklore, local legends, and lower caste religious practices, is largely absent from mainstream narratives and it is only now that attempts are being made to undertake a rigorous study of the place of these sections of society in the anti-colonial struggle of 1857.

◆

The British succeeded in re-establishing their authority in almost all the areas where the uprising had taken place by the end of

---

[21]Sashi Bhushan Chaudhuri, *Civil Rebellion in the Indian Mutinies (1857-1859)*, Calcutta: World Press, 1957.

1858. During the winter of 1858–59 they carried out mopping-up operations against the few remaining pockets of resistance. The concluding phase of the suppression of the revolt coincided with a change in the manner in which the Indian empire was governed. In August 1858, parliament enacted legislation that brought to an end the long, dark era of company rule, but with little hope of light ahead.

THE COLONIAL SUBJUGATION OF INDIA

TEN

STRATEGIES OF IMPERIAL CONTROL

The constitutional arrangements in the metropole, by which the empire was administered by the East India Company, were drastically revised as the final campaigns against the rebels reached their conclusion. The crown directly took over the governance of India. The British monarch was now formally the sovereign ruler of the Indian empire. In practice this meant that Britain's Indian possessions were to be administered directly by the British cabinet. The Company, rather its court of directors, no longer had any role in this. The Company survived as a legal entity till 1874. The guaranteed 10.5 per cent dividend continued to be paid even after the crown directly took over the Government of India in 1858. As has been mentioned earlier, the Charter Act of 1833 had a provision whereby the British government could dissolve the Company after a period of forty years, prolonging its existence as a corporate entity till at least 1874. The government was to pay double the nominal price of each share if it took this step. Thus, the shareholders were assured that they would not suffer losses due to the takeover.

The 1858 Act abolished the board of control. The responsibility for administering India was given to a cabinet minister, designated as secretary of state for India. Policy relating to India was to be formulated by the secretary of state in consultation with a newly formed 'council of India' consisting of fifteen members (this council is not to be confused with the governor general's council). The council of India gradually became merely an advisory body, and had lost much of its relevance by the end of the century, though it remained in existence till 1935. The bureaucratic establishment attached to the secretary of state for India, the India Office, emerged over a period of time as the main instrument through which the Indian empire was controlled from London. This was a vast establishment, staffed by a large body of civil service officials and clerks. All these organs were, of course, ultimately subject to the authority of the British Parliament.

Decision-making in London, needless to say, involved consultations with the governor general. This process, which earlier took several months, was sped up by the completion of the project to connect India and Britain by telegraph. This was done by linking Bombay and London through cables located under the sea; in 1870, Bombay and London were connected by telegraph. This made possible almost instant communication between the metropolis and the colony, thereby making it easier for the secretary of state to monitor the functioning of the governor general and his council. At the same time, it has been pointed out, this technological advance exposed the colonial state to greater public scrutiny in England which, on occasion, actually slowed down the formulation of policy.[1]

◆

Following the enactment of legislation whereby the British government took over direct control over the Indian empire, Queen Victoria issued a proclamation in November 1858 in which all inhabitants of the empire, including princely rulers, were declared to be subjects of the crown (see Appendix, p. 290). This declaration was partly an attempt to resolve the tricky issue of sovereignty. The question of sovereignty had been a complicated one due to the ambiguous status of the East India Company. Although the Company owed its existence to royal charters granted by the British crown, in India it

---

[1]Deep Kanta Lahiri Choudhury, *Telegraphic Imperialism: Crisis and Panic in the Indian Empire, c. 1830-1920*, Basingstoke: Palgrave Macmillan, 2010.

was constitutionally subservient to the Mughal emperor. By the beginning of the nineteenth century this was only a matter of symbolic importance since the Mughal emperors no longer had any real power, yet right down to the middle of the century the Company had formally acknowledged the emperor as its overlord through various ceremonial gestures. The sham trial of Bahadur Shah Zafar in early 1858, in which the main charge against him was that he had committed high treason against the Company's state by agreeing to accept the leadership of the sipahis, was intended to publicly assert the Company's sovereignty and delegitimize the authority of the emperor. In an important essay published in 1922, F. W. Buckler had examined the various constitutional issues involved in the so-called trial and argued that 'the source of the Company's authority in India lay, not in the Charters of the King of England, nor in the Acts of the British Parliament, nor in the sword, but in the *farmans* of the Mughal Emperor'. He concluded that it was the Company that was the rebel, and that the sipahis were duty-bound to support the emperor: 'if in 1857 there were any mutineer, it was the East India Company'.[2]

From the point of view of the Mughals, the Company had been governing the empire on behalf of the emperor. As for the East India Company, it would appear that it preferred ambiguity on the question of sovereignty. Categorically disowning the sovereign status of the Mughal emperor would have implied acknowledgement in unequivocal terms of the sovereignty of the British crown over the Indian empire. In effect, this would have meant greater parliamentary intervention. The question was decisively resolved only in 1858 when the crown directly assumed charge of the Indian territories hitherto governed by the East India Company, reducing simultaneously rulers of all princely states to the status of subjects of the British crown.

---

[2]F. W. Buckler, 'The Political Theory of the Indian Mutiny', *Transactions of the Royal Historical Society*, London, 1922, pp. 74, 75.

Even at this stage the Company did not give up without a fight. Its position was forcefully articulated by John Stuart Mill who was particularly critical of Palmerston for the abolition of company rule. Mill was strongly opposed to the interference of parliament in Indian affairs, carrying forward some of the arguments advanced by prominent Company administrators of the early nineteenth century such as Thomas Munro and John Malcolm. Specialized knowledge of the Indian empire was supposedly essential for governing the empire well, and this was knowledge that parliament did not possess. Such knowledge could only be acquired through 'prolonged and intimate contact with the difficulties of ruling an area different in many respects from Britain'.[3]

Another objective of Victoria's proclamation was to assure rulers of princely states that their territories would remain intact and that there would be no interference in matters relating to adoption or succession. This was in keeping with the British policy of enlisting the support of feudal elites and the landed aristocracy to strengthen the colonial state in the post-revolt period. Princely rulers and feudal elites were supposed to constitute the main audience to which the proclamation was addressed since they were regarded as the 'natural leaders' of Indian society. The queen announced that the governor general would be the monarch's representative in India, and would as the deputy of the monarch have the additional title of 'viceroy'. This title, for which there was no statutory provision, came to be increasingly favoured by governors general due to its imperial connotations. The title literally means 'in place of king'; it was borrowed from the ancient Romans who used it for governors of provinces of the empire, and from the Spanish who gave this designation to the foremost administrative functionaries of their overseas possessions in Latin America. It should be kept

---

[3]Cited in Lynn Zastoupil, *John Stuart Mill and India,* Stanford: Stanford University Press, 1994, p. 183.

in mind that by this time the British were projecting themselves as inheritors of Roman imperial traditions. This was made apparent particularly in the use of the phrase 'Pax Britannica' (the British peace), in imitation of 'Pax Romana' (the Roman peace), while referring to Britain's colonial dominance over the world.

Further, the proclamation promised the queen's Indian subjects that there would be no interference in their religious observances or social customs, and that they would be treated with equality irrespective of their faith. Opportunities for employment in government jobs would be open to everyone, 'of whatever race or creed', subject to applicants having the necessary qualifications. Finally, the proclamation declared a general pardon for those charged with participation in the revolt, unless they were guilty of violence, especially against Europeans. Most of these pronouncements were just empty promises.

In order to portray the queen as a benevolent and compassionate monarch, the proclamation contained an amnesty clause which pardoned all rebels, 'save and except those who have been, or shall be, convicted of having directly taken part in the murder of British subjects'. The question of excluding those guilty of the killing of British subjects from the amnesty provisions of the proclamation had to be resolved by clarifying who was to be considered a British subject. Members of the governor general's council and senior law officers had to figure out 'whether the term "British subjects" used in the exceptional clause of the amnesty was to be interpreted in its restricted sense as "European British subjects" or in its wider sense as to extend to all subjects of the crown'.[4]

The consensus which emerged was that what was available to 'native subjects' was an inferior form of subjecthood. The proclamation promised fair treatment to all subjects of the

[4]Suparna Sengupta, 'The Sovereign Exception: Interpreting "British Subjects" in the Queen's Amnesty of 1858', *Social Scientist*, Vol. 46, No. 5–6, 2018, pp. 22–23.

Indian empire. This was not so in practice—India was after all a non-white colony. The two legal luminaries who shaped the judicial mechanism in the immediate post-revolt period in their capacity as members of the governor general's council, Henry Maine and James Fitzjames Stephen, 'had embedded racial difference in the law. They left behind them a legal code that bore little relation to the paternal rhetoric of the queen's proclamation of 1858'.[5]

◆

Within India itself the 1858 Act did not modify the existing administrative structure. The continuation of Canning as governor general (till 1862) ensured a fairly smooth transition from company rule to crown rule and allowed continuity between the two phases. It was in 1861 that some significant changes were made through the Indian Councils Act. This was part of a more comprehensive endeavour to reorganize various organs of the colonial state in view of the abolition of the Company's rule. One might mention that the Indian Penal Code, which became the basis for colonial criminal law, was introduced in 1860.

The Indian Councils Act of 1861 was an important step because it created the framework for a legislative machinery which by the beginning of the twentieth century was to be developed into a central legislature with some elected Indian representatives. As noted earlier, the Charter Act of 1833 had added a law member to the governor general's council who was supposed to be present when the council took up legislative matters. Subsequently, the Charter Act of 1853 modified the composition of the governor general's council when it met for legislative purposes. In order to have adequate inputs from the various presidencies and provinces, as well as from the judiciary,

[5]Miles Taylor, *The English Maharani: Queen Victoria and India*, Gurgaon: Penguin/Viking, 2018, p. 95.

six more members were added to the council.

The 1861 Act increased the number of ordinary members of the governor general's council (including the law member) from four to five. There was now a finance member, usually referred to as the 'fourth member'. The commander-in-chief could attend as an extraordinary member (i.e., without the right to vote). The more significant provisions of the Act related to the constitution of the council when it met for legislative business. On these occasions the council was to be a larger body, comprising a minimum of six and a maximum of twelve 'additional' members. Half of these additional members had to be non-official persons (those not in government service), some of whom could be Indians. The councils of governors of presidencies were required to have four to eight additional members (half of them non-official) when these councils took up legislative matters.

The Act deliberately avoided describing the council, when it met for legislative purposes, as a legislative council. Thus there was no notion of there being two distinct entities, an executive council and a legislative council. As the secretary of state, Charles Wood, pointed out to Governor General Elgin (governor general, 1862–63), 'You have a Council which occasionally makes laws, and when it makes laws, certain other people sit with your Ordinary Councillors. But your Council is one and the same Council.'[6] The British did not, at this stage, want to give the impression that they were creating an embryonic legislature as an initial step towards self-government. As a further safeguard, members of the council, when the body met for legislative purposes, could not 'without the previous sanction of the Governor-General'[7] discuss any matter pertaining to public debt and revenues, religious rights

[6] J. L. Morison, 'Lord Elgin in India, 1862-63', *Cambridge Historical Journal*, Vol. I, No. 2, 1924, p. 188.
[7] *The Indian Councils Act and the Acts Amending It..., etc.*, Madras: National Press, 1893, p. 10.

and usages, military or naval forces, and relations with foreign powers. Crucial areas of colonial governance therefore remained outside the purview of the council. Nevertheless, it was through subsequent modifications in the composition and functioning of the council, when meeting to transact legislative business, that an imperial legislative council (as distinct from the governor general's executive council) evolved.

The possibility of appointing Indians as additional members was considered to be a major concession. Colonial policymakers were of the view that the absence of a formal mechanism for consulting Indians while making laws was one of the major underlying causes of the revolt. Since the British Indian government was not properly informed about 'native' opinion, it did not always know which laws were likely to produce resentment. Had such a mechanism existed prior to 1857, the government might have avoided, according to this line of thinking, enacting legislation that was seen by the East India Company's subjects as amounting to interference in social customs or religious practices. The inclusion of a few Indians in the council when it met for legislative purposes was intended to avoid the repetition of such a situation. These members were invariably selected from among those whom the British regarded as 'natural leaders' of Indian society, which meant that they belonged to the landed aristocracy or were princely rulers. The first three Indians nominated to the council were Narinder Singh (ruler of Patiala), Ishwari Prasad Narayan Singh (titular raja of Banaras), and Dinkar Rao, who had held the position of diwan in the Gwalior state during the revolt. There was a similar pattern in the nomination of Indians to the Madras and Bombay councils.

The next stage in the evolution of the governor general's council, and the provincial councils, was the Indian Councils Act of 1892 which amended some of the provisions of the 1861 Act. With the growth of nationalist activity in the last quarter of the nineteenth century, colonial officialdom tried to give the impression that it was formally consulting a larger number of Indians as part of the decision-making processes of the state. For this purpose, the councils were expanded by increasing the strength of non-official additional members. Further, even though these members were still technically selected through nomination, nevertheless it was understood that the government would go 'beyond mere nomination'. In other words, for the first time, an elective principle, very vaguely defined, was introduced for selecting additional members of the legislative councils. This principle was actually to be experimented with in the provincial councils and only in a severely restricted manner in the governor general's council. The relevant regulations for selecting the additional members for the respective councils were finalized in 1893. The Madras and Bombay councils were to have twenty additional members each, half of them non-official. The Bengal council (i.e., the council of the lieutenant governor of Bengal) was also to have twenty additional members, half of them non-official. The legislative council of the North-Western Provinces was to consist of fifteen members, eight of them non-official, selected by the lieutenant governor of the province (other provinces did not have councils). The non-official additional members were to be representatives of the bodies or associations that elected them; members would represent 'types and classes rather than areas and numbers' as in a modern democracy. The regulations specified the bodies and associations that were to elect the additional members: municipal corporations (e.g. the Corporation of Calcutta); municipal boards and committees; district boards; associations of merchants and manufacturers; university senates (e.g. Senate of the University of Calcutta); and big landowners. In the case of the governor general's council, the number of additional members was increased to sixteen, ten of whom had to be non-official. Four of the non-official additional members were to be selected, respectively, from among the non-official additional members of the four provincial councils. One member was to be elected by the European-dominated Calcutta Chamber of Commerce. The remaining five non-official additional members were to be selected by the governor general at his discretion in such a way that other parts of the Indian empire too had some token representation. The elective principle notwithstanding it was made clear that 'ultimate selection of all Additional Members rests with the Government, and not with the electors. The function of the latter will be that of recommendation only.'[8] Apart from the changes in the composition of the councils, there was also some modification in their functioning. It was now possible for the members to discuss financial matters and ask questions by way of seeking information from the government on various matters. More substantial changes in the composition and functioning of the councils were made under the provisions of the Acts of 1909 and 1919.

[8]Henry Lansdowne, 'His Excellency Lord Lansdowne's speech on the Rules under the Indian Councils Act (1892)', reproduced in *The Indian Councils Act, and the Acts Amending It*, Madras: The National Press, 1893, p. 51.

THE COLONIAL SUBJUGATION OF INDIA

ELEVEN

MILITARY ORGANIZATION

O nce the revolt had been suppressed, reorganization of the East India Company's army became a matter of priority, especially as the Bengal Army had almost ceased to exist. For this purpose a royal commission was set up in 1858. The commission was headed by Jonathan Peel, the secretary of state for war, and included several leading military officials of Britain. A major task before the commission was to identify social groups and regions from which 'loyal' soldiers could be recruited for the colonial army in India. The recommendations of the commission provided the blueprint for the military structure of the colonial state in the post-revolt period. It may be recalled that at this time the Company's army was merged with the royal army and ceased to exist as a separate formation.

One of the key recommendations of the commission was that the proportion of European troops in the British Indian army[1] be increased substantially. In the case of the Bengal Army, the proportion of Europeans to Indians was to be 1:2; and 1:3 for the Madras and Bombay armies. The three armies were to be kept separate and distinct. The experience of the revolt had demonstrated the usefulness of not encouraging cohesiveness of the three components. Recruitment of Indian troops into the scientifically most advanced units, such as the artillery, was to be entirely stopped.

[1]Although the nomenclature 'British Indian' army is, strictly speaking, inaccurate, it has been used here as a convenient shorthand. By the end of the nineteenth century the three presidency armies were merged to form the 'Indian Army'.

There was, however, no easy solution to the problem of recruitment. It was obvious that a fairly large number of soldiers had to be recruited from the Indian subcontinent. The expense of bringing troops entirely from Britain was prohibitive, even assuming that a sufficient number of soldiers were available for enlistment at home. According to one estimate, the cost of maintaining a regiment of European infantrymen was more than twice that of a similar contingent of Indian soldiers. The commission received numerous suggestions, including one for employing mercenaries from various parts of Asia. Ultimately, the commission was unable to come up with any specific proposal. Only a general recommendation was made for recruitment from a wider social base: 'the Native army should be composed of different nationalities and castes, and as a general rule, mixed promiscuously through each regiment'. This essentially implied that sipahis for the Bengal Army were no longer to be recruited exclusively from among the upper castes of Awadh and Bhojpur; the Madras Army and the Bombay Army were already recruiting sipahis from diverse social groups.

The overwhelming majority of the sipahi units had rebelled in 1857. Almost all of the Bengal Army had to be rebuilt once the revolt had been suppressed. Many of the existing units were reconstituted, with those soldiers who had remained loyal comprising their nucleus. Recruitment in the Ganga–Jamuna Doab was not abandoned. Instead, many of the fresh recruits came from lower castes. Thus the soldiers from eastern Uttar Pradesh and western Bihar continued to serve in the British Indian army in large numbers. Further, greater Punjab now became a major catchment area for the Bengal Army. The East India Company had begun tapping into the huge military labour market of this region following the two Punjab wars. Two regular infantry regiments had been formed in Punjab as early as 1846–47. The process of absorbing soldiers from the disbanded army of the erstwhile Lahore kingdom gathered momentum after 1849. The Company was keen to acquire the best contingents of the formidable army that had been left behind by Ranjit Singh. The annexation of Punjab had rendered nearly 60,000 well-trained soldiers unemployed. It was from among these that sipahis began to be recruited in large numbers into the Bengal Army in the early 1850s. Initially, the British were wary of employing these troopers because the army of the Lahore kingdom had been so hostile to them. It was only in 1851 that 'the lid on the recruitment of Punjabis into the regular corps of the Bengal Army was officially lifted'.[2] Even then there were restrictions on the number of Punjabis who could be recruited into contingents of the army. They were not to exceed one-fifth of the total number of sipahis in a regiment. But usually just a handful of Punjabi soldiers were to be found in each regiment prior to 1857. During and after the revolt a steadily increasing number of sipahis from Punjab began to be recruited into the Bengal Army, both to replenish the units and to counterbalance the purabiya troops. The Gurkhas of Nepal became another important component of the Bengal Army in the post-revolt period (their recruitment had commenced circa 1815, following the Anglo-Nepalese War).

Not only were Indian soldiers from different areas encouraged to maintain their distinctive identities, but animosity among the various ethnic groups was actively fostered as a matter of official policy. Colonial officials were convinced of the necessity of strictly adhering to the principle of 'divide and rule'. 'As regards Armies and Regiments in India', stated Charles Wood in 1861, 'I am for "*Divide et impera*"'.[3] The secretary of state for India was merely reiterating what was already settled policy since at least 1859. One of the recommendations of the Peel Commission had been that soldiers should be made to serve in the respective areas from which they had been

---

[2]Tan Tai Yong, *The Garrison State: The Military, Government and Society in Colonial Punjab, 1849-1947,* New Delhi: Sage, 2005, p. 38.
[3]Letter of Charles Wood, 8 April 1861, cited in R. J. Moore, *Sir Charles Wood's India Policy, 1853-66,* Manchester: Manchester University Press, 1966, p. 224.

recruited. In other words, soldiers recruited from the Awadh and Bhojpur region should be posted in that region itself. This was to ensure that strong bonds did not develop between the different regional/ethnic components of the army.

During the 1860s and 1870s, the trend towards recruitment from Punjab and the foothills of the Himalayas in northern India became more pronounced. Apart from the Gurkhas, the Dogra Rajputs became another preferred community from which sipahis were sought for contingents of the Bengal Army. By the end of the 1870s, the Bombay Army and the Madras Army were looked upon as being definitely inferior to the Bengal Army. A commission set up in 1879 to examine the military organization of the Indian empire, of which Ashley Eden (lieutenant governor of Bengal) was the chairperson, by and large reiterated the guidelines that had been framed on the basis of the recommendations of the Peel Commission. Significantly, the Eden Commission recommended that the strength of the Madras Army, regarded by now as quite mediocre in terms of military ability, be reduced. Stephen Cohen in his authoritative history of the British Indian army has noted that the 'decline of the Madras Army dates from this time'.[4] It would appear that the larger expense involved in recruiting soldiers from the south was an additional factor that contributed to the decline of the Madras Army: 'The labour market in the south was much more diverse than that in the newly annexed north, and hence the costs of employing and victualling Madras recruits far exceeded those which were accrued in recruiting from, for example, Punjab'.[5] The commission expressed its general disapproval of the tendency to recruit sipahis from areas lying outside the zones of operation of particular contingents. For instance, the Bombay Army enlisted troopers from the north to

[4] Stephen P. Cohen, *The Indian Army: Its Contribution to the Development of a Nation*, Berkeley: University of California Press, 1971, p. 41.
[5] Gavin Rand, 'Reconstructing the Imperial Military after the Rebellion', *Mutiny at the Margins, IV*, p. 104.

make up for deficiencies in recruitment from western India. This practice was frowned upon as it went against the basic principles of localized recruitment enunciated by the Peel Commission. The Eden Commission also recommended that the three armies be reorganized into four regional commands, a measure that was implemented towards the end of the century. In the 1890s, the three armies were merged and four regional commands (Punjab, Bengal, Madras, and Bombay) were created for the unified British Indian army.

A qualitative change in policies of recruitment began to take place from the mid-1880s onwards. By the last quarter of the nineteenth century, the British were firmly entrenched in India and there appeared to be no serious challenge to colonial rule for the time being. The anxieties of the immediate post-revolt period had given way to imperialist confidence and aggressiveness. For nearly two decades after the 1857 uprising had been brutally put down, maintaining internal security was regarded as the main task of the army. Priorities began to change by the 1880s. This was partly due to the intensification of imperialist rivalries at the international level. Britain and other imperialist powers (including new competitors such as Germany, Italy, and the USA) were attempting to seize new territories all over the world. Most of Africa had been colonized by the end of the century. In Central Asia, Britain was engaged in a contest with the expanding Russian empire. As part of its endeavour to acquire a strong base in order to thwart Russian designs in the region, Britain launched yet another offensive to establish control over Afghanistan. It may be recalled that the First Anglo-Afghan War had resulted in one of the worst military disasters for the British. The Second Anglo-Afghan War (1878–80) achieved nothing substantial, though it was accompanied by massive violence. Frederick Roberts, the officer who led the British force in the concluding phase of the Afghan War, was subsequently instrumental in formulating the position that henceforth the Indian army should be trained to take on a

European power. A prominent section of policymakers, both in England and India, had been creating hysteria over a supposed Russian threat to the Indian empire. Were the Russians to enter northern Afghanistan through the portions of Central Asia that they had recently annexed, it was argued, they could easily reach the northwestern frontier of the Indian empire. It was therefore necessary to station a powerful fighting force in the region to thwart a possible Russian invasion. These fears were highly exaggerated. Nevertheless, they provided the justification for a major overhaul of the British Indian army. The Bengal Army was expected to play a crucial role in protecting the northwestern frontier of the Indian empire. Strengthening this army now became the main focus of colonial military policy.

During the 1880s, a novel doctrine was being spelt out which divided Indian society into two broad categories: martial and non-martial. A few select communities came to be perceived as being martial 'races', while the bulk of the inhabitants of the Indian subcontinent were labelled as non-martial. The term 'race' was used in the sense of a well-defined group that had several common physical features, which in turn gave to them certain inherent, naturally acquired behavioural traits. *All* the members of the community, it was imagined, shared these traits. Courage was not, for example, an aspect of an individual's personality but a racial quality. If one belonged to a community that was 'racially' brave, only then could one be courageous; otherwise you would be biologically timid irrespective of your personal abilities. Likewise, someone born into a so-called 'criminal tribe' would invariably be a criminal. According to this perverse doctrine, specific contexts, historical conditions, social milieu, and personal temperament did not determine individual behaviour. Moreover, 'racial' behaviour corresponded to physical features such as complexion of the skin, shape of the head, shape of the nose, height, structure of the limbs, contours of the eyes, colour of the hair, thickness/thinness of the lips, etc. Broadly speaking, dark complexioned, short-statured, relatively flat-nosed, and thick lipped people were classified as inferior racial types. Communities in which these were typical features could not be expected to possess much intelligence or 'higher' sentiments. It should be emphasized that there is no scientific basis whatsoever for any of these notions.

The ideas of race as they evolved in the latter half of the nineteenth century assumed that the human species was divided into races, and that these races were arranged hierarchically. The most evolved races were to be found in the west, especially in the northern parts of western Europe. Races became progressively inferior as you moved to the east and the south. Asia was inhabited by inferior racial types. The people of southern and central Africa were regarded as being at the lowest level of evolution! Another element in this kind of thinking was that those groups which spoke Indo-European languages (which included Latin, Greek, Sanskrit, and the Germanic languages—from which English is descended) belonged to a common Aryan race, thereby equating a linguistic group with a racial type. The main 'racial' characteristics of Aryans were very fair complexion, tall stature, broad forehead, narrow high-built nose, and relatively thin lips. Those who spoke the languages belonging to the Indo-European family were supposed to belong to the Aryan race, of which the most evolved types were the people who lived in the coldest parts of western Europe (e.g., England, Scotland, Germany, Scandinavia). Many of these ideas were elaborated upon in academic institutions in German states where they were closely linked to the study of philology (study of the historical development of languages). There were several variants of this understanding of the human species, though broadly speaking it was considered axiomatic that non-Europeans were physically and intellectually inferior to Europeans.

Some communities in India were identified as sharing Aryan characteristics, and therefore being racially superior to other inhabitants of the subcontinent. The discovery that

Sanskrit, Latin, and German were closely related in terms of their grammar and vocabulary led to the view that speakers of these languages belonged to the Aryan 'race', which had originated from a common homeland. Whereas the Aryans who had settled in Europe had retained their racial characteristics, those who had moved into northern India had lost many of these characteristics over a period of time. The cold climate of northern and central Europe had allowed the Aryans inhabiting these areas to fully develop their physical and mental potential, while the warmer climate of the north Indian plains had caused deterioration of the Aryans who had migrated to this area. People living in a hot climate tended to be lazy, given to sensual pleasures, and intellectually inferior. Nevertheless, the Aryans of the Indian subcontinent did have some of the qualities of their race and were racially closer to the British. More importantly, they had martial characteristics. This made them superior to other subjects of the empire. Moreover, it was believed that caste endogamy (marrying within one's caste) had enabled Indian Aryans to preserve racial purity to some extent. Sikhs, Jats, Pathans, Rajputs, and Dogras were identified as the most prominent martial races, having conspicuously Aryan 'racial traits'. Interestingly, the term 'race' was applied in a very confusing manner to what were actually religious and/or ethnic communities and/or *jatis*. In addition to these groups, the Gurkhas were identified as a martial race. As they hailed from cold, mountainous areas they were considered to be hardy and courageous soldiers.

The tenure of Frederick Roberts as commander-in-chief (1885–93) saw a major reorientation in practices of recruitment. The doctrine of martial races was now formally declared to be the basis upon which soldiers were enlisted; the Bengal Army acquired a special status while the Bombay and Madras armies were further downgraded; and Punjab henceforth became the most favoured province of the British Indian army. The bulk of the recruitment under Roberts was from Punjab—mainly

Sikhs, Pathans, and a few selected Muslim communities. Besides, Gurkha and Dogra recruitment was stepped up. By the end of the nineteenth century, more than half the sipahis in the British Indian army were from Punjab. Between 1862 and 1914, the number of infantry units raised in Punjab had risen from twenty-eight to fifty-seven; and Gurkha units increased from five to twenty. Over the same period, the number of infantry units in the Bombay Army and the Madras Army was drastically reduced, from thirty to eighteen in the case of the former and from forty to eleven in the latter. The Bengal Army eventually had three components: soldiers recruited from the Ganga–Jamuna Doab (purabiyas); soldiers recruited from Punjab; and Gurkhas. The three components were expected to act as a check on each other. This was in keeping with the official policy of 'divide and rule' that the army was constantly urged to follow.

By the 1890s, mixed regiments were being replaced by ethnically uniform regiments. Regiments were the key units of the military organization. In keeping with the recommendations of the Peel Commission, regiments in the post-revolt period tended to be constituted on the basis of what came to be known as the 'class company' system. The company was the main sub-unit of a regiment; a regiment comprised several companies. Under the 'class company' system, a company would be ethnically homogenous while a regiment might have a mixed composition, being formed of companies of different ethnic groups. A regiment might, for instance, be made up of some Ahir and some Jat companies. The term 'class' in this context could, rather indiscriminately, be applied to 'race', caste, locality, region, religious community/sect, or ethnic group. Once the doctrine of martial races became prevalent it was considered desirable to have 'racially' homogenous regiments, or 'class regiments' instead of 'class company regiments'. There were already a few class regiments in the Bengal Army, but whereas they had been an exception prior to the 1890s, they now became the norm. Recruiting stations for enlisting specific communities were set up in Punjab and the Doab. Peshawar was the main recruiting centre for Pathans of the northwestern frontier, Rawalpindi for Punjabi Muslims, Amritsar for the Sikhs, and Delhi for Jats.

Gavin Rand has recently argued that the Roberts era should not be seen as marking a complete departure from the views set out in the Peel Commission's proposals. The experience of the counter-insurgency operations of 1857–58 provided vital inputs for the scheme whereby recruitment was to be confined to communities designated as martial races. He sees a continuity in the policies of the period between 1857–58 and the early 1880s and those put in place during Roberts's tenure. The doctrine of martial races represented a systematization of the ethnographic data that had been assembled after the revolt. Ever since the Peel Commission a lot of emphasis was placed on observing and comprehending the ethnography of Indian soldiers. This information was necessary to determine the most suitable areas and communities for purposes of recruitment. A major function of the colonial state in the post-revolt period was the compilation and classification of ethnographic data which 'helped to prepare the ground for the reforms of [the] 1880s and 1890s'. 'The apparent discontinuity', Rand states, 'reflects more the problems associated with organising and processing knowledge in the aftermath of the rebellion (and the gradual resolution of these problems in the 1870s and 1880s) than it does a fundamental shift in nature of military administration'.[6] It may be mentioned that some of the communities that came to be seen as martial, such as the Sikhs and Gurkhas, had been frantically enlisted by the British during the campaigns of 1857–58. Nevertheless, a large number of scholars hold the view that there was a significant change from the mid-1880s onwards, and that the notion of martial races was related to

[6]Rand, 'Reconstructing the Imperial Military', pp. 93, 101.

ideas about race that became prevalent only in the last quarter of the nineteenth century.

Frederick Roberts emerged as the main proponent of the doctrine of martial races. The enormous prestige that Roberts and several other contemporary colonial military leaders enjoyed throughout the empire made their views extremely influential. As we have already noted, this was a period of large-scale imperialist expansion in Africa. The British carried out a series of aggressive military campaigns in southern and eastern Africa to bring large chunks of territory under their control. Roberts, and his disciple Horatio Herbert Kitchener (who was commander-in-chief of the British Indian army from 1902 to 1909), were central figures in these campaigns. They both acquired an international reputation largely for their bloody and ruthless exploits in Africa. Roberts served in India for over forty years. In 1892, he was honoured with the title 'Lord Roberts of Kandahar' in recognition of his services to Britain. After the Second Anglo-Afghan War, he was briefly posted in South Africa. Between 1881 and 1885 he was commander-in-chief of the Madras Army. The contempt that he developed for the sipahis of this army was the outcome of his deep-seated racial prejudice. In 1895, he was raised to the rank of field marshal. Roberts successfully led the British armed forces during the Second Anglo-Boer War (1899–1902), a gruesome imperialist war fought to establish British supremacy over the territories that today constitute South Africa. The main opponents of the British in this war were the Afrikaners, descendants of Dutch settlers in the region. Kitchener was Roberts's second-in-command in this war. He had already established himself as a formidable military leader—as the victor of Omdurman (Omdurman is located near Khartoum, in Sudan). The massacre carried out at Omdurman in 1898, by troops under the command of Kitchener, had given to the British control over Sudan. British forces were led by Kitchener in the final phase of the Second Anglo-Boer War. As a reward for his triumph he was made commander-in-chief of the British Indian army. Meanwhile, Roberts was appointed to the very high position of commander-in-chief of the British Army, a position he held till 1904 when the post itself was done away with as a result of various changes introduced in the military organization of the empire. Yet Roberts's eminence endured. When he passed away in 1914, his body was placed at Westminster Hall in London for people to pay their respects. This is a location where only bodies of members of the royal family lie in state before formal burial. Roberts was accorded this rare privilege even though he did not belong to the royal family. Winston Churchill (d. 1965) has been the one other exception in the twentieth century. This should give us some idea of the stature of Roberts.

How influential military ideologues were in the late nineteenth and early twentieth centuries may be gauged from an episode that occurred in 1904–1905 during the viceroyalty of George Nathaniel Curzon (governor general, 1899–1905). This was a dispute between Kitchener and Curzon, which Cohen refers to as 'the most important civilian-military dispute in the long history of British India'.[7] Sharp differences over the status of the military member of the governor general's council led to an almost irreconcilable conflict between the viceroy and the commander-in-chief. The military member held charge of the department that dealt with matters pertaining to the army. Military members were drawn from the army (they were senior non-serving military officers), but stood below the commander-in-chief in the military hierarchy. Within the council, however, his views on military matters had precedence over those of the commander-in-chief. Kitchener, with all the arrogance of a celebrated general who had won several imperialist wars, resented the subordination of his status to that of the military member in the council. He therefore demanded the abolition

[7]Cohen, The Indian Army, pp. 22–23.

of the position altogether so that the council would have to go by the opinion of the commander-in-chief on military matters. Curzon, an arch-imperialist and himself a very arrogant person, was unwilling to concede this demand. Kitchener was asserting his pre-eminence in military matters which would have amounted to diminishing the governor general's control over the army.

Whereas Curzon saw this as a question of civilian control over the army, Kitchener emphasized the ultimate authority of the secretary of state (and the British cabinet) in this matter: he 'persisted in his belief that the military should be under the control of the civilian authority in Britain, not India'.[8] It should, of course, be noted that in the context of the Indian empire 'civilian control' meant very little as the civilian authorities were not answerable to the Indian people. Kitchener was able to enlist the support of London (in spite of the fact that Curzon himself was politically very influential in Britain). The issue became a matter of prestige for the two officials and when the governor general offered to resign his office, the British cabinet preferred dispensing with him rather than with Kitchener. Curzon left India in 1905, within a year of his assumption of office as governor general for a second term. The position of the military member of the governor general's council was downgraded by confining his jurisdiction to matters pertaining to military supplies while all other aspects of the army came within the purview of the commander-in-chief.

◆

The racial character of the British Indian army was most evident in the almost complete exclusion of Indians from the officer cadre. As we have noted earlier, all officer-level positions in the British Indian army were held by Europeans. The highest rank that an Indian soldier could hope for was that of subedar-major

[8]Ibid., p. 26.

in the infantry and risaladar-major in the cavalry. Subedar-major/risaladar-major and subedar/risaladar (the corresponding lower ranks) were 'sepoy officers' or 'native officers' who rose to this rank through promotion after long years of service. A subedar-major would often be on the verge of retirement at the time of his promotion. It was not until after World War I that a handful of Indians began getting commissions in the army. In 1947, the three highest ranking Indian officers were still brigadiers, and were promoted to the rank of major general a few months before Independence in order to facilitate the transition.[9] It should be borne in mind that there are three substantial ranks above that of a brigadier. The sepoy officers were of course crucial for the organization and discipline of the army, and in the field, because of their extensive experience in dealing with sipahis of their respective companies (these officers rarely held regimental positions). The British officers commanding a company—for ultimate authority was always in the hands of British officers—would usually be too young and inexperienced whereas the 'sepoy officers' would have greater familiarity with the sipahis and better soldiering skills.

British officers were mostly products of military colleges or academies situated in Britain. The most prestigious of these institutions was the Royal Military College located at Sandhurst. It may be mentioned that the EIC's Military Seminary located at Addiscombe was shut down shortly after the revolt. A cadet passing out of Sandhurst was qualified to receive a commission as an officer—queen's/king's commissioned officer (QCO/KCO). As Indians were not admitted to Sandhurst (or Addiscombe) there was no way in which an Indian could receive a commission as an officer. From the late nineteenth century an inferior commission, the viceroy's commission, was available for some of the senior sepoy officers who upon receiving the commission

[9]K. M. Cariappa, Muhammad Akbar Khan, and Rajendrasinhji, were promoted in July 1947.

were designated viceroy's commissioned officers (VCOs).

During Curzon's tenure a limited and largely meaningless opening was provided to a few young men from princely families and the landed aristocracy when an Imperial Cadet Corps (ICC) was constituted in 1901. An institution was set up at Dehradun to impart training that would enable successful candidates to enter the army as officers. Those admitted to the ICC had to undergo a three-year course. The third year was optional. Very little professional military training was imparted in the first two years; the real training was reserved for the third year. Candidates were selected through a process of nomination by British officials. Sixty-eight candidates were admitted to the corps during its existence.

To accommodate these officers another layer was added in the military hierarchy, somewhat lower than the queen's/king's commission but higher than the viceroy's commission, namely, a king's commission in 'His Majesty's Native Indian Land Forces'. This implied that the commission was relevant only for military units with Indian troops, and like the VCOs these officers could only command Indian soldiers. Nevertheless, the officers were denied regimental postings. They were mainly attached to the general staff, and were usually given parade duties on ceremonial occasions. These officers did not actually command any soldiers.

The ICC should be seen as part of Curzon's policy of binding the princely states more tightly to the empire. Cohen has observed that the corps was 'a military counterpart to the Statutory Civil Service', particularly as it sought recruits from among the feudal elite (see Chapter XII).[10] As was the case with the statutory civil service, an inferior version of the covenanted service, this class was not interested in professional careers in the army as second-rate officers. In contrast, those who might have been attracted to the ICC, young men from families of

[10]Cohen, *The Indian Army,* 64n15.

professionals who had received a western-style education, were debarred because they were perceived as being non-martial. The scheme produced eleven commissioned officers in all. The experiment thus ended in failure. In any case, it was not designed to succeed; it was abandoned in 1914.

It was against the backdrop of World War I and mounting nationalist pressure that the British took some steps for rigidly controlled 'Indianization' of the officer cadre, i.e. recruitment of Indians to upper-level officer positions. According to Partha Sarathi Gupta, this was essentially a 'token' gesture.[11] A large number of Indian soldiers were deployed in several theatres of the war. Some gesture was required for encouraging more active Indian participation in the campaigns. The criticism by nationalists that Indians were only used to fight in Britain's military campaigns but denied access to responsible posts in the army too needed to be addressed, even if through inconsequential concessions. Under the Montagu–Chelmsford scheme, ten seats at Sandhurst were earmarked for Indians from 1918 onwards; Indian graduates of Sandhurst would qualify for superior commissions. For the first time in the colonial era Indians could be KCOs. Besides, nine ICC officers received regular commissions.

Simultaneously, a military college was to be established at Indore (Daly Cadet College). The cadets who graduated from Daly Cadet College too were eligible to be KCOs. The first Indian commander-in-chief after Independence, K. M. Cariappa, was a product of this college. The Indore institution soon folded up. During the 1920s, the Sandhurst quota of ten seats was the sole path whereby an Indian might acquire a substantial commission. Not surprisingly, the rate of failure was high: almost one-third of the Indian candidates were unsuccessful,

[11]Partha Sarathi Gupta, 'The Debate on Indianization, 1918-39', Partha Sarathi Gupta and Anirudh Deshpande, eds., *The British Raj and Its Indian Armed Forces, 1857-1939'*, New Delhi: Oxford University Press, 2002, p. 228.

nearly ten times the figure for Europeans. Sandhurst was an elite institution, entry into which had always been jealously guarded. There was much hostility there, and in imperial military circles in Britain generally, to the quota, which was regarded as an unacceptable violation of exclusive upper-class white privilege. The racial prejudice which Indian graduates had to face as KCOs was even more blatant. They were frequently prohibited from entering officers' clubs, or certain spaces (such as swimming pools) in these clubs. Their presence at the dining table in the officers' mess too was resented. Given the problems that Indians faced at Sandhurst, the Dehradun institution was revived in 1922–23 as the Prince of Wales Royal Indian Military College for imparting preliminary training to Sandhurst aspirants.

In the late 1920s, Sir P. S. Sivaswamy Aiyar, a member of the Central Legislative Assembly formed under the Government of India Act of 1919, consistently raised the issue of the 'Indianization' of the officer cadre of the British Indian army. His interventions and those of another member, B. Venkatapati Raju, eventually led to the formation in 1925 of a committee to go into the 'Indian Sandhurst' question. Most of the members of the committee, which was headed by Lieutenant General Andrew Skeen, were Indians including nationalist leaders such as Motilal Nehru. The committee produced a very radical report in 1927. Its recommendations, had they been accepted, would have resulted in the speedier induction of Indians into the officer cadre. As might have been expected, the recommendations were mostly ignored by the London authorities. There was, however, one concrete outcome that the Skeen committee's report had— the establishment in India of an institution along the lines of Sandhurst. This institution, the Indian Military Academy (IMA) located in Dehradun, began functioning in 1932. The IMA now became the principal route whereby an Indian could become a full-fledged commissioned officer in the colonial army. Simultaneously, the Sandhurst quota was withdrawn. Graduates of the Dehradun academy were styled Indian commissioned officers, and were not equivalent to KCOs. As the Sandhurst route was blocked, Indians could no longer be KCOs. They could henceforth be commissioned officers at a slightly lower level with fewer perquisites and lesser allowances.

TWELVE

THE BUREAUCRATIC APPARATUS

In the absence of modern democratic institutions that would allow the people to participate in governance and decision-making processes, the colonial state mainly relied, till at least the first quarter of the twentieth century, on a strong bureaucracy to administer the Indian empire. As a matter of policy, Europeans almost completely monopolized the highest positions in the civil service before World War I. It was argued that since India had no democratic traditions, the civil service would provide leadership to society and for this reason had to be British ('English') in character. Strictly speaking, Indians were not debarred from entering the upper levels of the civil service (the covenanted civil service) once the system of selection through public examinations was introduced in 1855. Victoria's proclamation of 1858 reiterated that Indians could aspire for these positions provided they had the necessary qualifications. Nevertheless, the system worked in a manner that ensured British dominance. Just a handful of Indians managed to clear the examinations in fifty years after the new procedure for selection was introduced. Between 1868 and 1875 no more than eleven candidates were successful, of whom one—Surendranath Banerjee—was promptly dismissed soon after his appointment on a flimsy charge.

Some of the clauses of the Charter Act of 1853 had provided for changes in the mode of recruitment for the covenanted service, which was henceforth to be on the basis of an open competition. As has been mentioned already, the Act divested the directors of the EIC of the right to recommend candidates for appointment as writers in the Company's civil service. The introduction of open competition implied that new rules had to be formulated for admitting prospective officials for undergoing the two-year training course at Haileybury. This task devolved upon the board of control. Charles Wood as president of the board constituted a five-member committee chaired by Thomas Macaulay to advise the board on this question. The committee included the eminent classical scholar Benjamin Jowett who taught at Balliol College (Oxford),[1] and the principal of Haileybury, Henry Melvill. Jowett's intellectual guidance was important in shaping the recommendations of the committee, especially the emphasis on high academic standards for civil service aspirants. The committee presented its report in November 1854, and almost all its key recommendations were promptly accepted by the board of control. A notification was issued at the beginning of 1855 inviting applications for a public examination, to be held in May 1855. Twenty appointments were to be made through this new mode of selection. The first batch of covenanted servants began arriving in India towards the end of 1856 after having successfully completed the probationary period at Haileybury. This batch included C. U. Aitchison whose career in India as a bureaucrat spanned over three decades and who would himself be a crucial figure in the history of the covenanted service as the chairperson of a major commission set up in 1886 to examine comprehensively the administrative apparatus of the British Indian government.

The Macaulay committee in its report on the modalities for recruitment to the covenanted civil service through open competitive examinations had recommended that candidates should possess a broad general education, equipping them with knowledge about advances in various disciplines. Candidates

[1] In 1855, he was appointed as Regius Professor of Greek, a prestigious academic position at the University of Oxford. He became vice-chancellor of the university in 1882, and continued to take a great deal of personal interest in issues relating to civil services, especially the covenanted service.

were expected to have acquired a university education (graduation was not an essential requirement; it was a desirable qualification), and acquaintance with recent trends in various branches of knowledge. Specialization could come later on. The objective that the Macaulay committee had in mind was to attract the best products of universities, especially Oxford and Cambridge. An important consideration in recommending eighteen as the minimum age was that students would have had the time to acquire a university degree before appearing for the civil services examination. An indirect consequence of the Macaulay committee's recommendations was the closure of Haileybury in 1858 (Haileybury later reopened as a public school in 1862, which is still in existence). The committee had suggested that teaching and residential facilities at the East India College be upgraded since it would have to cater to trainees who were university products, rather than boys who had just been to school. The government decided to close down the institution rather than attempt making the kind of changes which were envisaged by the Macaulay committee.

After the shutting down of Haileybury, public examinations for recruiting covenanted servants were conducted by the civil service commissioners, a board constituted by the British government for the purpose of assisting with the recruitment of administrative personnel for various government departments, including the India Office. From 1858 onwards, the commissioners looked after the examinations for the covenanted service on behalf of the India Office. Rules and regulations pertaining to the examination, and qualifications of candidates, were however determined by the India Office. It may be mentioned here that in the 1850s the British (Home) civil service too was being reformed, though in Britain open competition for recruitment to the civil services was not introduced till the 1870s. However, there was considerable similarity in the views of the committees set up by the government to examine these issues in the 1850s.

Candidates who passed the competitive public examination (held in London) for recruitment to the covenanted service had to clear another set of examinations within a maximum period of two years in subjects that pertained specifically to their work in India. Till then they were referred to as probationers. The probationers had to learn an Indian language, familiarize themselves with Indian history, acquire knowledge of law and jurisprudence, and of official rules. They also had to undergo physical endurance tests (such as horse riding). Upon arrival in India, the probationers had to undergo a further period of training in a district, and it was only after they had cleared the relevant departmental examinations that they got their substantial postings. The candidates who made it to the top of the merit list in the initial public examination in Britain were posted to the Bengal Presidency; the Madras service came next in the hierarchy, followed by Bombay.

During the first decade of its existence, the new system was dominated by graduates of Oxford and Cambridge. Subsequently, there was a decline in the intake of graduates from these two elite universities specifically, and university products generally. This was partly due to the lowering of the maximum age from twenty-three to twenty-two in 1860, and the minimum age from eighteen to seventeen in 1865. A section of colonial policymakers advocated lowering the maximum age as those candidates who cleared the initial examination at the age of twenty-three, would be twenty-five by the time they set out for India and nearly twenty-seven years old by the time they were confirmed in their appointments. This, it was felt, was not a suitable age for learning new languages; people pick up languages faster when they are younger. Also, it was not very easy to mould their ideas and behaviour by the time they had reached this age. The preference increasingly was for young men freshly out of school. In 1876, the Macaulay scheme for recruitment was modified by Salisbury, the secretary of state for India. The Salisbury scheme remained in place till further changes were introduced in 1892. Between 1876 and 1891 candidates were recruited from the seventeen to nineteen year age group.

J. M. Compton has observed that the Macaulay scheme was designed to attract 'gentlemen' from the upper classes of British society for employment as civil servants in India, and was in its conception inegalitarian: 'Macaulay's committee certainly did not intend to give an equal chance to all clever young men.'[2] The committee's preference was for Oxford–Cambridge graduates with a public school background. By the mid-1860s, however, along with the decline in the intake from premier universities there was a relative decline in the number of successful candidates from elite British public schools such as Eton, Harrow, and Winchester. There was an increase in the number of successful candidates who were products of grammar schools. Grammar schools catered to students belonging to less privileged social groups. Their origins dated back to the middle ages and traditionally, as the name indicates, these schools provided instruction in languages, i.e., classical languages (mainly Latin). In the early nineteenth century many of these schools began teaching modern languages (e.g., English and French), and arithmetic as well. The decade of the sixties witnessed significant changes in the system of school education in Britain. The management and curriculum of both public schools and grammar schools was reformed. To a great extent this was in response to the pressure exerted by the middle class, and sections of the working class, for improving the standard of school education. Some of the public schools too shifted their focus from classical learning to modern languages, 'commercial' subjects, mathematics, and science. These subjects were more useful for clearing the civil service examinations.

Simultaneously, private institutions—somewhat like present-day coaching centres—that specialized in preparing candidates

[2]J. M. Compton, 'Open Competition and the Indian Civil Service, 1854-1876', *The English Historical Review,* Vol. 83, No. 327, April 1968, p. 266.

for these examinations came into existence. These were colloquially known as 'crammers' due to their emphasis on rote learning and memorizing. Two of the most well-known of these preparatory institutions were Wren and Gurney and the crammer of W. B. Scoones. Both were located in London. Students aspiring for a career in the civil service of the British Indian government would, immediately after leaving school, spend some time at a crammer, or study on their own for a couple of months, and then appear for the competitive examination. This became the usual pattern in the last quarter of the nineteenth century. Overall, there was a change in the social composition of the civil service, with quite a few recruits now coming from humble backgrounds. Boys from families of lower clergymen, petty shopkeepers, clerks, farmers, and occasionally even coachmen were able to make it to the civil service.

Under the Salisbury scheme successful candidates had to spend two years as probationers in Britain before proceeding to India. They had to formally enrol as students at universities designated for the purpose (these included Oxford and Cambridge) and clear examinations in the courses they were pursuing. Probationers received a special allowance for the duration of their study. There were a separate set of examinations for the probationers. The successful probationers were declared eligible for appointment as civil servants. A probationer could, if he so desired (the civil service was entirely male), spend an additional year at the university in order to acquire a degree, though the loss of allowances for one year and of seniority were disincentives for those keen on a university degree.

Anil Seal has argued that the demand for more government jobs, especially higher-level positions, by sections of Indian elites who had acquired western learning is crucial for understanding early nationalist activity.[3] Indeed, in the late nineteenth century

[3] Anil Seal, *The Emergence of Indian Nationalism: Competition and Collaboration in the Later Nineteenth Century*, Cambridge: Cambridge University Press, 1971 (first published, 1968).

nationalists vigorously took up the issue of 'Indianization' of the civil services. It needs to be mentioned here that the term 'Indianization' is somewhat misleading in this context. What was being demanded at this stage was greater representation for Indians in the civil services. Indianization in its broader sense would have implied working in the interests of India and not of Britain. Given that the bureaucracy was geared to serve the interests of British imperialism this would not have been possible. Such an objective could only have been achieved by subverting the functioning of the government from within. This was clearly not the intention of the nationalists in this era. Their demand was for appointing more Indians at the uppermost levels of the bureaucracy.

Though from 1855 onwards Indians could enter the civil services if they were able to compete successfully in the recruitment examinations, actually by the 1880s barely twelve had managed to gain entry. Satyendranath Tagore was the first Indian to be recruited (1864). Apart from colonial prejudice, which was a very serious impediment to success, there were two major problems with which Indian aspirants were confronted. First, their families had to be sufficiently affluent to be able to bear the expense of their travel to London, where the examinations were held, and their maintenance in England for the duration of their stay. Second, the candidates had to be proficient in the subjects in which they were examined, which included classical languages such as Greek and Latin that gave a clear advantage to candidates who had had their schooling in Britain. There was a strong emphasis on classical learning in the curriculum for the preliminary examinations. As Phiroze Vasunia has shown, by the 1890s over 60 per cent, or even higher, of the total marks were allocated for papers in Greek and Latin (language, literature, history, philosophy, and political thought). This tilted the balance in favour of Oxford candidates. Mathematics was next in terms of the total marks allocated to it, giving a distinct advantage to Cambridge products given that this was an area in which the university was particularly strong. It is not surprising then that between 1892 and World War I, Oxford accounted for nearly half the candidates, and Cambridge for one-third. Most of the successful Oxford candidates had studied classics, and Cambridge candidates had studied mathematics.[4]

The steady reduction in the maximum and minimum ages for candidates, coming down to nineteen and seventeen respectively by 1876, made it even more difficult for Indians to sit for the examinations. There was no tradition of sons of well-to-do families undertaking the journey from India to Britain at such a young age. Upon reaching London these candidates had to adjust themselves culturally to a new way of life, which required time. Moreover, formal schooling in India often started late, and a year or two could make a big difference. Not surprisingly, between 1879 and 1883 only one Indian, out of twenty-eight who had appeared for the examinations, was successful. From the point of view of the nationalists the reduction in upper and lower ages for candidates was aimed at keeping Indians out of the civil services. Modifying the age requirement so as to facilitate Indian recruitment became one of the key demands of many of the nationalists in this period. The age requirement was revised upwards in 1892, but for reasons that had more to do with criticism of the system in the British context rather than to allow more Indians to become higher level civil servants. As far as the British were concerned, 'Indianization' was a minor issue.

Colonial policymakers were certainly not interested in filling the top, roughly one thousand, positions in the civil services with a large number of Indians. At best they were willing to tolerate a handful of them at the higher levels of the bureaucracy.

[4]Phiroze Vasunia, 'Greek, Latin and the Indian Civil Service', *The Cambridge Classical Journal*, Vol. 55, 2005, pp. 51–56. A wide choice was available to candidates, who could opt for various combinations of papers or sets of papers. But this was nullified by the differing weightage given to the papers.

Further, competitive examinations were not regarded as the most appropriate means for recruiting Indians since social conditions in eastern societies, unlike the West, supposedly prevented the selection of the most suitable persons through this method. Limited competition, rather than open competition, closely supervised by British officials, was considered to be a better mode of recruitment. These officials would have a role to play in nominating candidates who would then compete among themselves. The final selection would not necessarily be on the basis of merit, but personal assessment by European civil servants. Their intervention was necessary to ensure that the right persons were chosen. These principles determined the manner in which, down to the 1920s and even beyond, Indians were recruited for the middle-ranking government jobs, and a few higher-level positions in the civil service. This was apart from the few Indians who were successful in the competitive examinations held in London. It is these men who made it to the upper levels of the bureaucracy.

We should bear in mind that in the latter half of the nineteenth century the colonial state was enlarging the scope of its activities so that administrative and/or managerial positions were becoming available for a limited number of Indians in the railways, postal, and telegraph services, public works department, forest department, municipal bodies, educational institutions, and organizations such as the Archaeological Survey. An Act passed by the British Parliament in 1870 authorized the British Indian government to set aside for Indians a small number of positions in the civil service which had so far been filled through competitive examinations. Recruitment for these positions was to be through nomination. Nevertheless, it was only in 1879 that the relevant posts were identified, and rules framed for selection in this manner. In 1879, a new category of colonial bureaucrats was introduced in the shape of the statutory civil service. About 20 per cent of the positions earlier earmarked for covenanted civil servants were now thrown open for the statutory civil service. Indians from among so-called natural leaders of society were to be nominated for this service by provincial governments; recruits were to be selected from the lists of candidates drawn up by these governments. That this was intended to be somewhat inferior to the covenanted civil service was indicated by the lower pay scales in the statutory civil service—two-thirds of corresponding scales for covenanted servants.

This experiment proved to be unsuccessful. The statutory civil service was expected to attract, in the words of Governor General Lytton, 'young men of good family and social position',[5] which invariably meant young men from families of the landed aristocracy and the feudal elite. The first person to be appointed to the service was Rameshwar Singh of the Darbhanga estate. Rameshwar Singh initially held the position of assistant magistrate of Darbhanga. In all, sixty-nine persons were inducted into the statutory civil service during the twelve years that it was in existence. The social groups that the British Indian government wished to attract to the service showed no enthusiasm for joining it, the more so as the service was seen as an inferior version of the covenanted civil service. At the same time, sons of families of professionals (lawyers, doctors, teachers, journalists) who might have been interested in joining the service were deliberately kept out due to the contempt that the colonial state had for this class. Eventually the service was dismantled by 1892.

The question of Indian recruitment in the civil services was examined in some detail by a commission set up in 1886. The fifteen-member commission was headed by C. U. Aitchison, then the lieutenant governor of Punjab, and it included six Indians. The Aitchison Commission, which presented its report

[5]Lady Betty Balfour, *The History of Lord Lytton's Indian Administration, 1876 to 1880: Compiled from Letters and Official Papers*, London: Longmans, Green, and Co., 1899, p. 534.

in 1887, recommended several major changes in the structure of the civil services. A substantial portion of the report is concerned with the unconvenanted service. The existing two-tier structure based upon the division between covenanted and uncovenanted servants was to be replaced by a three-tier structure in which the covenanted civil service became a smaller and even more exclusive body. There were to be two lower-level services corresponding to the uncovenanted civil service: the provincial civil service and the subordinate civil service. The commission proposed that the statutory civil service be abolished. The demand for holding simultaneous examinations for the covenanted civil service in India was not conceded. Most of the recommendations of the commission were accepted and implemented from 1892 onwards.

The covenanted civil service, henceforth known as the civil service of India or Indian civil service (ICS) remained an elite service, almost completely monopolized by Europeans till the 1920s. Recruitment into it continued to be through examinations held in Britain for which Indians too could appear. Minimum and maximum ages for candidates were increased to twenty-one and twenty-three, respectively. Some of the posts hitherto reserved for the covenanted civil service were transferred to the provincial civil service, thereby reducing the number of annual covenanted appointments (about fifty to sixty every year) and rendering competition for the ICS much tougher. Personnel for the provincial civil service were recruited in India. These included deputy collectors, deputy magistrates, tahsildars, and munsifs (the munsif was the key judicial official of the sub-district). The report of the commission noted that more than 97 per cent of these positions were held by Indians.[6] This was a lesser service for which the mode of recruitment was a mixture of nomination by the respective provincial governments

---

[6]About 2,600 in all; the number of covenanted servants in the mid-1880s was 940.

(each province/presidency had its own provincial civil service), and limited competition among nominated candidates. It was occasionally possible for highly experienced senior members of the provincial civil service to be inducted into the ICS through promotion. The subordinate civil service was the lowest rung of the bureaucracy in the presidencies and provinces. Personnel for this service were recruited in a manner similar to that of the provincial civil service, though requiring lesser qualifications. It was also a feeder service for the provincial services of respective provinces.

One might note that soon after the Aitchison Commission's recommendations became operative in 1892, the House of Commons passed a resolution in support of simultaneous examinations for the ICS in India. Dadabhai Naoroji, who was a member of the house at this time, was instrumental in the adoption of this resolution. It took three decades for the resolution to be implemented. Although the House of Commons had accepted in principle the idea of having examinations in India, colonial officialdom was strongly opposed to acting upon the resolution. Furthermore, there were sections of Indian society which were opposed to such a move as it was felt that candidates from Bengal, especially those belonging to upper castes, would be the main beneficiaries of simultaneous examinations held in India. The British played upon these fears, constantly projecting themselves as guardians of the interests of the Indian people as a whole, rather than of certain privileged communities. Even among the different strands of nationalist opinion there was no unanimity on this issue. Consequently, it was possible to postpone the introduction of simultaneous examinations till the early 1920s.

In 1912, another commission was appointed to review the question of recruitment into the civil services and related issues. Lord Islington, who had been governor of New Zealand, was the chairperson of this ten-member commission (with three Indians as members). The report of the Islington Commission was finalized in 1915 but was published two years later due to the disturbed conditions created by World War I. The commission's recommendations were superseded by the Montagu–Chelmsford proposals which led to the Government of India Act of 1919. The Islington report is mainly of academic interest. Nevertheless, it provides an insight into the thinking of colonial policymakers in the pre-war period. The suggestion of simultaneous examinations in India was once again rejected. An increase in the pace of Indian recruitment was visualized, although the increase was to be gradual and cautious. On the eve of the outbreak of World War I, Indians accounted for about 5 per cent of the higher-level civil servants. The commission recommended that in order to increase the intake of Indians, 25 per cent of the appointments should be made in India—mainly through nominations. In other words, the commission's report did not mark any significant shift in the colonial attitude towards Indian recruitment in the civil services.

The next stage in the evolution of the colonial bureaucracy was the implementation of the Montagu–Chelmsford report. The report recommended that Indian recruitment should be increased by 1.5 per cent annually until one-third of the civil servants were Indian. Competitive examinations were to be held in India (in addition to those held in England) so as to facilitate achieving this goal. The examinations commenced in 1922. They were held initially at Allahabad; the venue was later shifted to Delhi. T. H. Beaglehole in his study of the changes in the pattern of recruitment during the 1920s has noted that in the immediate post-war years there was a decline in European recruitment and that the British in these years were more concerned about making the ICS more attractive to Europeans.[7] It was only after another commission, the Lee Commission (appointed in 1923; report presented in 1924), re-

[7]T. H. Beaglehole, 'From Rulers to Servants: The I.C.S. and the British Demission of Power in India', *Modern Asian Studies,* Vol. 11, No. 2, 1977, pp. 239–40.

examined the issue and made its recommendations that Indian recruitment gathered momentum. The scheme proposed by the Lee Commission was that 80 per cent of the annual recruitment for the ICS should be through competitive examinations, half of these (i.e., 40 per cent of the total) being Indian, the other half British. The remaining 20 per cent were to be enlisted through promotions from the provincial civil service. Indians could appear for the London examinations as well, although Europeans (including those residing in India) could not sit for the examinations held in India. The aim was to achieve parity between European and Indian officials within a few years, a target that was actually attained by the beginning of the 1940s. This new scheme was introduced in 1925. Initially, there was reluctance to implement the scheme with sincerity. There was considerable room for manipulating the selection process which was ultimately controlled by senior colonial officials in Britain. Tampering with merit lists was one way of doing this; being biased in favour of European candidates at the interview stage was another. According to Beaglehole, between 1925 and 1930 whereas there were on an average sixty vacancies every year, the average of actual vacancies filled annually through the Delhi examination was nine.[8] All vacancies earmarked for Indians were not necessarily filled through examinations. The British Indian government could use its discretion to make appointments through nominations so that various communities were nominally, if not adequately, represented in the ICS. Moreover, there was a move to discourage too many Indian candidates from appearing for the London examination. In 1935, the secretary of state for India stipulated that only those Indians who had graduated from a British university could henceforth compete in London.

Indian recruitment into the ICS was not merely a question of relative numbers. There was a tendency to retain the principal

[8]Beaglehole, 'From Rulers to Servants', p. 241.

superior positions, especially at the centre, for Europeans. Moreover, it was considered comparatively safer to appoint Indian civil servants to the judicial branch of the service, rather than to executive posts. Nearly one-third of the judiciary at the higher levels, and most of it at the district level, was staffed by members of the ICS. Finally, there was one branch of the bureaucracy that remained virtually closed to Indians down to 1947. This was the 'political service' which dealt with the princely states. The political service too was a fairly large service. W. Murray Hogben has drawn attention to the systematic exclusion, from the 1870s onwards, of Indians from the political service. The few who were appointed held low-level positions. The main reason for the 'reluctant Indianization of the Indian Political Service' was 'the distrust of Indians in the elite role of diplomatic agents and guardians'.[9] This distrust, as we have seen, was even more conspicuous in the case of the army.

[9]W. Murray Hogben, 'An Imperial Dilemma: The Reluctant Indianization of the Indian Political Service', *Modern Asian Studies,* Vol. 15, No. 4, 1981, p. 768.

THIRTEEN

'NATIVE' STATES

As has been mentioned earlier (chapter VIII), only three-fifths of the Indian empire was governed directly by the British Indian government. The remaining 40 per cent of its area was under numerous princely rulers who ruled over political entities referred to as 'native states'. In the latter half of the nineteenth century, the British Indian government sought to codify the relationship, while at the same time keeping it fluid. We have noted that following the revolt of 1857, the British increasingly relied on the support of princely rulers to stabilize their position in India. It was therefore in their interest to allow some degree of autonomy, and real power, to the states. This made possible the cooption of the princes by the colonial state, as junior partners. The actual extent of power that a state enjoyed was determined by various factors, most importantly by its size, the specific historical context of its incorporation into the Indian empire, and the role that its ruling family had played in the revolt. Thus Hyderabad, which was the largest princely state, had a long history of collaboration with the British, and had remained steadfastly loyal in 1857, could be governed by its rulers without much interference. Nevertheless, rulers of princely states had no authority in matters pertaining to defence, communications, and foreign relations. Foreign relations included relations with other princely states.

The theory articulated by colonial officials in the latter half of the nineteenth century was that sovereignty over the Indian empire, including the 'native' states, vested in the British crown. The governor general in his capacity as viceroy was the representative of the crown in its dealings with the princely states. As the sovereign power the crown was paramount, and had overriding authority. The principle of 'paramountcy', as elaborated upon in the writings of Henry Maine, William Lee-Warner, and Charles Tupper, implied that the crown reserved for itself the right to determine the way in which respective states were to be governed and to intervene in their affairs as and when necessary. According to Maine, a leading imperial ideologue and constitutional expert, sovereignty was divisible and princely rulers had *some* sovereign rights. But they were not independent rulers as they did not possess *all* the attributes of sovereignty. They were subordinate to the British crown which had 'an almost unlimited right of interference for the better order of the States'.[1] This understanding provided the theoretical framework for the arguments developed subsequently by Lee-Warner and Tupper to underscore the subordinate status of the princely states. Simultaneously, the relationship between the paramount power and the princely states was guided, it was argued, by 'usage', i.e. the actual manner in which relations had been historically conducted with a particular state. This varied from state to state and was not necessarily derived from written agreements or treaties. The extent to which sovereignty was shared with a state was based on 'usage'. In the words of Maine, 'The mode or degree in which sovereignty is distributed between the British Government and any given Native State is always a question of fact, which has to be separately decided in each case, and to which no general rules apply.'[2]

There were, of course, attempts to systematize the relationship by referring to written agreements and treaties, one prominent example of which was the publication of C. U. Aitchison's several volume compilation *A Collection of Treaties, Engagements and*

[1]Henry Maine, 'Minute on Kathiawar', in M. E. Grant Duff, *Sir Henry Maine: A Brief Memoir of His Life (With Some of His Indian Speeches and Minutes, selected and edited by Whitley Stokes)*, New York: Henry Holt, 1892, p. 324.
[2]Ibid., p. 323.

Sanads Relating to India and Neighbouring Countries, which placed the relevant documents in the public domain. Besides, there were gazetteers that provided comprehensive information about each princely state (history, physical features, natural resources, economy, administration, caste, religion, culture), and census reports (from 1872 onwards). The act of placing these texts in the public domain itself somewhat reduced the element of fluidity in the relationship between the British and the princely states. Given the enormous diversity of these political entities, especially in terms of their size and prominence, it was not easy to define with any precision or uniformity their place within the empire. From the 1860s onwards a semblance of coherence was imposed upon the disparate arrangements governing their presence within the Indian empire by organizing the princes into a feudal hierarchy. At the lowest level there were the tiny principalities of Gujarat, followed by assorted petty chiefdoms in central India and Orissa. Then there were the middle-ranking states of Travancore, Patiala, Rampur, Indore, Bahawalpur, Junagarh, Bhopal, Manipur, Tripura, Rewa, and the states of Rajasthan (Udaipur, Jaipur, Jodhpur, Bikaner, Bharatpur, Jaisalmer). At the top were the five most important states: Hyderabad, Mysore, Kashmir, Baroda, and Gwalior. Of these five states, Hyderabad enjoyed a special status that gave the nizam pre-eminence over all other rulers. Whereas the form of address for most of the other princely rulers was 'his/her highness', the nizam had the distinction of being referred to as 'his *exalted* highness'. Personal loyalty tied each ruler individually to his or her suzerain, the British monarch, through the viceroy who was the suzerain's deputy in India.

This hierarchy, with the monarch at the apex, was made 'visible' and 'actual' by resorting to public gestures—referred to as 'ornamentalism' by David Cannadine—that included gun salutes, ostentatious parades, and conferring of honours and titles on princely rulers.[3] Institutions, symbols, and rituals borrowed from the medieval past of Europe were improvised to signify the feudal character of the structure into which the rulers were accommodated. For instance, in 1861 the British established an order of knighthood, the Order of the Star of India, as an exclusive association of twenty-five princes with Queen Victoria as its head. There were traditionally several 'orders' in Britain, and being made a member of one of them was a way of bestowing official honour. The Order of the Garter, which dated back to the mid-fourteenth century, was the premier order among these. These orders were inspired by chivalric orders of the middles ages which were societies of knights initially formed against the backdrop of the Crusades (e.g. Knights Templar, Teutonic Knights) and incorporated many of their symbols and rituals. Membership of an order involved an elaborate investiture ceremony. In the case of the Order of the Star of India the investiture ceremony required the person being honoured to pay personal homage to the viceroy who was designated 'Grand Master of the Order of the Star of India' (GMSI). The other members of the order were called 'knight companions'. The original 'knight companions' included the rulers of Hyderabad, Kashmir, Gwalior, Baroda, Indore, Bhopal, Travancore, Rampur, Patiala, and Kapurthala as well as some colonial officials. The order was subsequently expanded by creating a hierarchy within it (knight grand commander, knight commander, and companion). This further reinforced the feudal principle upon which it was based. Later, prominent officials and public figures too were felicitated with these honours, mostly as a reward for loyalty.

The number of gun salutes that a ruler was entitled to was the most obvious indicator of his or her (there were a few women rulers, such as Shahjahan Begum of Bhopal) position

[3]David Cannadine, *Ornamentalism: How the British Saw Their Empire,* New York: Oxford University Press, 2001, p. 122.

in the hierarchy. This had become, by the end of the nineteenth century, 'the principal determinant of precedence'.[4] The gun salute for the British monarch was 101, while the viceroy was entitled to a thirty-one-gun salute. Gun salutes for the princely rulers ranged between nine and twenty-one. The official 'table of salutes' of the British Indian government that regulated the firing of gun salutes was first prepared in the mid-nineteenth century, and underwent several revisions till the 1920s. To begin with, the twenty-one-gun salute was reserved for just three states, namely, Hyderabad, Mysore, and Baroda, and later extended to five. There was a process of negotiation here as well. At times there could be serious disputes on this issue. Dick Kooiman has described the protracted tussle between the colonial government and the state of Travancore, which was a nineteen-gun salute state, over the claim of the state to a twenty-one-gun-salute status.

A grand 'durbar' organized by Lord Lytton in Delhi in 1877 provided an occasion for announcing publicly the kind of structure that the British had devised to make the princely rulers allies of the colonial state. This durbar, an assemblage of princely rulers both big and small, was held to announce Victoria's new title of 'empress of India', rendered for the 'natives' as 'Qaisar-i-Hind' (Caesar of India), which she had assumed in 1876 following the enactment of the Royal Titles Act of that year. The title was added in 1876, at the nudging of Victoria herself, to the other titles borne by the British monarch. It was specific to India. Victoria remained queen in the context of the United Kingdom. Hence the somewhat awkward comprehensive title borne by her, 'queen-empress' ('king-emperor' in the case of male monarchs). In his study of the durbar, Bernard Cohn has unravelled the several layers

---

[4]Dick Kooiman, 'The Guns of Travancore or How Much Powder May a Maharaja Blaze Away?', *Indian Economic and Social History Review*, Vol. 43, No. 3, 2006, p. 305.

of political and cultural meanings of this spectacle, the key to which was the assertion of the sovereignty vested in the British crown and the status of the princely rulers as vassals of the monarch.[5] The venue of the event was the area lying north of the ridge, close to the present campus of the University of Delhi. It was here that the viceroy's camp was set up. Around it, for a long distance, were the tents of the princes. The position of a state in the hierarchy determined the distance of its ruler's tent from the viceregal camp. On the day of the durbar (1 January 1877), there was a grand assembly at which Lytton was seated on a large dais with all the princes facing him. The seating arrangements placed the rulers of Hyderabad, Mysore, and Baroda in the front row and the other princes in a semi-circle behind them strictly according to rank. Considerable attention was placed on the seating arrangements as these were intended to declare for the first time at a public event the status of each ruler within the all-India hierarchy, a hierarchy literally invented by the British.

Cohn draws attention to various other devices used by colonial officials on this occasion to make the princes resemble feudal nobility along European lines. They went to such absurd lengths as to fabricate coats of arms (the distinctive emblems of noble families in the form of a shield) for nearly eighty states. This was an 'invention of tradition' as these coats of arms were entirely European in design and conception, and had little to do with the kind of insignia that were associated with royalty in the Indian subcontinent. For that matter, even the translation of Victoria's new title, officially empress of India (or Indiae Imperatrix in Latin), was a clumsy invention. The title was translated for the Indian audience as Qaisar-i-Hind on the assumption that it would evoke the notion of imperial

[5]Bernard Cohn, 'Representing Authority in Victorian India', *An Anthropologist Among the Historians and Other Essays,* New Delhi: Oxford University Press, 1998, pp. 633–82.

majesty whereas it had no such resonance for Indians who were more familiar with titles such as shahanshah or badshah. The Indian version of Victoria's title was adapted from one used in medieval West Asia for the Byzantine emperor, Qaisar-i-Rum.

All this ceremony went hand in hand with, and facilitated, greater colonial penetration in the territories of the states. Princely states should not be regarded as being absolutely distinct from 'British India', i.e. from the directly administered portions of the Indian empire. They were closely connected with other parts of the subcontinent and there was often little to distinguish them economically, socially, or culturally from the directly administered territories of the regions in which the respective states were located. It is just that they were controlled in a different mode, with much reliance being placed on the indigenous elites within the states (in this case princely rulers) for assisting the colonial state in exercising control. We should bear in mind that even in the directly administered territories, the British sought out indigenous elites, 'natural leaders of society', as collaborators. The formal position maintained since the suppression of the revolt was that the British had a policy of non-interference insofar as the princely states were concerned. This was not true at least till World War I. One might mention that even as late as 1946 the British were prepared to take the drastic step of deposing a ruler, Gulab Singh of Rewa— not entirely an insignificant state. Officials specifically deputed by the British Indian government for the purpose, monitored the affairs of each state. Higher-ranking states had a resident stationed at their respective capitals, while states of lesser importance were usually grouped together and placed under the supervision of a political agent. These officials constituted what was called the political service of the government. The political service had a reputation for being anti-democratic and conservative in its outlook.

Residents and political agents often interfered in the day-to-day administration of the states, thereby undermining whatever autonomy they theoretically possessed. Curzon's tenure as governor general witnessed aggressive intrusion by the paramount power. Curzon visited a large number of states, delivering sermons to the princes on 'good' governance. In his public speeches during these visits he spoke to them like a school teacher reminding his students of their responsibilities. In the colonial perception, the rulers of princely states were pupils who had to be taught how to govern. In his time, over sixty states were temporarily placed under administrators appointed by the British Indian government. By the time Curzon departed from India in 1905 the growing strength of the anti-colonial struggle, in the wake of his decision to partition Bengal along communal lines, was compelling colonial officials to view the princes as allies in their attempt to curb nationalist agitation. It was against the backdrop of the swadeshi movement that Lord Minto announced in 1909 that the British Indian government would henceforth pursue a policy of laissez-faire (abstaining from interference) with regard to the princely states. Nevertheless, the British maintained rigid control over the princes down to 1947.

Since the beginning of the nineteenth century the British had tried to regulate succession in the princely states. Succession disputes were invariably used to meddle in the affairs of princely courts, especially when rival factions tried to enlist the support of colonial officials in their tussles. Dalhousie's policy of disallowing succession of adopted heirs, and using the doctrine of lapse for annexation of such states, was an aggressive assertion of the prerogative of the paramount power to determine legitimate succession. Even though Victoria's 1858 proclamation had assured the princes that succession would be allowed to adopted heirs, and that the states would be free to manage their internal affairs, every succession (of adopted heirs or otherwise) required confirmation by the British Indian government. The recognition of a successor by the paramount power had to be formally announced at a public durbar. Some states had to pay a special monetary tribute at the time of succession. The threat of withholding imperial recognition, especially when there was some internal conflict, helped the British to tighten their grip over such states with each succession. When a successor happened to be a minor, the British Indian government constituted a council of regency for governing the state till the time that its ruler came of age. These councils were packed with loyalists and toadies. Mayo was alive to the possibilities that these situations presented for ensuring colonial influence and emphasized the need to intervene forcefully during 'minority administrations' when a state was, for all practical purposes, under direct rule. Incidentally, adopted heirs were permitted to succeed only in states that had been granted adoption sanads or deeds after 1857.

The economies of princely states were vulnerable to colonial exploitation as they were required to allow free trade with other parts of the Indian empire and not impose any restrictions of their own on the free movement of goods. The currency of the British Indian state was legal tender throughout the empire, though some states were permitted to have their own parallel currency. The development of communications further integrated the states into the colonial economy, giving easier access to their natural resources and agricultural produce. The states located in central India and Orissa, for example, were major sources of raw materials, especially minerals and forest produce. The Berar region of the Hyderabad state was a cotton-producing area. The Malwa states supplied large quantities of opium for the China market while Rajasthan was an important source of salt. It may be mentioned that the government had a monopoly over salt. The resources of princely states were appropriated in the form of tribute as well. About two hundred states were obliged to pay tribute to the British. Towards the end of the century, Mysore was paying a tribute of Rs 35 lakhs annually. Besides, states had to pay for their 'protection' by funding contingents of the British Indian army stationed in their territories. The payment of tribute was also a public acknowledgement of the paramountcy of the British crown.

The underlying tensions between the princely states and the British could occasionally result in open confrontation. The most well-known example is that of Baroda which from the 1870s tried to resist British high-handedness, at times quite successfully. Relations between the British Indian government and Baroda began to deteriorate during the reign of Malhar Rao Gaikwad (1870–75), reaching a breaking point in 1874. One of the reasons for this was the overbearing manner of the resident, Colonel Robert Phayre, and his support to a faction at the court which was hostile to the maharaja. The diwan of the state at this time was Dadabhai Naoroji—the first of several committed nationalists who served in Baroda. Naoroji had been appointed by Malhar Rao with the objective of reforming the administration of the state. The resident was not pleased with this appointment. The hurdles created by him made it difficult for the diwan to function. Then, in November 1874, the resident precipitated a crisis by accusing Malhar Rao of attempting to poison him. The government set up a commission, comprising three Europeans and three Indians (the rulers of Gwalior and Jaipur, and Dinkar Rao who had earlier been diwan of Gwalior), to enquire into the allegation. This commission conducted a public trial of Malhar Rao, something that was extraordinary in the post-1857 scenario. Since there was no satisfactory evidence against Malhar Rao, the three Indian members of the commission expressed the opinion that the charge had not been substantiated. The European members of the commission were of the view that the maharaja was guilty. Under the circumstances, the government could not punish Malhar Rao for trying to assassinate the resident. Yet it was unwilling to allow him to continue as the ruler of Baroda. In a blatant assertion of their authority, the British deposed Malhar Rao in 1875 and exiled him to Madras. Phayre, whose recall, prompted by a letter from the maharaja, was being considered by the governor general even before the November incident, was removed from his position at Baroda. There was a proposal to annex the state so that its fate might be a lesson to other princes. Eventually Baroda survived because colonial policymakers felt that the annexation of such a major state would result in widespread discontent. A more subtle strategy could be employed to control the state. However, Malhar Rao's successor, Sayaji Rao III (1875–1939), was even harder to tackle due to his ability to project himself as the kind of 'model' prince that the British claimed their empire was seeking to produce. He did not conform to the colonial stereotype of the inept and unenlightened native ruler incapable of introducing modern governance. The main ideological justification for colonial rule was, after all, that it was meant for the good of Indians who by themselves could not progress in the direction of modernity. 'Progress' and 'modernity' were of course defined in colonial terms, being equated largely with achievements of the West. Rulers such as Sayaji Rao threatened the status quo as they undermined colonial stereotypes. At the same time, the steps undertaken by such rulers to make their states 'modern' did not really destabilize British rule because the scope they had for independent action was severely limited.

With Malhar Rao having been deposed, a search was launched for an acceptable successor as the erstwhile maharaja had no direct heir. A child from another branch of the clan was selected and placed on the throne in 1875 with the title Sayaji Rao Gaikwad III. Sayaji assumed full powers in 1881. In the history of princely rulers of the late colonial period, his reign was somewhat exceptional in the range of measures initiated for changes in the pattern of governance. Manu Bhagavan has noted that Sayaji made good use of whatever autonomy was available to the state, especially in the fields of education and culture, to create a 'sovereign sphere'.[6] The colonial attempt to

[6]Manu Bhagavan, *Sovereign Spheres: Princes, Education, and Empire in Colonial India,* Delhi: Oxford University Press, 2003.

monopolize modernity could thus be challenged. In 'reclaiming' modernity, he was offering a critique of colonialism which aligned the state with anti-colonial nationalism.

The ideas of Sayaji were to some extent shaped by nationalists associated with Baroda. We have already referred to Naoroji's brief tenure as diwan. In the early 1890s, Aurobindo Ghosh was invited to join the maharaja's government. During the thirteen years that he was in the state he held various positions, including that of secretary to the maharaja and the vice-principalship of Baroda College. R. C. Dutt, one of the earliest proponents of economic nationalism in India, was invited to Baroda a few years after his retirement from the ICS. He was made a member of the Baroda State Council with the designation amatya (minister; more specifically, minister looking after finances of a state), sharing some of the responsibilities of the diwan. Dutt took up his assignment in 1904, and died in 1909 while still in office. It was during his tenure that several schemes were initiated. Perhaps the most significant of these was the introduction of free compulsory primary education in the whole state in 1906. The scholarship granted by Baroda to Dr B. R. Ambedkar for pursuing higher education at Bombay must be seen as part of its educational and social initiatives. Subsequently, in 1913, with the financial support of the state, he went to the US to study for his MA. Upon his return, he was appointed military secretary by Sayaji Rao, though Dr Ambedkar resigned from his post after a short while due to the caste discrimination he faced at the hands of the administrative staff.

Relations between Baroda and the British were not cordial during this phase. Curzon was convinced that Sayaji was not loyal to the crown. The maharaja's defiance of instructions issued by the governor general in 1900 requiring rulers of princely states to seek prior sanction of the British Indian government before travelling abroad aggravated tensions between Calcutta and Baroda. Sayaji ignored the circular and proceeded on a voyage to England without bothering to obtain permission from the government. Allegations that Baroda was extending support to nationalists was another cause of friction. There might have been some substance in this charge since Ghosh was involved in some subversive activities while at Baroda, activities that Sayaji was either not aware of or preferred to disregard.

Given that Baroda was a leading princely state, ranking third in the imperial hierarchy, it was sensible policy to avoid a public showdown with it, the more so as its ruler had demonstrated that he was a 'model' prince. It is for this reason that a major transgression of Sayaji was overlooked in 1911 (Hardinge was governor general at this time). On the occasion of the coronation durbar held at Delhi in that year to proclaim George V as the new king-emperor, rulers of princely states had to declare their acceptance of the overlordship of the British monarch through appropriate ceremonial gestures. Princes had to walk up to the king-emperor one by one and bow thrice before him, returning to their seats without turning their backs towards their acknowledged feudal master. To begin with, Sayaji did not wear his ceremonial dress on this occasion. And he did not bow the third time while paying obeisance to George V. Finally, he turned his back upon the king-emperor as he returned to his seat. This misdemeanour was officially attributed to the maharaja's inadequate comprehension of the ceremonial requirements. Whether or not it amounted to rebelliousness remains a matter of debate. A film of the event has survived which can be used to recreate the episode, but it is difficult to figure out the motives of the maharaja's behaviour from such visual evidence.

One other state, namely Mysore, could lay claim to being a 'model' state. In fact, at the beginning of the twentieth century the British hailed it as the best administered princely state. Here too the colonial model was creatively adapted so as to achieve real autonomy in some aspects of governance. This in turn created possibilities for questioning colonial domination—a possibility that was not entirely realized. Unlike Baroda, the relationship between Mysore and the British during the late colonial period, when a series of reforms were initiated by rulers of the state, was remarkably friendly all through. Interestingly, it was after the British loosened their grip over Mysore in the 1880s that these reforms were introduced. The state had a chequered history in the nineteenth century. Following the death of Tipu Sultan, a substantial portion of his territories, as described earlier, was annexed by the East India Company and a truncated Mysore was constituted as a princely state under Krishnaraja Wodeyar III. Krishnaraja was invested with full powers in 1810.

Krishnaraja passed away in 1868. A few years before his death he had adopted his eldest daughter's son as his heir, securing British recognition for this arrangement in 1867. The new maharaja succeeded Krishnaraja in 1868 with the title Chamaraja Wodeyar. Chamaraja (r. 1881–94) was a minor at the time of his accession; he was invested with full powers in 1881. This was the year in which direct control over the administration of the state was relinquished, an action officially referred to as the 'rendition' (handing back) of Mysore, signifying that this was an act of generosity by the paramount power. The tribute due from the state was increased to Rs 35 lakhs annually, though the payment of the enhanced amount was postponed for a few years. Nevertheless, the colonial appropriation of the resources of the state in the form of tribute continued to be the central problem for its economy. Under the circumstances, Chamaraja and his successor Krishnaraja IV (1895–1940) saw state-sponsored modernization of the economy as being crucial for its survival. Janaki Nair in her study of the ways in which Mysore defined its modernity observes that for its elites the stress was on economic development rather than political democracy.[7]

Chamaraja laid the foundations through initiatives in

---

[7]Janaki Nair, *Mysore Modern: Rethinking the Region under Princely Rule*, New Delhi: Orient Blackswan, 2012.

the field of school education. These initiatives were carried forward by Krishnaraja under whom free compulsory primary education was introduced in 1913 but the scheme could not be implemented successfully for financial reasons. Krishnaraja is better known for promoting institutions of higher learning. In 1909, the Indian Institute of Science was set up at Bangalore (it remains India's premier institution for cutting-edge research in science). Mysore became the first princely state to have its own university, i.e., the University of Mysore which was founded in 1916. Higher education was tightly regulated by the British, and colleges located in princely states had to be affiliated to universities in British India. Between 1857, when the three presidency universities were established, and 1916, no princely state had been permitted to have a university of its own. With its public libraries, colleges, university, and other institutions of higher learning and research, early twentieth century Mysore became, intellectually, a very vibrant state.

Krishnaraja could count on the assistance of able administrative personnel who gravitated towards Mysore as it acquired the reputation of a 'model' state. We may mention two particularly outstanding figures who served the maharaja successively as diwans in the twentieth century: M. Visvesvaraya (diwan, 1912–18) and his protégé Mirza Muhammad Ismail (diwan, 1926–41). Visvesvaraya was an engineer by profession while Mirza Ismail belonged to a group which had emerged in the late colonial period, that of specialist administrators employed by princely states. Many of those who belonged to this group were extremely competent, were highly regarded for their integrity, and rotated between several states (Mirza Ismail became diwan of Jaipur and subsequently of Hyderabad after departing from Mysore upon the death of Krishnaraja).

Visvesvaraya was instrumental in building a network of irrigation canals to facilitate agricultural growth. These canals helped boost the production of sugarcane and paddy rice in the state. He designed and supervised the construction of the massive Krishnaraja Sagar Dam across the Kaveri River for irrigation, supply of drinking water to Mysore and Bangalore, and generating hydro-electric power. In the absence of a sizeable entrepreneurial class with sufficient access to capital, it was the state that took the lead in investing in industrial development. A sandalwood oil factory was set up at Mysore in 1916, followed by a soap factory in Bangalore (1918). A more ambitious venture was the establishment of the Mysore Wood Distillation and Iron Works in 1918 at Bhadravati. This was a sector of the economy that the British regarded as their exclusive preserve. The wood distillation plant was intended for producing charcoal which was then used as fuel for making iron. In the mid-thirties, the enterprise progressed to steel production and in 1936, was renamed as Mysore Iron and Steel Works. These efforts were combined with the creation of infrastructure for technical education. Several engineering and agricultural institutes were set up, of which Government Engineering College, Bangalore (1917) was among the more noteworthy institutions for technical education.

The long experience of dealing with diverse princely states had made available a wide range of options to the British for subordinating them. None of these options, including military intervention or partial annexation, was discarded after the 1857 revolt. The most brazen use of naked armed force was that which was deployed in the case of Manipur. The princely state was placed under colonial military occupation between 1891 and 1907. A succession dispute, which was far from being violent, was exploited by the British to create a situation in which it could carry out a military campaign to ruthlessly suppress anti-colonial resistance in the state. The dispute broke out after the death of Maharaja Chandrakirti Singh (r. 1834–44; 1850–86). Chandrakirti Singh was succeeded by his eldest son, Surchandra, in 1886. Within four years, Surchandra was deposed by Tikendrajit, a younger son of the late maharaja. Whereas Tikendrajit acquired de facto authority, he installed

Kulachandra, another son of Chandrakirti, as the ruler of Manipur. Tikendrajit was able to consolidate his position by securing the support of the army through its very able military leader, Thangal 'General'. Meanwhile, Surchandra had rushed to secure the support of the British for his restoration.

The British Indian government and its local officials seem to have worked out a devious scheme to use this dispute to gain more effective control over Manipur. It was announced that Kulachandra would be recognized as the new ruler, but would have to hand over Tikendrajit to the British authorities. The chief commissioner of Assam, J. W. Quinton, was sent to Imphal to enforce this demand. An armed clash ensued in which Quinton and a few other officers were killed, whereupon the British rushed reinforcements to the state. Tikendrajit, along with Thangal and a large number of their armed supporters, resisted the onslaught for several weeks. Eventually, Manipur was subdued by the end of April 1891. Tikendrajit and Thangal were hanged publicly in Imphal. Kulachandra was exiled. Somewhat surprisingly, Surchandra was not reinstalled. Instead, an infant from the ruling family was made the maharaja. The British thus got an opportunity to directly administer the state for the next nearly two decades. Kangla Fort in Imphal, the traditional residence of the rulers of Manipur, was taken over, symbolically indicating the powerlessness of the native chief. The state remained under British military occupation till 1907. Such harsh treatment of the state over a dynastic problem which had initially not posed any direct threat to the paramount power had the larger purpose of serving as a warning to other princes. It was to be understood that the British could, if they so wished, punish a state severely were it to be disobedient. Resorting to the option of military occupation once in a while was a way of disciplining other states by example.

Furthermore, outright annexation of territories of princely states was not entirely given up. This was, however, a step that was taken very rarely, with much circumspection, and invariably related only to portions of the territories of certain states. One conspicuous example is that of Hyderabad. What makes this example particularly significant is that Hyderabad occupied the topmost position in the princely hierarchy constructed by the British. In the early 1850s, the cotton-producing Berar districts of the Hyderabad state (situated in present-day eastern Maharashtra) came under the direct control of the EIC against payment of arrears that were owed to it by the nizam for maintaining British armed contingents. This was one of the regions supplying raw cotton for the textile industry in England and to the cotton mills of Bombay. Railway lines linking Berar with Bombay were laid in the 1860s, their construction gathering momentum during the Lancashire 'cotton famine' when the American Civil War (1861–65) cut off supplies of raw cotton to England, and Bombay emerged as a major port for exporting the commodity. As we have seen, the districts were taken over 'in trust' by the Company in 1853. The possession was confirmed by a treaty signed in 1860. Then in 1902, a new arrangement was made during Curzon's tenure whereby Berar (Hyderabad Assigned Districts) was leased to the British in perpetuity for an annual rent of Rs 25 lakhs. The following year it was attached to the Central Provinces, and in 1936 Central Provinces was renamed as 'Central Provinces and Berar' amounting to a formal appropriation of the name of the region by the British. As a personal concession to the nizam he was henceforth referred to as 'his exalted highness'. Another sop was the permission to allow the Hyderabad state flag to be hoisted at Amravati (administrative headquarters of Berar) once a year on the occasion of the nizam's birthday. Finally, by way of acknowledging that formally Berar belonged to Hyderabad, the heir apparent of the state was styled, from 1936 onwards, as Prince of Berar in imitation of the practice in the United Kingdom of designating the heir apparent as Prince of Wales. We may see here a process of continuous negotiation in which symbolic gestures had to be conceded even if substantially it was the paramount power that gained.

Paramountcy denoted British superiority in the relationship with princely states. The notion of the paramountcy of the crown was designed to deny agency to the states. All action was seen to spring from the crown, or its representatives, so that even the limited autonomy enjoyed by princely states was supposed to have been gifted to them. Placing a territory under indirect rule was, in the colonial conception, an option exercised by the paramount power as its special prerogative. Such an understanding of indirect rule reflects, as Hira Singh has pointed out, 'the tendency in historical analysis to privilege the metropolis'. In his words, 'The problematic assumption is that the agency of doing, or not doing, anything in India... rested exclusively with European political economy.' Such a perspective can only give us a 'one-sided view of the colonial encounter in which the Indian subjects are represented as mere objects of manipulation by the colonial-capitalist forces...'.[8] In his critique of the concept of indirect rule, Singh remarks that 'indirect rule' suggests a one-way process in which the princely states, both rulers and subjects, played no role at all. Any meaningful analysis of the place of princely states in the British Indian empire has to take into account both resistance and collaboration by the indigenous elites of these states, which, in turn, were determined by the balance of class forces within the respective states. Yet it may be suggested that the term has its uses, particularly as a convenient way of referring to the relationship between the British and the princely states.

[8]Hira Singh, 'Colonial and Postcolonial Historiography and the Princely States: Relations of Power and Rituals of Legitimation', Waltraud Ernst and Biswamoy Pati, eds., *India's Princely States: People, Princes and Colonialism*, London: Routledge, 2007, pp. 18–19.

FOURTEEN

EPILOGUE: PAX BRITANNICA!

Queen Victoria passed away in away in 1901. Her lengthy reign (1837–1901) had witnessed massive territorial expansion of the British empire, and the climax of British imperial power. This historical circumstance, and Victoria's own longevity, gave her a unique status. The queen symbolized colonial omnipotence in a manner that no other monarch of the modern era could aspire to. She could easily be projected as being semi-divine, and her cult was vigorously promoted throughout the empire. The end of the Victorian era also coincided with the decline of British power. Yet, the empire went about its business, as if it would still endure for long. To most contemporaries, other than the more astute observers, it appeared that Pax Britannica would prevail at least till the end of the new century, if not longer. Such an impression was reinforced by the plethora of grand edifices built at the turn of the century symbolizing imperial permanence. Of these the most imposing was perhaps the monumental architecture of the new capital of the Indian empire. The project remained unfinished, though its most imposing structures were in place by the time India attained freedom.

Shortly before the outbreak of World War I (1914–18), three major projects for building capital cities were launched in the British empire. Two of these, Canberra and Pretoria were for newly constituted colonial entities within the empire, respectively the Commonwealth of Australia and the Union of South Africa. The third was the project for the new imperial capital for India, New Delhi. All reflected their specific historical contexts, which were quite dissimilar. Yet all drew on ideas from diverse sources across the world, and occasionally from each other, giving these ventures a global character.

Of the three, Canberra was the most democratic in its conception. As a white settler colony Australia enjoyed greater autonomy, 'self-government' in the real sense of the term. Most of the issues that the federation, consisting of six self-governing British colonies that came together in 1901, had to grapple with had to do with the integration of these units, rather than involving serious contestations with the metropolis. The federal parliament was central to the constitutional arrangements of the Commonwealth of Australia; Canberra was to be the site for the federal legislature and administration. The plan for the federal capital of Australia, selected in 1912 through a competition, was prepared by the American architect and town planner Walter Griffin, in collaboration with Marion Mahony. In this plan, never executed in its entirety, the zone containing the key government buildings, the 'parliamentary triangle' as it is known today, the people were symbolically placed at a higher level than the 'capitol'. The central axis of the complex culminated at the summit of Capital Hill, which was, significantly, not intended to be the location for the legislature. The Griffin design for the apex of the triangle, where the central axis intersected the diagonals of the triangle, envisaged a ceremonial building for public events, confusingly named the Capitol, along with a public park. For this building, Griffin had in mind a 'stepped pinnacle treatment in lieu of the inevitable dome'.[1] Eventually, a parliament house was built on Capital Hill towards the end of the twentieth century, incorporating some of Griffin's ideas, especially in making the top of the building accessible to the public so that the people could literally stand above the legislators. Incidentally, in the original design, the residences of the governor general and the prime minister were placed on

[1]Walter Griffin cited in Lawrence J. Vale, *Architecture, Power and National Identity,* second edition, Abingdon: Routledge, 2008, p. 89.

either side of the proposed Capitol.

In the case of Pretoria, the capitol complex project was intertwined with political manoeuvres of the Afrikaner leadership of Transvaal on the one hand, and British imperial ambitions on the other. The violent and bloody conflict of 1899–1902, the Second Anglo-Boer War, had ended in a decisive victory for Britain. However, the realities of the South African situation had led to a frantic search for a formula that would accommodate both British and Afrikaner interests. Colonial policymakers in Britain realized that, for the time being at least, they would have to establish a working relationship with sections of the Afrikaner elite, particularly in Transvaal, for exercising some degree of control over the region. It is against this backdrop that negotiations to form a union comprising Transvaal, the Orange River Colony, Cape Colony, and Natal proceeded apace between 1907 and 1909. By the beginning of 1909 most issues had been resolved, and constitutional formalities were being finalized. The question of whether Cape Town would be the capital of the Union or whether Pretoria would have this honour, had provoked much acrimonious debate. An agreement could only be reached by conceding the claims of both: Pretoria would be the seat of government, while the legislature would be located in Cape Town. Nevertheless, Louis Botha, prime minister of Transvaal in the transitional phase before union, and his colleague Jan Smuts, still hoped that Pretoria might become *the* capital of South Africa after the union was formed. Hence the speed with which they went ahead with their scheme for a capitol complex in Pretoria.

A prominent British architect, Herbert Baker, who had been working in the Cape since the 1890s was commissioned to design the complex even before the constitution for South Africa was passed by the British Parliament. Baker's initial design of 1909 placed a domed structure at the top of the hill, Meintjes Kop, chosen as the site for the complex. It was thought that this building would house the legislature, though Baker was reluctant to admit publicly that this was what he had in mind. Rather, he referred to it as 'a Temple of Peace dedicated to the ultimate consolidation and happy union of the two races of South Africa',[2] namely the Afrikaners and the British. However, the structure was never built. The overwhelming majority of those who lived in South Africa were completely excluded from all organs of the state when the Union came into existence in 1910. Africans had no place at all in the new dispensation, and would be physically excluded from the capital for a long time to come. There was therefore no acknowledgement of their presence, symbolic or otherwise, in the design for the capitol complex. Later, Baker got an opportunity to develop some of his ideas on a lavish scale when he was invited to join the team which was being put together to design the imperial capital in Delhi.

In order to comprehend the historical process whereby, at the turn of the century, Delhi came to be perceived as the most suitable location for constructing a grand residence for the governor general, surpassing every building erected by the British in India so far, it is necessary to refer to the role of imperial assemblages or durbars in articulating the imperial idea. The template was provided by Lytton's durbar of 1877 held in Delhi—not, it needs to be underlined, in Calcutta. The 1877 durbar, as we have seen, was a monumental spectacle organized to announce Queen Victoria's pompous new title, Indiae Imperatrix or Qaisar-i-Hind. With this event, the city came to be firmly lodged in the official colonial imagination as the appropriate site for imperial spectacles.

In its ceremonial aspects and symbols the 1877 assemblage combined imperial ingredients from ancient Rome, medieval Europe, and India's past to signify that the British empire embodied, and was carrying forward, all these traditions. The

---

[2]Herbert Baker cited in Roger C. Fisher, 'The Union Buildings: Reflections on Herbert Baker's Design Intentions and Unrealised Designs', *South African Journal of Art History*, No. 19, 2004, p. 44.

practice of organizing such durbars continued under Curzon and Hardinge. Curzon held a durbar in 1903, again in Delhi, to announce the coronation of Victoria's successor, Edward VII (r. 1901–10). Princes were the main invitees to these events as well. The ostentatious assemblages of 1877 and 1903 were instrumental in establishing the status of Delhi as the foremost imperial city of the Indian empire. The last and grandest durbar was held in 1911, during Hardinge's tenure. George V (r. 1910–36), the new British monarch, was present at this durbar lending additional prestige to the assemblage. It was at this durbar that the decision to transfer the capital of the British Indian empire from Calcutta to Delhi was announced. Largely due to nationalist outrage over the extravagance which such assemblages entailed, no durbar took place upon the accession of George VI as king-emperor.

Work on the new capital commenced almost immediately. A committee was constituted to devise a plan for the project, provide professional advice on technical matters and oversee the execution of the plan. Edwin Lutyens, a distinguished British architect, was invited to be on the committee and became the guiding spirit of the venture; he was joined by Herbert Baker. Lutyens was well known as an architect who had designed several charming country residences for the aristocracy. These were picturesque and pretty houses in rural settings, which were supposed to blend harmoniously with the English countryside. In designing them Lutyens attempted to emphasize their Englishness by incorporating local traditions and building material. Attention to detail was his forte, as is evident in his grandest creation in Delhi, the viceregal palace (Government House).

A vast tract of agricultural land on the outskirts of the 'native' town was acquired by the colonial government for the project. The imperial capital was not exactly contiguous with the existing urban settlement of Delhi. The nucleus of that settlement was the Mughal capital built in the early seventeenth century, named Shahjahanabad. Shahjahanabad was a walled city; ample space intervened between New Delhi and the walls of the old city, underlining distance between ruler and ruled. In this segregation, Lutyens's capital retained the typical form of the colonial city which made a clear distinction spatially between European and native quarters.

The main axis of the city was imagined as a Roman processional path, a via sacra, running east to west with a length of over 2 kilometres. This axis was exactly parallel to the axis of the old city. A statue of George V, placed under a canopy, would mark the eastern end of the processional path. This would terminate in the west on a hill, Raisina Hill, where Government House was to be located. The height of the Raisina Hill, named after the village which had been situated there before it was appropriated and the inhabitants turned out, was artificially raised in order to place the building on a higher eminence than was allowed by its natural formation. Little progress on the project was made during World War I, giving Lutyens an opportunity to develop his ideas for the imperial capital, especially the capitol complex. Work resumed in 1920 by which time a war memorial had to be added to the design. A massive triumphal arch, inspired by the Arch of Titus in Rome and the Arch of Triumph in Paris, was placed adjacent to the statue of George V, so that the processional path proceeding from the statue would pass under the Arch.[3] Names of a number of Indian soldiers who had fallen in the war, were engraved on the stones of the Arch, thereby giving Indians some symbolic presence in the complex. Nearly 1.5 million Indian soldiers had been deployed in various theatres of the war, mainly in Europe and Turkey; the Arch was a cheap substitute for the self-government which Indians were demanding and had hoped for as a reward for sacrifices made by the men fighting for an alien cause. The foundation stone of the Arch was laid

[3]Titus, Roman emperor, 79–81 CE.

in 1921, around the time Mahatma Gandhi launched a major mass movement against British rule.

It was Government House that consumed most of Lutyens's energy. What he produced had, strictly speaking, no predecessor. The main building is approached by traversing a vast open gravelled forecourt. A flight of steps leads to an imposing portico. The design for the portico is ultimately descended from the portico of the Parthenon at Athens with its Doric columns, via what is referred to as the Tuscan order, a more austere variant of the Doric. However, Lutyens creatively placed twelve columns at the front, exceeding those in the Parthenon by four. To the Doric–Tuscan columns he added his own flourish, a capital with a stylized acanthus, and temple bells carved in stone on the four corners of the capital, inventing the so-called 'Delhi order' of columns. This embellishment was intended to be a minor concession to 'native' sentiment.

There are two other features of the design for the palace which may be noted. One is the huge column which dominates the forecourt. In fact, before the processional path reaches its final destination on the summit of the hill, this is the only structure that is encountered after leaving the war memorial. The column combines elements of an Egyptian obelisk with those of the column of Trajan in Rome. It is surmounted by a giant metal star, the 'Star of India'.[4]

The other significant feature is the design for the dome. This is the only component of the style evolved by Lutyens for the palace which is substantially influenced by an Indian building, the Sanchi Stupa, located in central India.[5] This was one of the very few buildings which impressed Lutyens, who was otherwise quite contemptuous of Indian architectural traditions.

[4]Trajan, Roman emperor, 98–117 CE.
[5]The Sanchi Stupa is a famous historical site located in central India. A stupa is a Buddhist shrine, a structure usually hemispherical in shape which houses sacred relics. The stupa at Sanchi was built in several phases between the mid-third and first century BCE.

Once again, it was the sheer simplicity of the structure which appealed to him. He was so fascinated by the Sanchi Stupa that he also replicated the railings which surround the hemisphere. Apart from the exterior of the dome, no other element derived from Indian traditions finds a place in the overall design of Government House. Flourishes such as small domed pavilions or elephants carved in stone are mere ornamentation.

In the division of labour between Baker and Lutyens, Baker was assigned the administrative block which was to be part of the capitol complex. In his design for the secretariat he more or less repeated the design of the Union Buildings in Pretoria, replacing some of the elements derived from the Cape Dutch style with Indian motifs. Together, Government House and the Secretariat Buildings comprise a whole. What is noteworthy is the manner in which the two are juxtaposed. Unlike in Pretoria, where the two wings of the Union Buildings are connected by a semi-circular colonnade symbolizing unification, on Raisina Hill, the two rectangular blocks are separated by the processional path which begins its ascent to the summit at the base of the Secretariat Buildings. The two wings of the secretariat act as a screen for the palace. Only a portion of the dome and the column in the forecourt, are visible from a distance. This adds a sense of mystery to the scene.

Despite obvious differences, the imprint of Baker's vision for the capitol complex in Pretoria is unmistakable in the overall conception of the complex in Delhi. One may be startled by the similarity while looking at Baker's preliminary sketch for Pretoria. In this sketch, the Union Buildings are placed about halfway up the summit of Meintjes Kop, where they were indeed built. The summit has a domed structure, which was intended to be for the legislature but was never constructed. In India, this was substituted by the Government House; the legislature in India was a powerless institution which served a decorative function and therefore does not figure prominently in the design either of Lutyens or of Baker. It is inconspicuously tucked away in a corner, as if it were an afterthought.

The connections between Pretoria and New Delhi are not irrelevant. The designs for both were based on colonial ideas which assumed the superiority of the West. This was sufficient justification for the exclusions inherent in the projects for the two colonial capital cities. Unlike Griffin's Canberra or, for that matter, Edward Bennett's 1915 plan for Ottawa, which looked forward to a more democratic future, Baker's Pretoria and Lutyens's Delhi were both firmly rooted in the past. In terms of city planning, they represented historical dead ends. It is only with Indian independence in 1947 that something could be retrieved in the case of New Delhi, while Pretoria's Union Buildings would have to wait till the 1990s to be of any use to the vast majority of the people of South Africa.

◆

By the end of World War I, the old imperialist powers, particularly Britain and France, were exhausted and much weakened. They could no longer rule over their colonies with the same coercive methods that they had employed for nearly two centuries. It is not surprising that there were mass upheavals extending from Egypt to China in the years immediately following the end of the war.

In India, there was growing resentment during World War I over the massive use of India's resources in a war that was being fought for furthering Britain's imperial interests. Apart from money and supplies, India was forced to contribute, as we have noted, nearly 1.5 million soldiers as part of its war effort. The soldiers fought in distant theatres, in the killing fields of Europe, Ypres (in present-day Belgium) for instance, under the most appalling conditions, for a cause that would ultimately prolong the subjugation of the Indian people. About 75,000 Indian soldiers were killed in the fighting. The colonial authorities resorted to coercive measures to procure supplies of Indian soldiers as cannon fodder. Informally, conscription was introduced in major recruiting zones such as Punjab, where quotas for enlistment were imposed on villages. Recruitment was stepped up from mid-1917 onwards, and by April 1918 it was expected that the number of soldiers sent by the province would reach the figure of 200,000. Village and tahsil officials became hated recruiting agents. All this led to widespread disaffection that would become a significant factor in the popular anti-colonial post-war upsurge in Punjab and other parts of India.

During the war, Ghadar revolutionaries played an active role in trying to mobilize people in Punjab against forced military recruitment. The Ghadar Party was founded by nationalists in San Francisco/California in 1913, under the leadership of Baba Sohan Singh Bhakna and Lala Har Dayal. Within a short time, the Ghadarites were able to extend the scope of their activities to Indian migrant labour in Canada, the Caribbean, Philippines, and Singapore. The Ghadarites linked the struggle against inhuman conditions in which Indian migrants in North America and Southeast Asia had to work, and the racial discrimination they faced, to the larger struggle against colonial rule and for the liberation of India. As a result of the infamous *Komagata Maru* episode of 1914, in which the Canadian authorities demonstrated their racial bigotry by denying entry to Indian passengers aboard the ship when it reached Vancouver after a long and arduous journey from Hong Kong, and the violence unleashed against the passengers by British authorities at Budge Budge in Calcutta when the *Komagata Maru* arrived in India upon being forced to return from Canada, the Gadhar movement acquired a militant character. With the outbreak of the war the Gadharites intensified their activities in several parts of the Indian subcontinent, especially among peasants in Punjab. In Punjab, they strove to undermine the authority of the British raj, making it difficult for colonial officials to recruit soldiers in the province. Attempts were made to rally Indian soldiers for a mutiny in the British Indian armed forces. The plan did not succeed and provided the pretext for brutal repression of the Ghadarites. The Defence of India Act of 1915 was a legislative measure directed mainly against the Ghadarites. About fifty Ghadarites were executed, while several more were sentenced to transportation for life, or sentenced to life imprisonment. The martyrdom of Kartar Singh Sarabha, who was barely nineteen years old when he was executed in 1915, was to inspire an entire generation of young revolutionaries of whom Bhagat Singh was the most prominent. The 1915 Act was used to imprison large numbers of revolutionaries for several years without trial.

It was against this backdrop that the British government announced that some concession would be made to nationalist sentiment after the war. In August 1917, Edwin Montagu, as secretary of state for India, officially declared in the House of Commons that Britain was committed to 'the gradual development of self-governing institutions with a view to the progressive realization of responsible government in India'. This was followed by the Montagu–Chelmsford Report of 1918, which in turn led to the Government of India Act of 1919. The key feature of the report and the Act was a constitutional scheme of limited autonomy for provincial governments. These governments were supposedly answerable to provincial legislative assemblies, elected on the basis of a severely restricted franchise. In practice, the provincial governments remained firmly under British control. A few subjects, such as education and health, were 'transferred' to these governments. In any case, the colonial state hardly had any interest in these areas of governance.

The timing of the Montagu declaration and the Montagu–Chelmsford Report is noteworthy. The declaration came within a few months of the February 1917 Revolution in Russia. It may be mentioned that the February Revolution was the prelude to the October Revolution of 1917. The so-called 'reforms' which the report offered were seen as a necessary sop to prevent the radicalization of the national movement under Bolshevik influence.

While on the one hand the British attempted to put the brakes on the radicalization of the nationalist movement by offering some minor concessions in the form of the Montagu–Chelmsford proposals and the Government of India Act of 1919, on the other hand, they widened the scope of the Defence of India Act of 1915 through the more draconian and stringent provisions of the Anarchical and Revolutionary Crimes Act (Act XI of 1919), better known as the Rowlatt Act. This is how Indians were rewarded for their outstanding (albeit largely involuntary) contribution to the Allied victory in World War I. It needs to be underlined that the main objective of the Act, and of the continuing repressive measures to stamp out 'revolutionary crimes' (the wording of the title of the Act is significant), was to restrain the rising tide of popular resistance and revolutionary mobilization. This, however, was no longer possible to achieve without violent repression.

Massive participation in the anti-Rowlatt agitation launched towards the end of March 1919 was a reflection of the anger which the Act had aroused. More importantly, such participation clearly showed that conditions were now ripe for mass mobilization against British rule. The countrywide hartal of 6 April 1919 to protest against the Rowlatt measures was a huge success. Punjab was the epicentre of the agitation where Amritsar, Lahore, and Gujranwala were the key locations of the agitation. Events at Amritsar unfolded rapidly in the second week of April. Violence erupted on 10 April, but was quickly contained. Yet, it became the official justification for all the brutality that Amritsar and other parts of Punjab had to suffer for several months thereafter, including the killings at Jallianwala Bagh on 13 April. Amritsar was placed under martial law on 11 April, even though it was formally declared four days later. A distinction between civil and military authority is spurious here, since this was not a democratically elected government answerable to the people.

What has generally been ignored in historical accounts of the Jallianwala Bagh massacre is the unhappy fate of the wounded, those who were injured either in the firing, or in the stampede, or both. With utter callousness, the administration left the wounded to die in the Bagh and the streets surrounding it. There was no one to tend to them, no succour, no ambulance, no medical help, and no access of relatives or friends to the area due to curfew. Hundreds of wounded victims, including infants, lay groaning in pain, helpless, stupefied, crying out for water, throughout the long, dark night (electricity had already been cut off in Amritsar). A large proportion of the injured just perished, while those who were able to make it to their homes had to remain in hiding so that they were not apprehended as criminals. In the absence of medical assistance many of these victims lingered on in agony till their death. We are not even approximately close to a realistic estimate of the dead.

The horrific massacre has often been attributed merely to the aberrant personal conduct of Reginald Dyer. Dyer was the commanding officer of Amritsar, and was personally present at Jallianwala Bagh; he personally gave the order to open firing. A total of 1,650 rounds were fired on unarmed and peaceful protestors. The actions of Dyer have to be seen in the context of the brutally repressive regime imposed on Punjab during the war, and the relentless persecution of Ghadarite and other revolutionaries. Jallianwala Bagh was meant to be a lesson to opponents of British authority. Historically, it is immaterial whether it was an individual decision or had the general sanction of Dyer's superiors. The entire colonial machinery was complicit in the massacre, as was made more than apparent by the exoneration of Dyer and the endorsement of his action in white racist circles. What could have been a better illustration of this than the provocative gesture of collecting nearly £27,000 to be given to the 'butcher of Amritsar' by way of felicitating him?

The anti-Rowlatt agitation and the wave of popular unrest that followed the Jallianwala Bagh massacre ushered in an era of mass mobilization against colonial rule. It goes without saying that Gandhi played a major role hereafter in shaping the national movement, and leading it for the next two decades. The Non-Cooperation Movement of 1920–22, the Civil Disobedience Movement, which began in 1930, and the Quit India Movement launched in 1942, were indeed huge mass movements. Gandhi was their architect and foremost leader. The movements were unprecedented in their scope, and had an all-India spread.

By the early 1920s, it had become difficult for the British to ignore nationalist demands. From time to time they declared that India would be granted self-government in the distant future. Self-government was never defined in precise terms. For thirty years, between 1917 and 1947, colonial policymakers kept up the pretence that the Indian empire would be given, sooner rather than later, the status of a self-governing dominion (within the British empire obviously), and that Britain had some kind of blueprint or timetable for this purpose. In fact, the possibility was considered so remote that no one ever got down to preparing any such blueprint.

In Britain itself, the Conservative Party with its strong commitment to the preservation of empire, was in power for the entire period (brief interludes apart), from the end of World War I to the end of the British rule in India. For the last two years of British rule a Labour Party government was in office. The new ministry had to quickly sort out the mess left behind by the Conservatives. To begin with, existing constitutional arrangements had to be undone by qualitatively altering the structure of governance created by the Government of India Act of 1935, which had been designed to provide a new constitutional framework for governing the Indian empire without relinquishing control—the final exercise in colonial constitution-making prior to 1947. The problem was that the Act had given rise to a situation in which it was almost impossible to produce a practical formula: 'The 1935 Act had created all the requirements for stasis. It set the princes, Muslim League and Congress in architectural opposition to each other.'[6] Ironically, the legislation had been strongly opposed by the right wing of the Conservative Party led by Winston Churchill who aggressively campaigned against it. Churchill fulminated against the India Bill inside Parliament, and tried to mobilize public opinion against it outside through platforms such as the ultra-reactionary Indian Empire Society. The bill triggered a civil war among the Conservatives, ending in a convincing victory for the official faction headed by Prime Minister Stanley Baldwin. Yet, the 1935 Act was hardly a progressive measure. It envisaged a federal scheme which on the one hand had the objective of strengthening the position of princely rulers vis-à-vis nationalists, and on the other was intended to prevent the Congress from having any say at the centre.

A more disquieting aim of the Act was to foster divisions based on religious identity. The years following the 1935 Act were precisely the years in which the British worked assiduously to actually wreck its severely limited democratic elements by aiding the resurrection, under Muhammad Ali Jinnah, of the All India Muslim League, a political formation based exclusively on religious identity; and propping up princes in the name of federation. The outbreak of the war in 1939 provided a wonderful opportunity to carry this work forward, especially through the seven-year-long (1936–43), relentless onslaught of Governor General Lord Linlithgow. The top leadership of the Congress was incarcerated from 1942 onwards following the launch of the Quit India Movement. Linlithgow's own personal contribution to what happened in 1947 has unfortunately not received adequate attention in historical research. However,

[6]Walter Reid, *Keeping the Jewel in the Crown: The British Betrayal of India*, Delhi: Penguin/Viking, 2016, p. 124.

Sir Stafford Cripps seems to have been sincere in his endeavour, during his official visit to India in 1942 on behalf of the British cabinet, to move forward on the question of Indian independence. Cripps, who belonged to the left wing of the Labour Party, was then a high-ranking minister in the War Cabinet of Churchill. His efforts, however, were bound to fail as both Churchill and Linlithgow, respectively prime minister and governor general, made sure that Cripps's mission did not achieve a breakthrough. Churchill and Linlithgow were united in their steadfastness to the idea of an empire that would endure.

It was only around 1944–45 that a section of policymakers began to think in terms of a concrete plan for substituting direct British control with some sort of self-governance. Astonishingly, there was still no sense of urgency. Cripps and Archibald Wavell (the penultimate British governor general), were perhaps the only two political figures of some consequence who, in the final days of the Raj, attempted to grapple with the issue of logistics, showing an awareness of the huge amount of spadework that might be required for a smooth transition. The much celebrated Louis Mountbatten, last British governor general of India, merely got by with charisma combined with constant improvisation. Thus an exasperated Cyril Radcliffe who was given the job of demarcating the boundaries of India and Pakistan with barely five weeks to carry out the task remarked, referring to the utter lack of prior planning, 'Strange chaps. [They] just didn't do their homework.'[7] This terse remark sums up, very effectively, the callousness with which the Indian subcontinent was abandoned to its fate in August 1947.

At the end of World War II (the war ended in Europe in May 1945) the British Indian government invited leaders of the Indian National Congress, the Muslim League, and representatives of a few other political formations for several rounds of talks at a conference moderated by the British. The conference

[7]Cited in Reid, *Keeping the Jewel in the Crown*, p. 249.

was to discuss the manner in which the subcontinent would be constituted and governed once it achieved independence; independence for India was now officially on the agenda. Congress leaders were released from prison to enable them to participate in the conference. These talks commenced on 25 June 1945, and were held at Simla (now Shimla). Governor General Wavell presided over the conference. Although Gandhi did not formally participate in the conference, he was present in Simla on this occasion for informal consultations, and to assist the leaders of the Indian National Congress; he stayed on in Simla till the end of the deliberations.

Gandhi reached Simla on 24 June 1945, one day before the conference commenced. On the same day, he held talks with Wavell at the viceregal lodge. The Indian National Congress was officially represented at the conference by its president, Abul Kalam Azad. Jawaharlal Nehru too was present in Simla, though he also did not participate in the official deliberations.

The Congress delegation included Dr Khan Sahib (premier of North-West Frontier Province), Govind Ballabh Pant (former premier of the United Provinces), and Bhulabhai Desai (leader of the Congress party in the Central Legislative Assembly). The Unionist Party was represented by Khizr Hyat Khan Tiwana (premier of Punjab). C. Rajagopalachari was invited as the former premier of Madras. He had headed the Congress ministry in the province between 1937 and 1939. Rajagopalachari later became the first Indian governor general of independent India (June 1948 to 26 January 1950). N. Sivaraj, a prominent Dalit leader, represented the 'Depressed Classes' at the conference. Sivaraj was a senior member of the imperial legislative council. Muhammad Ali Jinnah, president of the All India Muslim League, represented his party.

On 14 July, it was officially announced that the Simla conference had been unsuccessful. The failure to arrive at any agreement on the crucial issue of the reconstitution of the executive council of the governor general, the main cause for the collapse of the consultative process, was largely due to the insistence of the All India Muslim League that it should have the exclusive right to decide on the names of 'Muslim' members of the council. This led to a stalemate as the Congress would not agree to such an unreasonable demand. The failure of the conference made it increasingly difficult to evolve a consensus in the following period on the question of constitutional arrangements.

In much of the historiography on the closing years of British rule, there has been a general tendency to ignore the post-war mass upsurge. The focus has been mainly on top-level negotiations that preceded Independence and Partition. Left-wing political groups, especially communists (none of whom were part of the ongoing negotiations), were engaged in popular mobilization against colonial rule in these years. As P. C. Joshi, the then general secretary of the Communist Party of India (CPI) put it, this was the 'final bid for power' by the people.[8] The communists were at the forefront of the major popular movements of the years 1945–47. In some cases, these movements began almost spontaneously, and acquired a radical character under the influence of the CPI, trade unions, and peasant organizations, as they progressed. The Tebhaga movement in Bengal, the Telangana movement in the state of Hyderabad, and the Punnapra–Vayalar uprising in Travancore, to name the most significant of these popular struggles, were all mainly agrarian movements. The struggles during 1945 and 1946 in support of prisoners of the Indian National Army (the liberation force formed under the leadership of Subhas Chandra Bose), and the mutiny of Indian ratings of the Royal Indian Navy, were essentially urban-based, involving students, workers, and sections of the middle class. Overall, the popular movements of 1945–47 played a crucial role in the fight against

[8]P. C. Joshi, *For the Final Bid for Power!: Freedom Programme of Indian Communists*, Bombay: People's Publishing House, 1946.

imperialism at this critical juncture, and their pressure explains, to some extent, the haste with which negotiations attempted to deal with the complex issues of independence.

In the first general elections held in Great Britain after World War II, the Conservative Party led by Winston Churchill (who had been prime minister throughout the war), was defeated decisively. Results of the election were announced on 26 July 1945; the Labour Party won a landslide victory. Clement Attlee became the new prime minister.

At the beginning of 1946, Attlee announced that three senior cabinet ministers would proceed to India for further consultations regarding constitutional arrangements for moving towards independence. An interim government was to be formed prior to British withdrawal from the subcontinent. The cabinet delegation was to consist of Frederick Pethick-Lawrence (secretary of state for India), Stafford Cripps (president of the Board of Trade), and A. V. Alexander (First Lord of the Admiralty, i.e., minister in charge of the navy). The Quit India Movement, which had been launched in 1942, and the massive popular anti-colonial agitation throughout India at the end of World War II forced the British to eventually concede the demand for freedom.

The Cabinet Mission (as the visit of the cabinet delegation is generally referred to) began talks with representatives of various political formations and some individuals, such as rulers of a few princely states at Delhi, in the last week of March 1946. As part of the Cabinet Mission's consultative process, a tripartite conference was convened at Simla (this is also referred to as the second Simla Conference), at which delegates of the Congress and the Muslim League, along with the three British cabinet ministers, were to discuss the modalities for the formation of an interim government and related constitutional issues. The second Simla conference commenced on 5 May 1946. This time too Gandhi was present in Simla to informally assist with the negotiations.

The following extract from a newspaper report describes vividly the arrival of the delegates at the venue of the conference. It conveys the mood of anticipation which prevailed at the beginning of the conference; the collapse of the conference was to dash hopes of a peaceful transition to freedom, with momentous consequences for the subcontinent.

All roads in Simla led to the Viceroy's House this morning. The weather was bright, the sun shining gloriously over pine-clad Simla. There was considerable activity since daybreak. After an early breakfast everybody hurried to the main gates of the Viceroy's House, to catch a glimpse of the leaders proceeding to attend the Tripartite conference. The Congress members assembled at the 'The Retreat', Maulana Azad's residence at 9 o'clock. Pandit Jawaharlal Nehru, Sardar Vallabhbhai Patel and Abdul Ghaffar Khan walked right along the main road to the Viceroy's House. The Congress President drove in a rickshaw decorated with a tricolour flag. The Congress leaders were lustily cheered by the public who lined the route. Mr Jawaharlal Nehru wore a chocolate coloured sherwani, white churidhar, and white khaddar cap. He carried a Simla walking stick in his hand. By his side walked the tall, dignified Frontier leader, Khan Abdul Ghaffar Khan. The 70-year old Sardar Patel, attired in spotless white Khadi walked briskly carrying a yellow file in his hand. At the Viceregal Lodge the three British Ministers and their secretaries appeared at the steps of the main entrance punctually at a quarter to ten. Maulana Azad was the earliest to arrive. He drove straight to the portico where the Cabinet Ministers came down the steps to receive him. Maulana Azad greeted them in English as he alighted from the rickshaw. Lord Pethick-Lawrence was the first to shake hands with him very warmly. The other members, Sir S. Cripps and Mr A. V. Alexander came forward next to greet the Congress President. The group was then photographed after which the Secretary of State led the way to the conference room. Five minutes later, Pandit Nehru, Khan Abdul Ghaffar Khan and Sardar Patel also reached the Viceregal Lodge walking, when Sir S. Cripps and Mr A. V. Alexander came once again to the portico to receive them. They exchanged greetings and chatted pleasantly for a few minutes before they went in. The Congress delegates took their seats at the conference table by five minutes to ten. At the stroke of ten, the four Muslim League delegates, Mr Jinnah, Nawabzada Liaquat Ali Khan, Nawab Mahomed Ismail and Mr Abdul Rab Nishtar drove into the Viceregal Lodge in a military car.[9]

The tripartite conference concluded on 12 May 1946 without achieving any breakthrough on crucial constitutional matters. On 16 May, the Cabinet Mission announced its own proposals, known as the Cabinet Mission Plan. This was eventually rejected by the Muslim League, paving the way for the formation of two independent nation-states following the liberation of the Indian subcontinent from colonial rule in August 1947. As for the princely states, the British quite mischievously declared that the paramountcy of the crown would lapse once British rule came to an end, and that all princely states would become fully sovereign entities upon the lapse of paramountcy. The long history of the subjugation of princely states, and colonial penetration of their economies, deprived them of the means of existing, at least in the short run, as viable independent entities. Thus it did not really take very long for the respective states to be incorporated into either India or Pakistan. Not a single state was able to exercise the option, illusory as it turned out, of *not* acceding to one of the two dominions. A few states seriously attempted to do so; none of them succeeded. The overwhelming majority of the states, more than 500 of them, the borders of which were contiguous with those of India,

[9]*The Hindu*, report dated 5 May 1946, Rangaswami Parthasarathy, ed., *A Hundred Years of The Hindu: The Epic Story of Indian Nationalism*, Madras: Kasturi and Sons Ltd., n.d., p. 616.

became part of independent India within a few months of Independence, while the rest signed instruments of accession shortly thereafter. Popular movements in the states helped accelerate the integration of princely states.

◆

What happened in 1947 was not a mere 'transfer of power'. Rather, India attained freedom through a long and sustained struggle extending over nearly two centuries. The history of resistance since Plassey is an integral part of the history of anti-colonial struggle in India. The revolt of 1857 was an important moment of resistance. The national liberation movement of the period between the 1920s and 1947 marked a qualitatively new stage in this prolonged struggle. It was this that culminated in Independence on 15 August 1947—representing the triumph of anti-colonial Indian nationalism over British imperialism.

APPENDIX

A NOTE ON THE MAKING OF THE PERMANENT SETTLEMENT SCHEME[1]

The Permanent Settlement of 1793, the land revenue system introduced in the Bengal Presidency under Cornwallis, was the product of ideas that evolved over a period of more than two decades. Under the settlement, the revenue demand was made perpetual. Within just five years of the acquisition of diwani (1765), it had become obvious to careful observers that the East India Company's ascendancy in Bengal following Plassey had been disastrous for the economy of the region. The devastating famine of 1770 prompted colonial officials and political economists to put forth proposals for policies that would lead to a revival of the economy on a long-term basis. Of these, the most comprehensive was a plan drawn up by Philip Francis in 1776. Francis's plan was profoundly influenced by physiocratic ideas of the late eighteenth century. Theorists of the physiocratic school, such as François Quesnay (1694–1774), regarded agricultural production as the source of the wealth of a society; it was only through agricultural production that value was created. Unlike the mercantilists, who gave primacy to commercial activity and a favourable balance of trade, agriculture was of central importance in physiocratic theses.

[1]The brief outline provided in this appendix is based on Ranajit Guha's classic study, the most authoritative work on the subject: *A Rule of Property for Bengal: An Essay on the Idea of Permanent Settlement*, Delhi: Orient Longman, 1982 (first published, Paris, 1963).

Further, the physiocrats were strongly opposed to monopolies of all kinds, as well as to feudal privileges which, under the Ancien Régime in France, made it difficult for agriculture to realize its full potential—essentially due to the insecurity of property. A programme for strengthening of property rights in land figured prominently in physiocratic prescriptions.

Francis's view was that that the policies pursued by the Company since 1765 had resulted in seriously undermining property rights. This was the root cause of the ills afflicting Bengal. The system of farming out lands for very short durations to the highest bidder for purposes of revenue collection, introduced under Warren Hastings, had intensified the problem and received particularly severe criticism. The remedy lay in restoring traditional rights in landed property. Contrary to the understanding of a large number of colonial officials, including Hastings, that in India all land was traditionally the property of the ruler, Francis was convinced of the existence of private property prior to the establishment of the Company's rule. His statements on this question owed much to Voltaire's argument that evidence of hereditary succession pointed towards the existence of private property, an outright rejection of François Bernier's very widely accepted contention that the ruler was the sole proprietor of land in India. The Mughal conquest of Bengal did not, Francis argued, lead to the dispossession of landowners. It was the Company that had steadily undermined property rights after 1765. Moreover, under the farming system, landowners had no incentive to augment production as the surplus was liable to be taken away from them by revenue farmers. Revenue farmers, for their part, were only interested in appropriating as much of the produce as they could so that they could recover the revenue payable to the state and make a profit for themselves as quickly as possible. Such a situation was not conducive to the development of the agrarian economy. The solution lay in doing away with the farming system and making landed property stable by introducing a settlement that was permanent. The state's demand had to be moderate, but as the settlement would be permanent and perpetual the possibility of an increase in production, which Francis took for granted, had to be factored in as the state would forego any subsequent increase in revenue demand.

The zamindars, as holders of superior rights in land, were identified as the class which the state was to make answerable for the payment of revenue. Francis assumed that this would amount to a *restoration* of their 'ancient' rights. Once landed property was made secure, the zamindar, now assured that the revenue demand would not be enhanced, could look forward to enjoying the fruits of endeavours to improve production. He had in mind the model prevalent in contemporary England wherein the capitalist farmer took the initiative to develop agriculture through investment in improved methods and techniques. The zamindar as landlord–entrepreneur would, by the magic of secure property rights, become an improving agricultural capitalist in Bengal. The 'ryot' or peasant–cultivator was to play the role assigned to the yeoman farmer in the English model. Taking this line of reasoning to its logical conclusion, Francis insisted that the state ought to leave the zamindar free to settle the terms on which the ryot would cultivate the land. The government had no business to interfere in the relationship between the zamindar and the ryot. His assumption was that the terms would, in the long run, be determined by the laws of supply and demand. It may be mentioned in passing that given the scarcity of labour in the 1770s as a result of the extensive dislocation and loss of life caused by famine there was a favourable land–man ratio in this period.

Ranajit Guha, in *A Rule of Property for Bengal*, has drawn attention to the influence which economic ideas of the Scottish physiocrat Henry Pattullo had on Francis's formulations.[2] Although the details of Pattullo's life are somewhat obscure,

[2]Ibid., pp. 42–49.

it would seem that he was a political exile who lived in France for several years between the 1750s and 1770s where he was associated with the intellectual circle of Quesnay and other French physiocrats. He tried to popularize English agricultural methods in France and published a tract on the subject. It was in this context that he wrote an essay on 'The Cultivation of the Lands and Improvements of the Revenues of Bengal' (1772). Though Pattullo perhaps never visited India, he appears to have studied available writings on Bengal with great interest. We need to underline that contemporary analysts in the West were overwhelmingly of the view that the Company's policies in Bengal had been ruinous for its economy. Not surprisingly, therefore, economic thinkers such as Pattullo considered it worthwhile to suggest measures to bring about a revival. As noted earlier, the physiocrats likened conditions in Bengal to those in Ancien Régime France where the burden of arbitrary taxes and the insecurity of property had left the countryside impoverished. In keeping with physiocratic principles, Pattullo considered agricultural progress to be the key to economic development. In the case of Bengal he proposed a permanent settlement, which in turn would strengthen property rights and thereby stimulate agriculture.

Another intellectual precursor of Francis was the orientalist Alexander Dow, well known for his English translation of Firishta's *Tarikh* (a well-known historical account of medieval India), who approached the question from a mercantilist perspective. According to Dow, Bengal had flourished under the 'benevolent' despotism of the Mughals (both Dow and Francis discussed despotism in positive terms). The Mughals and their successors had encouraged international commerce, which had allowed the region to maintain a favourable balance of trade. Vast quantities of bullion and specie flowed in the direction of Bengal from different parts of the globe for the purchase of its manufacturers. The EIC, by subverting its commerce, had reversed this flow; wealth was now being 'drained' from Bengal.

The scarcity of money (with which Dow equated wealth) was responsible for the decline of the economy. One of the ways in which trade could be stimulated was by the introduction of paper money. More importantly for the history of the idea of permanent settlement, Dow suggested that all land (which he assumed to be entirely the property of the crown) in Bengal and Bihar should be disposed of 'in perpetuity, at an annual sum not less than the present rents'. In other words, the state should create property rights in land, rights that had not existed earlier. The sale of land would promote investment and thus result in the flow of money into Bengal. This would stimulate trade and commerce. For Dow, agriculture was an adjunct to trade, the ultimate aim of his proposals was to encourage commercial activity. Nevertheless, his proposals for the revival of agriculture were similar to those of Pattullo and Francis.

Francis was not able to get approval for his 1776 plan, the politics of which need not detain us. His ideas, however, remained in circulation and were reinforced by the opinion of several of the Company's revenue officials who were persuaded from their own experience of the feasibility of the plan. In the 1780s, Thomas Law, an official who had been posted for several years in Bihar, put forward a proposal that took the Francis plan further in the direction of capitalist farming. Whereas Francis was aware that strengthening of property rights would lead to a market in land, he was unwilling to recognize that this might undermine the 'ancient' rights of the zamindars. He would have preferred this class, 'the landed aristocracy of Bengal', with its 'great potentialities of social leadership' not yet exhausted, to retain its hold over land.[3] As Guha points out, there were remnants in his thinking of a feudal conception of the landlord, and he 'was a great believer in inequality'.[4] Law discarded these remnants to argue for the desirability of ousting inefficient

[3]Guha, *Rule of Property for Bengal*, p. 109.
[4]Ibid.

owners through the growth of a full-fledged market in land. This would put the agrarian economy of Bengal firmly on the path of capitalist development. Eventually of course, Cornwallis, a resolute supporter of permanent settlement, introduced the new scheme in 1793. There were some senior officials such as John Shore who had serious misgivings about the scheme as late as 1789–90. Shore was not in favour of a permanent settlement, contending instead that it should be for a limited period after which it might be reviewed. He was also not sure that the kind of ownership rights being vested in the zamindars actually belonged to them traditionally. A closer scrutiny of these rights would, according to him, be in order. Finally, and this was to become a major issue later, he felt that the state ought to have some say in regulating the relationship between the zamindars and the ryots.

QUEEN VICTORIA'S 1858 PROCLAMATION (EXTRACT)[5]

And we, reposing especial trust and confidence in the loyalty, ability, and judgement of our right trusty and well-beloved cousin and councillor, Charles John Viscount Canning, do hereby constitute and appoint him, the said Viscount Canning, to be our first Viceroy and Governor-General in and over our said territories, and to administer the government thereof in our name, and generally to act in our name and on our behalf, subject to such orders and regulations as he shall, from time to time, receive from us through one of our Principal Secretaries of State.

And we do hereby confirm in their several offices, civil and military, all persons now employed in the service of the Honourable East India Company, subject to our future pleasure, and to such laws and regulations as may hereafter be enacted.

[5]The full proclamation can be found at www.bl.uk/collection-items/proclamation-by-the-queen-in-council-to-the-princes-chiefs-and-people-of-india.

We hereby announce to the native Princes of India that all treaties and engagements made with them by or under the authority of the Honourable East India Company are by us accepted, and will be scrupulously maintained, and we look for the like observance on their part.

We desire no extension of our present territorial possessions; and, while we will permit no aggression upon our dominions or our rights to be attempted with impunity, we shall sanction no encroachment on those of others. We shall respect the rights, dignity and honour of native Princes as our own; and we desire that they, as well as our own subjects, should enjoy the prosperity and that social advancement which can only be secured by internal peace and good government.

We hold ourselves bound to the natives of our Indian territories by the same obligations of duty which bind us to all our other subjects, and those obligations...we shall faithfully and conscientiously fulfill.

...[W]e disclaim alike the right and desire to impose our convictions on any of our subjects. We declare it to be our royal will and pleasure that none be in anywise favoured, none molested or disquieted, by reason of their religious faith or observances, but that all alike shall enjoy the equal and impartial protection of the law; and we do strictly charge and enjoin all those who may be in authority under us that they abstain from all interference with the religious belief or worship of any of our subjects on pain of our highest displeasure.

And it is our further will that, so far as may be, our subjects, of whatever race or creed, be freely and impartially admitted to offices in our service, the duties of which they may be qualified, by their education, ability, and integrity, duly to discharge.

We know, and respect, the feelings of attachment with which the natives of India regard the lands inherited by them from their ancestors, and we desire to protect them in all rights connected therewith, subject to the equitable demands of the

State; and we will that generally, in framing and administering the law, due regard be paid to the ancient rights, usages, and customs of India.

...Our clemency will be extended to all offenders, save and except those who have been, or shall be, convicted of having directly taken part in the murder of British subjects. With regard to such the demands of justice forbid the exercise of mercy.

...When, by the blessing of Providence, internal tranquility shall be restored, it is our earnest duty to stimulate the peaceful industry of India, to promote works of public utility and improvement, and to administer its government for the benefit of all our subjects resident therein. In their prosperity will be our strength; in their contentment our security, and in their gratitude our best reward. And may the God of all power grant to us, and to those in authority under us, strength to carry out our wishes for the good of our people.

SELECTED BIBLIOGRAPHY

Alam, Muzaffar and Subrahmanyam, Sanjay, 'Trade and Politics in the Arcot *Nizāmat* (1700–1732)', Muzaffar Alam and Sanjay Subrahmanyam, *Writing the Mughal World: Studies in Culture and Politics*, New York, NY: Columbia University Press, pp. 339–95.

Brittlebank, Kate, *Tipu Sultan's Search for Legitimacy: Islam and Kingship in a Hindu Domain*, Delhi: Oxford University Press, 1997.

Buckler, F. W., 'The Political Theory of the Indian Mutiny', *Transactions of the Royal Historical Society*, Vol. 5, 1922, pp. 71–100.

Cannadine, David, *Ornamentalism: How the British Saw Their Empire*, New York: Oxford University Press, 2001.

Chatterjee, Partha, *The Black Hole of Empire: History of a Global Practice of Power*, South Asia edn, Ranikhet: Permanent Black, 2012.

Cohen, Stephen, *The Indian Army: Its Contribution to the Development of a Nation*, revised Indian edn, Delhi: Oxford University Press, 1990.

Cohn, Bernard, 'Representing Authority in Victorian India', Bernard Cohn, *An Anthropologist Among the Historians and Other Essays*, New Delhi: Oxford Unversity Press, 2001 (first published, 1987), pp. 632–82.

——'The Recruitment and Training of British Civil Servants in India, 1600–1860', Bernard Cohn, *An Anthropologist Among the Historians and Other Essays*, New Delhi: Oxford University Press, 2001 (first published, 1987), pp. 500–553.

Cooper, Randolf G. S., *The Anglo-Maratha Campaigns and the Contest for India: the Struggle for Control of the South Asian Military Economy*, South Asian edn, New Delhi: Cambridge University Press, 2005.

Dasgupta, Sabyasachi, *Sepoy Rebellions in the Nineteenth Century*, Delhi: Primus, 2015.

Derks, Hans, *History of the Opium Problem: The Assault on the East, ca. 1600–1950*, Leiden: Brill, 2012.

Deshpande, Anirudh, *Hope and Despair: Mutiny, Rebellion and Death in India, 1946*, Delhi: Primus, 2017.

Ehrlich, Joshua, 'The Crisis of Liberal Reform in India: Public opinion, pyrotechnics, and the Charter Act of 1833', *Modern Asian Studies*, Vol. 52, Issue 6, 2018, pp. 2013–55.

Faruqui, Munis D., 'At Empire's End: The Nizam, Hyderabad and Eighteenth-Century India, *Modern Asian Studies*, Vol. 43, No. 1, 2009, pp. 5–43.

Gandhi, Rajmohan, *Modern South India: A History from the 17th Century to Our Times*, Delhi: Aleph Book Company, 2018.

Gibbons, Brett, *The English Cartridge: Pattern 1853 Rifle-Musket Ammunition*, n.p., independently published, 2020.

Gilmour, David, *The Ruling Caste: Imperial Lives in the Victorian Raj*, London: John Murray, 2005.

Gupta, Narayani, *Delhi Between Two Empires,* Delhi: Oxford University Press, 1981.

Gupta, Partha Sarathi, 'The Debate on Indianization, 1918–39', Partha Sarathi Gupta and Anirudh Deshpande, eds., *The British Raj and Its Indian Armed Forces, 1857–1939'*, Delhi: Oxford University Press, 2002, pp. 228–70.

Hunt, Margaret R., 'The 1689 Mughal Siege of East India Company Bombay: Crisis and Historical Erasure', *History Workshop Journal*, Vol. 84, Autumn 2017, pp. 149–69.

Irving, R. G., *Indian Summer: Lutyens, Baker and Imperial Delhi*, New Haven: Yale University Press, 1981.

Markovits, Claude, ed., *A History of Modern India, 1450–1950*, London: Anthem Press, 2004 (English translation of French original published in 1994).

Marshall, P. J., *East Indian Fortunes: The British in Bengal in the Eighteenth Century*, Oxford: Oxford University Press, 1976.

Moon, Penderel, *The British Conquest and Dominion of India*, 2 vols., first Indian edn, New Delhi: India Research Press, 1999.

Mukherjee, Rudrangshu, *Awadh in Revolt, 1857–1858: A Study of Popular Resistance*, paperback edn, New Delhi: Oxford University Press, 2001 (first published, 1984).

Nair, Janaki, *Mysore Modern: Rethinking the Region under Princely Rule*, New Delhi: Orient Blackswan, 2012.

Potter, David, 'Manpower Shortage and the End of Colonialism: The Case of the Indian Civil Service', *Modern Asian Studies*, Vol. 7, No. 1, 1973, pp. 47–73.

Prakash, Om, *The New Cambridge History of India: European Commercial Enterprise in Pre-Colonial India*, Cambridge: Cambridge University Press, 1998.

Rajagopalan, Mrinalini, *Building Histories: The Archival and Affective Lives of Five Monuments in Modern Delhi*, Delhi: Primus Books, 2018.

Ramusack, Barbara N., *The Indian Princes and their States*, New Delhi: Cambridge University Press, 1978.

Rand, Gavin and Bates, Crispin, eds., *Mutiny at the Margins: New Perspectives on the Indian Uprising of 1857* (Volume 4: *Military Aspects of the Indian Uprising*), New Delhi: Sage, 2013.

Sen, Surendra Nath, *Eighteen Fifty-seven*, third reprint, Delhi: Publications Division, 1995 (first published, 1957).

Spangenberg, Bradford, 'The Problem of Recruitment for the Indian Civil Service During the Late Nineteenth Century', *Journal of Asian Studies*, Vol. 30, No. 2, 1971, pp. 341–60.

Subramanian, Lakshmi, *History of India, 1707–1857*, Hyderabad: Orient Blackswan, 2010.

Sundaram, Chandar S., *Indianization, the Officer Corps, and the Indian Army:*

The Forgotten Debate 1817–1917, Lanham, Md.: Lexington Books, 2019.

Trautman, Thomas R., *Aryans and British India*, Berkeley: University of California Press, 1997.

Vale, Lawrence J., *Architecture, Power and National Identity*, second edn, Abingdon: Routledge, 2008.

Vasunia, Phiroze, 'Greek, Latin and the Indian Civil Service', *The Cambridge Classical Journal*, Vol. 55, 2005, pp. 35–71.

Yong, Tan Tai, *The Garrison State: Military, Government and Society in Colonial Punjab, 1849–1947*, Delhi: Sage, 2005.

INDEX

joint-stock company, 6
Journey Through the Kingdom of Oude, 156
Karnatak Payanghat, 25, 28
Kaye, John W., 106, 164–66
Kaye's and Malleson's History of the Indian Mutiny, 165
Khan, Alivardi, 38–41
Khan, Bakht, 178–79
Khan, Murshid Quli, 38
Khan, Sidi Yaqut, 22–23
Kitchener, Horatio Herbert, 219–21
Komagata Maru, 271
Lancaster, James, 18–19
legislative council, 142, 205–207
Linlithgow, Lord, 276–77
Lutyens, Edwin, 266–70
mace, viii, 7, 8, 13
Madras Army, 57, 86, 173, 196, 210, 212, 217
Madras Presidency, 34, 53, 56, 67, 196
Mahal, Hazrat, 186–87, 191–92
Malabar, 1–3, 5, 13, 53
Malacca Straits, 3
Malleson, George B., 165
Malwa opium, 134–35
Marx, Karl, 142, 160
Middleton, Henry, 18
Mill, John Stuart, 143, 201–202
Minto, Lord, 249
Mohammad, Dost, 104–109, 124
Moluccas, 8
Montagu–Chelmsford, 224, 238–39, 272–73
Mountbatten, Louis, 277
Mughal empire, 21–30, 38, 44, 48, 66, 155, 177–80, 201
Mughal, Mirza, 178–79
Nair Eradi, 1
Naoroji, Dadabhai, 238, 251
native states, x, 89, 94, 144–45, 152, 242
Nepal, 89–93
Netherlands, vii, 6, 7, 10

Nicobar Islands, 7
Non-Cooperation Movement, 275
Northern Circars, 30, 33
North-Western Provinces, 63, 73, 142, 188, 190, 207
nutmeg, viii, 7–9, 13
Opium Wars, 131, 133, 135, 161, 171
opium, 13, 71, 132–37, 250
Order of the Star of India, 245
Orissa, 12, 32, 34–35, 38, 46, 65
Outram, James, 115, 157, 190–91
Padshahnama, 79
Palmerston, Lord, 161–62
Peel Commission, 212–13, 217–18
pepper, viii, 1, 5, 7–8, 10, 13, 19
Persian Gulf, vii, 2–4, 37
Pincott, Frederic, 165
policy of laissez-faire, 249
political service, 240–41, 248
Portugal, vii, 1, 5–6
princely states, 143–49, 152, 157, 201–202, 223, 242–44, 248–54, 256–57, 259–61, 282
provincial civil service, 236–37, 239
Punjab Wars, 121, 125, 174
Qaisar-i-Hind, 246–47, 265
Qasim, Mir, 43–45
Quilon, 5, 59
Quit India Movement, 275–76, 280
Radcliffe, Cyril, 277
Rao, Balaji Baji, 63
Red Dragon, 18
Regulating Act of 1773, 68–69
revolt of 1857, x, 143–44, 151, 159–98, 201
Roberts, Frederick, 213, 216–20
Rowlatt Act, 273, 275
Sahib, Chanda, 26, 28–30, 49
Sahib, Nana, 151, 168, 181–83, 187
Secretariat Buildings, 269
Shah, Maulvi Ahmadullah, 187, 192
Shah, Wajid Ali, 157
silk, 12–13, 35, 71, 132, 134